Responsibility for Refugee and Migrant Integration

Responsibility for Refugee and Migrant Integration

Edited by
S. Karly Kehoe, Eva Alisic, Jan-Christoph Heilinger

DE GRUYTER

ISBN 978-3-11-073686-1
e-ISBN (PDF) 978-3-11-062874-6
e-ISBN (EPUB) 978-3-11-062616-2

Library of Congress Cataloging in Publication Control Number: 2019936275

Bibliographic information published by the Deutsche Nationalbibliothek
The Deutsche Nationalbibliothek lists this publication in the Deutsche Nationalbibliografie; detailed bibliographic data are available on the Internet at http://dnb.dnb.de.

© 2020 Walter de Gruyter GmbH, Berlin/Boston
This volume is text- and page-identical with the hardback published in 2019.
Coverimage: akg-images / Sammlung Foedrowitz
Printing and binding: CPI books GmbH, Leck

www.degruyter.com

Foreword

The present volume contributes to the ongoing debate about the integration of newcomers into societies by gathering insights from different academic disciplines, experiences from migrants and newcomers, and comments from those engaged in the day-to-day work of integration. It focusses on the role and responsibility of individuals in the face of multi-faceted and complex global and social challenges of migration and integration. The volume is the outcome of an interdisciplinary collaboration that started as the *Global Migration and Human Rights* working group of the Global Young Academy, an international body of early- and mid-career academics from around the world. Several meetings, including a symposium at the Munich Center for Ethics, informed this collection. We wish to thank all the contributors, as well as those who have, through their support and advice, helped us along the way.

Firstly, we would not have had this volume or collaboration regarding responsibility had it not been for our Global Young Academy colleague Liav Orgad who stimulated an initial conversation in Berlin in 2016. We are also grateful to Sarah-Aylin Akgül, Jason Branford, Eva Parisi, and Eva Wintermantel for their helpful and comprehensive research assistance leading up to the workshop. Franziska Büchl, Anna-Maria Gramatte, Nicole Kaczmar, Jennifer Plaul, Veronika Sager, Paula Sarson and Christos Simis helped to make the workshop and this volume possible through their expert administrative, organisational and editorial assistance. All chapters went through peer-review and we are grateful to those who participated in that process. We thank de Gruyter editor Christoph Schirmer for his unwavering support. The creative energy within the Global Young Academy has been a constant source of inspiration to us and the seed funding it provided was an important facilitator for this project. Finally, this edited volume would not have come to fruition without the generous financial support that the Fritz Thyssen Foundation (Cologne) provided for the symposium.

Melbourne, February 2019
S. Karly Kehoe, Eva Alisic, Jan-Christoph Heilinger

Table of Contents

Responding

S. Karly Kehoe, Eva Alisic, Jan-Christoph Heilinger

Responsibility for integration

Introduction and overview

In Western Europe and in North America, the topic of refugee and migrant integration into host societies has become a pressing and much discussed issue.[1] Large numbers of people are seeking entry to a range of host countries as they flee war, persecution, and crippling poverty. They are pursuing safety, stability, and the opportunity to live their lives without fear. This edited collection considers various aspects of the process of migration and integration over time and place in several European countries and in Canada, but we are mindful of the fact that the majority of today's migrations are happening in the Global South. Currently, there are around 250 million international migrants globally (IOM 2017). Meanwhile, the number of forcibly displaced people is nearing 70 million (UNHCR 2018a). It may surprise some in the Global North to learn that the majority of the latter group remain within the boundaries of their own countries or close by in neighbouring ones. A significant proportion of the 5.6 million registered persons of concern, who have fled Syria since 2011, for example, have gone to Lebanon, Jordan, and Turkey, with Turkey hosting about 64 per cent of them, and in spite of this exodus, over 6 million people remain within Syria and are classified as 'internally displaced'.[2] Similarly, on the other side of the world in South America, the crisis that has been engulfing Venezuela since 2014 has led to the flight of more than 2.3 million people to bordering countries (Human Rights Watch 2018). While migrant numbers for countries in the Global

1 Throughout the book, contributors have used a range of terms to describe people who have been displaced and these include refugee, migrant, newcomer, and asylum seeker. There are technical differences between each term, often depending upon the rules and regulations of a given host country or period of time. The UNHCR's definition of a refugee, 'someone who is unable or unwilling to return to their country of origin owing to a well-founded fear of being persecuted for reasons of race, religion, nationality, membership of a particular social group, or political opinion,' was introduced in 1951 as a response to the mass displacement of people following the Second World War. This definition has been criticised as too narrow (Shacknove 1985), and it also does not work for and cannot be applied to past mass movements of people, as, for example, in the nineteenth century. The authors who contribute to this volume have given careful thought to the terms they employ and, in most cases, offer a justification for their terminological choice. If anything, these differences found within the pages of this book simply reflect the reality of the topic: when dealing with human beings on the move, there can be no one-size fits all.

2 See UNHCR 2018b; UNHCR 2019.

https://doi.org/10.1515/9783110628746-001

North might seem high – an impression often influenced by unhelpful media interventions – they are not exceptional when considered within the context of global migration. The movement of non-Europeans into the European Union and of non-Canadians into Canada has provoked serious debates about entry requirements, selection criteria and 'acceptable' numbers, but the actual number of migrants seeking entry to these countries is, by comparison, relatively small. On a deeper level, the migrant influx is exposing some major fissures in the host societies. We are learning about the prevalence of insecurity and anxiety about ideas of national identity, economic security, and so-called 'cultural purity', and we are witnessing how they can translate into xenophobia and outright hostility towards the 'other' with the idea that these 'other' groups have to be kept out in order to preserve one's own well-being, comfort, and privilege. Thus, some refer to what is taking place as more of a 'reception crisis' or 'solidarity crisis' than a 'migrant crisis'. The heated and often polarising debates, which occur at governmental levels, through mainstream media, among the wider public via social media, and within migrant communities, have made it difficult to understand, in measured and constructive ways, the actual challenges that host countries face in terms of realizing an integrated society. It is becoming difficult to separate genuine challenges from populist alarmism. The intensity of the debates also creates a degree of chaos, which obstructs deeper understandings of what it feels like to be a migrant in a new place where almost everything, including language, social norms, food products, and even weather, is unfamiliar.

The atmosphere of fear and confusion that is influencing the public debates across many of our societies can benefit significantly from interventions from the research community. There is an urgent need to share knowledge and expertise about the historical, social, and psychological processes inherent within the context of migration, so that nuanced and more critical analyses of some of the genuine challenges associated with migration and newcomer integration can emerge. Combining academic research with the concrete experiences of newcomers as well as with the awareness of those who engage with the practical work of integration on a day-to-day basis will enrich greatly our understanding of migrant integration because it includes important perspectives that are often overlooked or ignored. The chapters presented here come from a collaboration of researchers, witnesses, activists, advocates, and entrepreneurs – all of whom share an understanding of the pressing need to work in partnership. And while some of us are living as displaced persons, most of us have no idea what that actually feels like and probably never will. This is our uncomfortable and unequal reality, but in recognising this, we are trying to engage in a constructive dialogue that breaks down barriers and offers an opportunity for optimism in the face of despair. In working together on this book, in sharing our research and our stories, we have come together to explore practical responses to the task of newcomer integration.

This collection includes diverse perspectives, but the central theme connecting all of the chapters is the role and responsibilities of individual '*agents*' – citizens or residents of host countries and the newcomers themselves insofar as they can and do take *action*. This concentration is deliberate because all too often insufficient attention is paid to what people, as private agents, in contrast to official or institutional agents, are doing. Too often, the impact that individuals can have on major global challenges such as migration and integration is perceived as too small to be of any real relevance. Yet, we must not underestimate the importance of individual action because it can function as a powerful agent of change.

The potential of people to inspire and deliver change becomes obvious in situations where the institutional responses to challenges are, for one reason or another, absent or insufficient. The gaps that people fill in these instances shine a bright light on where we need institutional creations, reforms, or updates. As a number of the chapters show, individuals acting alone and in groups have offered support to refugees and migrants in numerous and multifaceted ways. They welcome newcomers upon arrival; they donate money, clothes, and furniture; and they dedicate time and energy to helping them to navigate an intimidating range of challenges in a new environment, including administrative structures such as education and healthcare. In the context of migration, civil society offers systematic support, often in collaboration with diaspora networks, and can take the form of language training, housing assistance, and in providing access to local social, economic, or legal systems. In some cases, civil society collaborates with or receives support from the state.[3] A number of the chapters emphasise the role that newcomers themselves play as active participants in the process of integration. In cases where trauma and other forms of adversity might require special consideration and support, recognising the personal agency of newcomers is imperative to recovery.

While the aim of this volume is to offer a critical and constructive exploration of the role that individuals and civil society can play in the process of integration, it is imperative to be mindful of the fact that individual engagement might lead to legitimising political and institutional *in*action. Where private individuals and civil society already take sufficient care of the needs of newcomers,

3 The Canadian private sponsorship programme to resettle refugee families from crisis zones to Canada is a particularly striking example. Valid critiques of Canada's program are noted by scholars who argue that what has emerged there in recent years resembles 'restrictive policy approaches that were pioneered in Europe' (Bauder/Lenard/Straehle 2014).

the state is unlikely to be compelled to develop and to finance adequate institutional responses. Clearly, private responses can and should complement and support public or state action, particularly in situations of acute or urgent need, but they must not serve as an excuse for replacing it. In the case of mass migrations, coordinated responses by the state and by appropriate international bodies are also needed urgently.

Yet, individual action is integral to successful newcomer integration. Integration needs to be understood as a collaborative enterprise, involving people interacting with one another; it cannot be realised by decree alone. In the past, integration was viewed as something to be achieved by newcomers; they were expected to adapt to host societies by assuming pre-existing cultural norms and values (Gordon 1964). More recently, however, a new understanding is emerging which sees integration as a process agreed as being bi-directional and reciprocal. This perspective fits much better with a twenty-first-century globalised reality. It is necessary to recognise integration as the peaceful co-existence and interaction of people from different backgrounds on a footing of equality. It is a two-way process requiring action and change from everyone (Ager/Strang 2008; Sam/Berry 2006).

The chapters in this volume approach the process of integration from different perspectives, but they do so with a *normative* impetus. They do not simply acknowledge and analyse the role that individuals play in the process of integration, either as facilitators of or as impediments to the realisation of a more just and more integrated society. Instead, they assume that the influence and importance of people's actions, with regard to the possible success or failure of achieving integrated societies, is something that we *should* all be aware of and aspire to realising. Underpinning this position is the conviction that responsibility exists not only between co-nationals, but also between all humans everywhere.[4]

The opening section, *Witnessing* includes three chapters that illuminate different aspects of migration and integration from first-person perspectives. *Alison Phipps* uses her own experiences in Calais in 2016 to argue for the necessity of bearing witness, when people suffer, as a first step towards solidarity and action. The following two chapters present first-hand understandings: *Yahya Al-Abdullah* reflects upon the experience of Syrian activists who, after having fled the civil war, find themselves in Paris, and on his ongoing film project, to emphasise

---

4 Recommendations about how such individual responsibility could be exercised can be found in the report that emerged from the workshop at which most of the present papers were initially discussed: Plaul et al. 2018. Further explorations of the idea of cosmopolitan responsibility can be found in Heilinger (forthcoming).

the importance of finding their voice and of being able to express their realities. *Debora Kayembe* discusses her work as an interpreter for refugees as a way of explaining how inadequate communication impedes integration and may, at times, put people's lives at risk in the new environment.

The second section, *Barriers and Challenges*, addresses a range of issues impeding integration from sociological, historical, and psychological perspectives. *Nasar Meer's* analysis of the legacy of colonialism and of racism on perceptions of belonging over time and space connects directly with *Karly Kehoe's* exploration of the ways in which black migrants were problematized by white colonial society in nineteenth-century Atlantic Canada. *Yves Frenette's* reflections upon the complex dynamics that shaped responses to migrants in French Canada also emphasises the long arm of the colonial experience. The next two chapters transition us from the historical to the psychological. *Niamh McLoughlin* and *Harriet Over's* discussion of research on prejudice, discrimination and dehumanisation towards immigrants and *Eva Alisic* and *Dzenana Kartal's* study of trauma and cultural distance between the refugee community and the host community shed important light on the delicate balance between human psychology and integration. In spite of these chapters' focus on barriers to successful integration, their intent is optimistic: if we know about and understand the challenges associated with integration, then we are better equipped to develop more constructive approaches to it in the future.

Section three highlighted a number of different possibilities and strategies associated with *Responding* to the different issues and challenges appearing in the context of migration and integration. *Jan-Christoph Heilinger* offers a philosophical exploration of the role and responsibilities of individual persons to get involved with and to accept individual responsibility for the social task of refugee integration. *André Grahle's* contribution contends that those in the host communities who engage in volunteer work should also become politically active and engage in activist work. Both chapters point to the importance of individual and political action to realise integration. In their chapter, co-authors *Jet G. Sanders*, *Elizabeth Castle*, *Karen Tan* and *Rob Jenkins* apply insights from behavioural science to the case of refugee integration and discuss whether and how nudging may help to enable more effective modes of integration. Evidence of how these ideas may translate into real-life action is offered by *Annemiek Dresen* and *Stephen Wordsworth. Dresen* shares a personal interpretation of global individual responsibility by describing her work as a social entrepreneur engaged in facilitating refugee access to the Dutch job market. Similarly, *Wordsworth* flags the work of Cara, The Council for At-Risk Academics, which was founded in 1933 in the United Kingdom to assist academics from around the world in escaping from persecution, violence, and conflict. The final chapter, co-authored by

Jason Branford, *André Grahle*, *Jan-Christoph Heilinger*, *Dennis Kalde*, *Max Muth*, *Eva Maria Parisi*, *Paula-Irene Villa* and *Verina Wild*, highlights the very real risk that those engaged in work with, for, or about refugees face as they confront increasing threats of online hate-attacks.

Across all of the volume's chapters, the possibility and the importance of individual agency is emphasised. When employed responsibly, it acts as an important source for social advancement and the realisation of integrated societies. Although made difficult by the extremely adverse circumstances of some, and by the complacency of others, that individuals can act and should always be treated as capable beings with dignity should never be forgotten. The book closes with a poem by *Alison Phipps* that was written after 'Day 1' of the two-day Munich Workshop that inspired this volume.

Bibliography

Ager, A./Strang, A. (2008): Understanding Integration: A Conceptual Framework. In: Journal of Refugee Studies 21(2), 166–191.

Bauder, H./Lenard, P./Straehle C. (2014): Lessons from Canada and Germany. In: Comparative Migration Studies 2(1), 1–7.

Gordon, M. M. (1964): Assimilation in American Life. New York: Oxford University Press.

Heilinger, J.-C. (forthcoming): Cosmopolitan Responsibility. Berlin/Boston: De Gruyter.

Human Rights Watch (2018): The Venezuelan Exodus: The Need for a Regional Response to an Unprecedented Migration Crisis. 3 September. https://www.hrw.org/report/2018/09/03/venezuelan-exodus/need-regional-response-unprecedented-migration-crisis (last accessed 20 February 2019).

IOM (2017): World Migration Report 2018. Geneva: IOM. https://publications.iom.int/system/files/pdf/wmr_2018_en.pdf (last accessed 20 February 2019).

Plaul, J./Kehoe, S.K./Alisic, E./Heilinger, J.-C. (2018): Global Individual Responsibility: The Role of the Citizen in Refugee Integration. Halle: Global Young Academy. https://globalyoungacademy.net/wp-content/uploads/2018/12/Global-Individual-Responsibility.pdf (last accessed 20 February 2019).

Sam, D. L./Berry, J. W. (eds.) (2006): The Cambridge Handbook of Acculturation Psychology. New York: Cambridge University Press.

Shacknove, A. E. (1985): Who Is a Refugee? In: Ethics 95(2), 274–284.

UNHCR (2018a): Global Trends: Forced Displacement in 2017. https://www.unhcr.org/en-au/statistics/unhcrstats/5b27be547/unhcr-global-trends-2017.html (last accessed 20 February 2019).

UNHCR (2018b): Syria Factsheet. Syria, February 2018. http://www.unhcr.org/sy/wp-content/uploads/sites/3/2018/02/Syria-Fact-Sheet-2017-2018.pdf (last accessed 20 February 2019).

UNHCR (2019): Operational Portal, Refugee Situations. Syria Regional Refugee Response Statistics. https://data2.unhcr.org/en/situations/syria#_ga=2.25196606.2094609381.1541512707–1075088928.1541512707 (last accessed 20 February 2019).

Witnessing

Alison Phipps

Bearing witness: The burden of individual responsibility and the rule of law

Abstract: When humans are caught up in systems that inflict great suffering upon them, people of conscience have a responsibility to bear witness and those having privileges and mandates should offer solidarity and engage in practical action. This paper focusses on the ethical public responsibility of *witness-bearing* as the uncomfortable and provoking response to such suffering. It discusses the influence of narratives, images, photography, media and the arts, reports and reflects personal experiences as an important element of knowledge, and makes the case for actively bearing witness and expressing solidarity.

1. Introduction

> It was when I called my family at home and described kneeling on the floor in the church, which now stands in the middle of a rased, bulldozed, mud bath of rubbish and devastation, that the tears came. The sound of the bulldozers coming ever closer, the presence of the bodies draped in the white Eritrean shawls (suria) at prayer beside me, the juxtaposition of the silent petitions of hope and peace alongside the violence of destruction and hopelessness were too much for the words which tried and failed to describe the scene. Witnessing became the witness of tears.

Since the 'reception crisis' more popularly known as the 'refugee crisis' began in Europe, there have been many different fact-finding missions. These have been visits to demonstrate solidarity and concern and humanitarian ventures to the flashpoints on the borders of Europe and also the border between France and the UK in Calais. There have also been visits designed to threaten and deter migrants and refugees as well as parachute visits, which allow for photo opportunities. A sustained series of visits from humanitarians and people in the public eye have enabled the situations in Calais, Lesvos, and Lampedusa to become a matter of public concern after years of obscurity.

At times of acute concern, and in the face of collapsing systems of justice and law in the European Union, where binding obligations are being set aside by states and local government in favour of security and emergency measures, the space for meaningful action is diminished.

Since 2016, UNHCR and Médecins sans frontières (MSF) have pulled out of working in 'reception' facilities in Greece in protest at the policies of refoulement

https://doi.org/10.1515/9783110628746-002

on the part of the European Union. Boats in the Mediterranean are being intercepted and turned back to Libya, where there are accurate witness reports of refugees being sold into slavery. Humanitarian actors are increasingly under threat of criminalisation and in need of legal protection, and witnesses to their intentions and their actions both on the seas and on land. A large worldwide movement has developed of people of conscience working as allies in various points of both acute need and reception. Most importantly those seeking protection and refuge have themselves made demands for their own rights under international law against the closing of borders and for decent conditions in reception centres.

Within this movement there has been substantial critical commentary. Humanitarian actors have been cast as naïve, or as 'white saviours' or overly charitable in intent; as diminishing refugee agency or as ineffectual, through to threats to state and European security. Large NGOs have struggled to respond quickly to what have been situations of acute humanitarian need for aid. Conditions within Europe's borders have been worse than in many areas of the world, where camp construction and reception facilities have had a much longer history. Politicians have been seen to both engage and abdicate responsibility.

In 2016, I was part of co-designing a visit which aimed to bear witness, rather than 'finding facts', in Calais, and to do so in such a way that was not about jumping to political conclusions, but developing and sustaining relationships with actors on the ground. This visit included a range of Scottish National Party Members of Parliament from the Home Affairs select committee, and academics, clinicians, campaigners, and those who have long experience in working with refugees in Scotland. These latter are all expert witnesses and experts at witnessing.

At times of chronic humanitarian crisis an active approach is that of bearing witness. Throughout the South African Apartheid years, courts, media, academic research, creative artworks, and government chambers provided spaces for bearing witness to the ways in which justice was undermined and human rights were violated, revealing publicly the structures at work to systematically destroy Black lives and undermine forms of resistance. Each domain was able to bear witness in distinctly different ways.

In Newton's laws of motion, the third law states that when one body exerts a force on a second body, the second body simultaneously exerts a force equal in magnitude and opposite in direction on the first body. In the struggles for migration justice and to honour the articles in the Refugee Convention and European Convention on Human Rights, there is indeed a sense in which the present situation is metaphorically caught in a struggle for and of motion, fraught with visceral emotion. The Refugees Welcome movement has been met with a rise of national populism, which is marked in particular by varieties of xenophobia and white supremacy, and with European measures to invest far greater sums in the Frontex operations on the borders than in the humanitarian aid, though some aid has been granted. Here we have pitted against each other agencies and populations determined to fix borders, stop movement, close exits, and others wishing to open the borders, free the movement, let movement flow. Within this metaphorical impasse, agency is exerted across the force field, and with it the act of witnessing has come to the fore.

2. Witness-bearing

Visits to situations of conflict and chronic humanitarian need have occurred in various situations in recent years. During the Decade to Overcome Violence, the World Council of Churches organised visits to bear witness to the suffering of peoples in Palestine-Israel, Nigeria, Sierra Leone, Liberia, Sri Lanka, and Indonesia, among others.[1] The visitors included those skilled in observation, writing, reporting, legal understanding, research, poetic practice, and medical knowledge, who had as part of their professional practice the ability to document and reveal something of the suffering with credibility and understanding.

In the context of Calais there has been an extraordinary mobilization of humanitarian aid from the UK, and especially from Scotland, with community groups leading where larger NGOs have been slow to follow and where local governments and states have failed to protect life and dignity. In addition, politicians and human rights celebrities have engaged in awareness raising and solidarity visits, which have highlighted the situation, and the BBC held 'Songs of Praise' from the Calais church during the summer of 2015.

Meanwhile MSF and Damien Carême, maire of Grande-Synthe, began the process of building a camp in the Calais area after the failure of the state and the local prefecture to act in accordance with their obligations. This was done for a fraction of the cost of the container detention camp put in place by state authorities under duress in Calais, and was done so non-violently and with a remarkably intelligent and striking approach which is distinctive and deserves the acclaim and interest it is beginning to attract, even in these first three weeks. The presence of the camps in the Calais/Grande-Synthe areas represented contested space for the state, the local administration, and for local residents as well as for the UK.

1 See http://www.overcomingviolence.org/en/peace-convocation/preparatory-process/living-letters-visits.html.

At times of great human suffering we see extraordinary courage and compassion. Communities across Scotland, and Europe more widely, have led with creativity, practical action, and costly generosity in Calais, Lesvos, and in receiving communities. In this there have been multiple acts of individuals taking responsibility and making a range of changes to their lives. Repeatedly, in the work I undertake with the UNESCO Chair Programme at the University of Glasgow I now hear discussions and presentations from individuals who begin by saying, "In September 2015, I..." The publication of the photograph of Aylan Kurdi, the Kurdish refugee boy drowned and washed up on a Turkish beach, was of such poignancy that it literally changed the course of individual responsibility in such large numbers it became the collective movement of welcoming refugees.

The generosity of these individuals is equalled and exceeded by that of those who are themselves seeking refuge, though it is also different. The communities of solidarity within those forced to migrate receive little attention, but are predominantly how and where assistance is found. Within national and ethnic groups of refugees, those from the same towns or local communities, those with similar experiences on the journey of detention, or hiding, or crossing land and seas borders, new clusters of solidarity grow around shared experiences and the responsibilities those seeking refuge take for those around them in their immediate families, but also in circles of solidarity and mutual support born of geography as much as kinship, and forged in extremis. The people have led where larger institutions and some governments have been slow, reluctant, and mired in outdated thinking and ineffective solutions.

At the same time, we have witnessed a vicious rise in xenophobia and structural violence against migration of all forms. This has happened in Europe before, and we have much to learn from the lessons of history. The last time Europe faced such numbers of refugees it failed (Arendt 1943). Facing its failure, the articles protecting human rights were created and these very articles are now in peril. The last time the people of Europe said never again. Bearing witness to this historical moment has become action in the present day. While the ending of the Second World War was a different historical moment and set of material circumstances to those of the present day and is by a long way not structurally or materially the same as the present moment in Europe, the symbolism of that moment in history and the creation of an ethic – particularly in Europe, and across humanitarian action – of witnessing and voicing solidarity has come to determine action, new ethical responsibilities, and how they are framed within the polity, particularly within groups of individuals.

Restatement of the moral code within the Refugees Welcome movement, and among the refugee actors themselves, runs as follows: when human beings are caught up in systems which inflict great suffering upon them, people of conscience have a responsibility to bear witness. When homes, livelihoods, dignity, and lives are destroyed, those of us with privilege and mandates should offer solidarity, practical action, and learn from those with direct experience, rather than relying on second-hand assumptions. There has been a great deal of voicing of solidarity since 2015. Much of it through media and the arts, public demonstrations, humanitarian endeavours, refugee-led agency, reluctant political change under a variety of pressures, legal actions, and non-violent direct action. In and of itself it represents the international, multilingual, and cultural work of bearing witness (Phipps 2017).

There is considerable technical academic work on the idea of the witness and of testimony in legal theory and jurisprudence (Scarry 2010; Choo 2015; Dennis 2017). There is not space in this chapter to go into this literature in detail. Instead, I wish to draw on the metaphorical power of the idea of witness-bearing as an action which expands on the idea of a visit or trip. Witness-bearing is not the same as visiting as it can occur in conditions which are not necessarily proximate. In her Nobel lecture, Judith Butler (2011) differentiates between actions responding ethically to suffering at a distance, and those which are proximate:

> The two questions that concern me are at first quite different from one another. The first is whether any of us have the capacity or inclination to respond ethically to suffering at a distance, and what makes that ethical encounter possible, when it does take place. The second is what it means for our ethical obligations when we are up against another person or group, find ourselves invariably joined to those we never chose.

This distinction is pertinent to teasing out the significance of witness-bearing as a response to suffering. In law the witness is usually in a proximate position, and it is often by chance that they are called up to offer, as an ethical civic duty, their best version of what they saw or experienced. The role of the witness is crucial to the work of justice, in the sense of the judgements of the law. But such an ethical obligation writes itself across the landscape of the Refugees Welcome movement as this same witnessing to images on screen, writings in newspapers, and artworks poses the same questions 'Will you bear witness? Will you use your body, time, intellect, memory, speech, writing, and actions to serve the rule of justice, the common good, the rights of humanity'? To do this in the legal setting is especially codified. To do this in the polity takes many forms, but is still undergirded by a sense of ethical responsibility. This ethical responsibility may also, it should be noted, be found in the structures of feeling common to individuals or groups protesting ethnic diversity bearing witness, however erroneously, as they do, to a sense of injustice against their own moral codes of ethnic purity.

Given the power unleased by the publication of the photograph of Aylan Kurdi – mentioned above as the defining moment in the narratives of individual responsibility in action for refugee justice – it is worth reflecting on the role played by artistry and photography in particular. Through the shared experience of the image in provoking the wave of responses as the image was seen and shared by millions worldwide. The question, 'Will you bear witness?' began to be answered by individuals, and individuals forming new collectives, in myriad ways. In a piece for the art journal *Drouth*, I reflect on this as follows:

> Photography is a form which intervenes in such situations in ways which have teased philosophers of the twentieth and twenty-first century. Susan Sontag has written of the ways photographers approach the question of the 'quintessential' experience of modernity, that of 'Being a spectator of calamities taking place in another country.' Her approach to the question as to what it means to be human, and a spectator of calamities is to separate out, not feeling from reason, but rather the act of bearing witness and the acts of artistry.
>
> "For photography of atrocity, people want the weight of witnessing without the taint of artistry, which is equated with insincerity or mere contrivance." (Sontag 2004, 26–27)

Sontag has also considered the way the camera itself, with its interventions on time with an image bound to fade, works with different temporal frames to that of words: 'A narrative seems likely to be more effective than an image. Partly it is a question of the length of time one is obliged to look, to feel' (Sontag 2004, 110).

While there is a difference in modes of witnessing and the place or otherwise of artistry in forms of witnessing, it is the metaphor of witness-bearing that is the idea of *bearing* which interests me here, that the working of witnessing, if chosen, must be borne, as an ethical public responsibility in the context of people seeking refuge. This means that the metaphor meets artistry and the work of bearing witness takes on a load, as individual responsibility which is borne, struggled under, which has weight. Donna Haraway (2016), in *Staying with the Trouble*, asks:

> How can we think in times of urgencies *without* the self-indulgent and self-fulfilling myths of apocalypse, when every fibre of our being is interlaced, even complicit, in the webs of processes that must somehow be engaged and repatterned?[2]

Feminist theologian Sallie McFague equally has written of metaphors as follows:

> Metaphor is, for human beings, what instinctual groping is for the rest of the universe – the power of getting from here to there. The imagination is the chief mover, setting the familiar in an unfamiliar context, so that new possibilities can be glimpsed. Metaphorical thinking

2 I'm indebted to Sarah Thomas for introducing me to Haraway's critical work on the Anthropocene and Le Guin's idea of 'rebearing' through her PhD research.

is the way human beings – selves not mere minds – move in all areas of discovery. (McFague 1975)

Bearing witness is both a present-time activity and an activity of memory. It changes those who are witnesses, often profoundly, as others who have made such visits will testify. The heaviness of witnessing to the erosion of and refusal of the rights of refugees weighs heavily in the polity and leads to individual actions which are outside of the ordinary, from opening up homes, to providing humanitarian assistance, to deliberately reorientating friendship groups around greater inclusion, to acts which border on and may well be illegal, but are seen as upholding natural justice. In this, individuals demonstrate a form of stoicism, a need not to flinch from the heaviness, the acute discomfort, even anger and helplessness, of witnessing to what, wittingly or unwittingly, our policies and voting habits, foreign and domestic, have done. Individuals weigh the questions of right and wrong for themselves, bear the weight of the judgement for themselves and then take on the task, which is invariably costly. Witnesses could be from within the populations of those seeking refuge and often are, and the most powerful testimonies often come from those who are experts by experience. Some testimonies of coming into a witness-bearing role highlight the suddenness of a compulsion to act, others of long being alongside so the witness-bearing is sustained.

3. Witness-bearing in Calais

Bearing witness is an uncomfortable and provoking activity. It means being present at the scene of a potential crime, and in Calais, this meant intentionally placing ourselves as a collective in a place where freedom of movement was intentionally frustrated, and where international laws, not to mention laws of motion, were potentially violated. It was to join other actors and witnesses and to offer up our testimony in a variety of ways. Following the visit to the Calais camps these testimonies from the witnesses came through in psychological medical reports, guidance for volunteers, fundraising actions, talks, speeches in Parliament, articles in academic journals (Piacentini 2014), keynote lectures, diary entries, votes, and committee procedures and motions, legal actions, visual documentation (Myers 2016), theoretical observations, and poetry. What follows is my own auto-ethnographic witness report, adapted and published in a national newspaper as a front-page exclusive, just days after the visit, and adapted here.

Calais, Day 1: Arrived in Calais and had first briefing meeting with SNP MPs from Home Affairs Select Committee and Médecins Sans Frontiers/Help Refugees UK. The catastrophe that is the European failure to uphold its own convention and the binding obligations member states have signed up to unfolds palpably before our eyes. The tenacity of the volunteers, the arrival of the British volunteers when states fail and willing hands are desperately needed, the courage of a local mayor against all the odds, the acute need for legal information and advice, the urgency of trauma support and the woeful inadequacy and failure of imagination for unaccompanied minors.

This is Europe 2016.

Briefings with local NGOs working hard to coordinate and systemise the incredible groundswell of volunteers from Britain immediately following the publication of the photograph of Aylan Kurdi, and the demand from visitors. Being in the presence of activists and veteran warriors in the struggle to manifest compassion is a familiar place. The individuals have qualities which are familiar to ourselves as witnesses, their tenacity, the rapid-fire, well-rehearsed phrases and facts, their clever understanding of the macro and micro politics, their seriousness and humour, their delight in questions which they have found answers of devastating simplicity and honesty, their willingness to share with those with whom they just know they are making common cause.

There is a need to share a great deal of information very quickly. The information is complex and is also important. The politicians ask question after question using every moment of what they are acutely aware is valuable time. Their questions about legal cases, about precedents, about management, about resources, about the humanitarian horrors, about the need to act with dignity and decency and care, and not get in the way of the day-to-day humanitarian and activist work in the camps.

We want to do it this way because it is not about political point-scoring, it is about learning so much on the ground so we can act.

We meet up with a guide from one of the relatively new organisations providing humanitarian assistance, legal education, entertainment, and advocacy in Calais. She is an activist and her habitus repeats as we meet more volunteers and guides. The slender figure is sprung, as if ready for action, emotion is on her face, tiredness is bright in her eyes, as is her readiness for the next task. This is known territory, the territory of work in a time of war. There is such beauty in her statement: 'I wear track suits and no make-up, there isn't time and I'm too tired, but I'm so energised by all of this.'

There is anger and admiration in the speech of those assembled, there is incredulity and an abiding lack of surprise. There is comparison with the work back home.

And there are the harrowing stories of those known of, those struggling, and of the agonizing injustice which is killing the spirits and killing the bodies and killing the souls.

We, the people of Europe. We did this.

Calais, Day 2: On a stone in the middle of the bulldozed 'Camp Sud' are graffitied the words 'veni, vidi, vici' famously deployed, so history has it, by Caesar after a rapid and complete victory. "I came, I saw, I conquered." So it seems with the 'victory' of the security state with its barbed wire and container-style detention camps, its sterile, lifeless systemising, and the constant activity of bulldozers and diggers uprooting every tree, levelling every dune, steamrolling every tent. I look down into the mud and there is a child's shoe, a boot; a broken pot – signs that people were given no chance to empty their homes of belongings. So many shoes – shoes and concentration camps in 2016 Europe, in a country, which should know better. Riot police are patrolling with tear gas, everywhere the vast acreage of £37 million fences and barbed wire all paid for by the UK taxpayer to keep out the people in the Calais camps.

The people we meet in the Camp Nord are entrepreneurs, cooks, bakers, accountants, professors, geologists, and then there are so many children and young people. They are people on their knees in a small, beautiful sanctified Eritrean church, praying. The people we are keeping from entering the UK greet us with smiles and with greetings of peace, with conversation and gratitude simply for having made the effort to visit them and to bring love and greetings from people back home. The people we keep from the UK with all the razor wire, bulldozing, and fire-raising are people with family who, as luck would have it, live in the UK. The people we keep at bay with tear gas and riot batons have a right to test their claim as having a well-founded fear of persecution, they have a right to a life, under EU law, of dignity and respect.

The people we meet and who are kept at bay by the multi-million pound border industry, which keeps shareholders in dividends, just want to be with their friends and families, as you or I might do. They are from countries with long connections to the UK, to its imperial history, victims of the line-drawing borders on maps a century ago, victims of the way states were not made for the Kurds or the Palestinians. The people in these camps are not those with ready connection of a similar nature to France and its state systems, they are not West African, North African, Chinese – they are indeed the UK's and Europe's responsibility, the result of our actions in history far and near.

There is everywhere a menacing presence of violence, overt and evident – it is the violence of a Europe which has lost its way and is lashing out against the most vulnerable in fear; it is the violence of the state as bully; it is the violence sanctioned by our lack of imagination and compassion and humanity; it is the violence which steps in, in place of the articles and declaration made when we said, in Europe, never again. It is 2016. Ecce Homo. We, the people of Europe. We did this.

Calais, Day 2, The Warehouse: I walk into the Warehouse and am met by the very distinctive sights and smells of my childhood – that of the jumble sale. On shelves with neat homemade labels, are piles and piles of clothes and bedding items. All around are volunteers who have come over from Britain. They are overwhelmingly female, student-aged young women and others the ages of their mothers. What brought them is what binds them in the flow of concentrated and good-humoured activity – care and a sense that this is indeed our responsibility to provide basic aid now that the UK and France have failed. On the tables in front of us are orange strips of duct-tape marked up 'Trousers – small, medium, large', 'tops, female; small, medium, large', etc. We get going. It doesn't take long, and cheesy pop music from the 80s is adding to the humour, conversation, and for some of us, nostalgia. Arms, hands, bodies moving almost as in a rhythmic dance sort the clothing into sizes, fold it, place it on the right shelf, and return to the sorting table. There is a murmur of conversation and a lot of laughter over some items. High-value items are sorted separately for different fundraising purposes. There is a tea break, and we sit in the watery sunshine outside sharing hand gel and feel a little overawed by the scale and careful logistics of the whole operation.

It's like an outpost of Britain on French soil. English spoken all around me. It reminds me of the atmosphere in the holiday camps I worked in as a student one summer. Only there is a worry here, and seriousness. Many have not been in to the camps themselves – keen not to get in the way, knowing what they can best do to help and to focus their volunteering on what they have been told needs doing.

The shift finished and we assemble again outside waiting for rides back. The group has formed around a common task, and we are laughing and chatting in between the sober conversations about what we are witnessing and becoming part of. As happens in so many groups where those seeking refuge and those taking up a responsibility where states or large NGOs have failed to act, or at least been slow to act, the formation of what the anthropologist Victor Turner calls 'communitats' – a levelled-out sense of social bond – takes shape (Turner 1995). Later that evening in a cramped room, we push aside chairs and sit on the floor so we can see one another clearly and one by one, in soft tones, or with anger, or with tears, or with bewilderment we tell one another what we have seen.

Calais, Day 3: On the side of the Mairie in Grande-Synthe – the municipal town council building – there is a banner opposing the Transatlantic Trade Agreement. We sit inside around a table and spend an hour with Maire Carême, the mayor, learning what a difference decisive, ecologically informed, and courageous political leadership can make. The conditions in the camp refugees had set up in woods on the outskirts of Grande-Synthe were 'epouvantable' – 'utterly disgraceful'. When MSF worker Michael Neuman gave a public lecture at the University of Glasgow in February 2016 he said he had never seen such terrible conditions in all his years of missions with MSF, not even in Chechnya. In coalition with MSF and festival organisers, the mayor had used the limited political power he had to move the people out of their miserable conditions and into sheds, which can sleep four people each, giving people the right to cook their own food, decorate the sheds and individualise them, mostly, as it turned out, with political statements about the misery of their conditions or the lamentable situations they had left behind.

We arrive at the new camp, and it's not the riot police approaching us with batons and questions as it was in Calais, but the local gendarmerie – community police – checking our papers, as is normal in France where you have to have your identity card with you at all times. The atmosphere is markedly different. The camp is only three weeks old but already the difference of good organisation, coordination, and also non-violent ways of working are palpable. There is not the menace of violence from the state that we had experienced in Calais, nor the overweening control. Children ride around on bikes everywhere; there is laughter and conversation. As we walk up and down and round the camp, people come up to us and ask us questions, request items, or tell us of their situation. Food, tea, and coffee are supplied, and we stand in the sunshine with a bag of salted sunflowers sharing them with a man from Iran. In Farsi, Turkish, some Arabic, and broken English we hold a conversation – one about hope and despair – not about the conditions in the camp but the politics of refugees in Europe. 'Where to, when no one will take you? Where to?' And I hear again the question asked by Jews fleeing Nazi Germany. And I hear the same answers: 'Not here, not here, not to us.'

Ninety per cent of the camp inhabitants are Kurds. There are many young men dying inside of frustration. They invite us to a meeting and tell us of Kurdistan, its history, the British involvement, the way lines were drawn on the map. They are begging the politicians to act. They are gracious, courteous; they arrange translation and greet us formally. Then the stories begin and I recognise them as those I have also heard from other desperate nations without states – from the Palestinians. The litany of historical events that must be recited carefully and correctly so that the audience understands the seriousness of the situation. The locations and sources of siege and suffering – Kirkuk; Dayesh. I realise that those speaking with such focus and careful urgency are desperate to find a way of telling the story, the epic story of their suffering, in a way that will communicate sufficiently that their suffering will end – for their suffering is intolerable and inhuman, and they cannot believe that it is one human beings can allow. So, the logic goes, there must be a way of telling the story, of giving testimony to those who bear witness, that will work, that will end the suffering. They try every angle. And I realise how I am utterly confounded, for there is not a way of communicating this story to those with power. I watch as those who are elected representatives in one of the richest countries in the world, bear the weight of witnessing and the individual responsibility which comes with their offices, to act, but in a Parliamentary democratic context where they can already see how hard it will be to bring even one of those asking for resettlement, to the UK. For all we are in the presence of politicians with real power who are determined to advocate and act, the kind of simple request for sanctuary has become unbearably complicated and difficult to address.

There is utter despair and suicidal hopelessness in the eyes of one of the men. I understand it. I have no words.

In Calais we had met a man who had known this despair and overcome it and learned to live from day to day with no hope. He said, 'I know there is nothing you can do. But it is enough that you have come to say hello to us.'

There is nothing we can do. Those with the power to make the physical camp conditions better have done it and done it courageously and in a way which contrasts completely with the simultaneous destruction of the camps. So here we are, one human being with another, individuals witnessing and bearing responsibility, in the state of exception that is the refugee camp in Europe in 2016, and we are united in a common understanding of the hopelessness of it all and thrown back on the most basic of human activities – that of the giving and receiving of hospitality, of meeting, greeting, and eating together. As we leave the camp, many of those with whom we had shared conversations accompanied us, giving us a written message and waiting until our rides back had arrived and waved goodbye. Europe 2016.

Calais, Day 4: It's our last day and time for a long, serious, and sustaining meeting with MSF workers about camp conditions, about the violence, sanitation, legal advice, the place of politics, well-being of volunteers, and what on earth can be done. It's time for commitments.

First-hand reports of random use by French riot police overnight of 500 tear gas canisters on the camp in Calais and of a young man from the camp crushed to death under a lorry.

At Calais-Fréthun, the Eurostar station, there is the presence of handguns with customs officers and of dogs as well as sub-machine guns – all part of the menacing atmosphere of the threat of state intervention under state of emergency powers.

The whole group is engaged in careful, considered discussion of what might be actions and how to create a future where the shame and impossible despair and entrapment of the camps is replaced by just futures and humane possibilities.

However well managed and constructed a camp, it is no solution, and certainly not a semi-permanent one. They are places of slow killing of body, mind, and spirit. To all intents and purposes they are death camps.

4. Bearing the witnessing

In her memoir (unpublished) and PhD thesis reflecting on the ecological disaster that is climate change, Sarah Thomas turns to Ursula Le Guin's writings on nature to consider the kinds of change wrought by metaphorical usages and emphasises: 'I am struck by how much we talk about rebirthing but never about *rebearing*... A door opens just by changing the name. We don't have to be reborn; we can *rebear*. This is part of the writer's job, either to rebear metaphors or refuse to use them' (Le Guin 1994, 107).

I have lived within the witness-bearing space with people seeking refuge for at least fifteen years. It was a choice and a commitment and a compulsion. It is a responsibility and at some level about both obeying the laws of motion and upholding the spirit and letter of international law, of the conventions and articles which give us protection. As an academic, this witness-bearing space is shaped and changed by artistry, advocacy, theory, and practice. It is linguistic and intercultural and fraught. It is also constantly in need of 'rebearing' in the sense that at times it can be light, feather-like, drifting on the breeze, it is joyous and optimistic and redolent with the ease that is responsibility satisfied, witnessing borne with and borne well. But it also needs to be borne in a heavier sense. It needs to find minds and bodies and souls which can hold it, especially when others cannot, or when respite is needed, or when the journey as stalled and stasis prevents any movement. The question posed at the outset here changes with an emphasis on the idea of 'bearing with', it moves it from the snapshot of the shutter click of Sontag's photography to the sustained temporalities of a narrative. 'Can you bear this witness?' as opposed to 'Will you bear witness?' is not a legal question of the subject but a question of tenacity, temporality, and faithfulness to the human being.

Bearing the witness of Calais, with its ongoing responsibilities and the ongoing bearing with the witness which began there, has had many consequences which bleed into my academic life and out again into my life as a subject. Philosopher and psychoanalyst Luce Irigaray makes an injunction to women to never abandon subjective experience as an element of knowledge (Irigaray 1994). The witness-bearing work in Calais did not last just a few days but has continued in both proximity and distance. The writing continues the witness, I meet unaccompanied minors resettled here in Scotland and support their families. My own foster daughter was in the Calais camps over ten years ago. I work with poets and photographers in their documenting of camp life, with academics, with NGOs developing resource materials, with lobbying groups trying to bring a change in UK law and policy.

The camp has closed, violently. The situation in the Pas-de-Calais is absolutely desperate. Reports reach me almost daily of NGOs at their wits' end as French and European policy tightens the noose around those who would dare to pose the question of sanctuary with their presence on European soil.

Bearing witness has brought me up sharp against my own limits, not least those as an academic but also as an activist and advocate. Bearing witness has not brought change, or very little it seems; the presence of powerful lawmakers and experts at witnessing did not prevent the violent destruction of the camp or the changing of policy in the UK government. For all the excellent, heartfelt, and expert witness speeches, the efforts were frustrated again and again. When some children were resettled, the press seized upon this as an opportunity to take photographs and question the age of the minors. More experts – dentists, paediatricians, teachers – were brought in to speak into a fraught public debate, that has lost all semblance of having ethical bearings.

Bearings. Bearing. One of things that happens in bearing witness to the treatment of people seeking asylum is that you lose you bearings. The laws you grew up with in Europe, the conventions and articles protecting freedom of movement and the right to claim asylum have been so chopped about with so-called arrangements for burden-sharing, and Dublin conventions, and the movement and fixing of certain bodies in certain places, preferably on the peripheries of Europe, that it's hard to trust to the Rule of Law and the International Articles in the long term, even though there is ample evidence that they have helped save lives and are one of our most reliable instruments of justice. There is a look about us, those of us who have been here for a long time, bearing with this, bearing this – allies and refugee actors alike – a grim and often smiling knowing that helps with the shouldering of the load.

5. Coda: The tradition of bearing

In the Western tradition, there is a story of a man who was pulled out of a crowd at a trial and execution and asked, when the prisoner was too weak, to carry his burden. It's a story which has entered into language in the idiom of resilience, and of distress: 'carry your cross'.

Friday – Hearkening

The story tells us
he was from a big city some distance away
and he was there;
and he did not say I cannot carry this
and he did not say I do not want the skelfs in my skin
and he did not say I do not have the strength
and he did not say I don't want to do this
and he did not say I will not travel with you
and he did not say I am afraid
and he did not say that the wood was sticky with your blood
and he did not say I despise you
and he did not say I do not want your shame upon my back
and he did not say he would not dig deep to find the strength
and he did not say his own suffering was great too
and he did not point first to his own burden
and he did not say that this was far too messy
and he did not say he was too good for the task
and he did not argue
and he did not ask why
and he did not say I do not want your suffering near me
and he did not say his kind did not help your kind
and he did not say that you should say sorry
and he did not say that you should be more careful
and he did not judge
and he did not hide his name
and he did not hide his home
and his name was Simon,
meaning hearkening, listening
and he was there

and he walked the way
and he carried it for a while.
And he was there.
And that is the story.
And that is all.

Bibliography

Arendt, H. (1943): We Refugees. In: Menorah Journal 31(1), 69–77.
Butler, J. (2011): Precarious Life: The Obligations of Proximity. Neale Wheeler Watson Lecture. 24 May. Nobel Museum, Svenska Akademiens Börssal.
Choo, A. (2015): Evidence. Oxford, Oxford University Press.
Dennis, I. H. (2017): The Law of Evidence. London: Sweet & Maxwell.
Haraway, D. (2016): Staying with the Trouble: Making Kin in the Chrhulucene. Durham: Duke University Press.
Irigaray, L. (1994): Thinking the Difference: For a Peaceful Revolution. London: Athlone.
Le Guin, U. (1994): Crossing Back from the Silence. In: J. White (ed.): Talking on the Water: Conversations about Nature and Creativity. San Franscisco: Sierra Club Books.
McFague, S. (1975): Speaking in Parables: A study in Metaphor and Theology. London: SCM Press.
Myers, A. (2016): Nothing Is Impossible Under the Sun. Sweden/Scotland: Sound of a Picture.
Phipps, A. (2017): Why Cultural Work with Refugees? E.P.C.o.C.a. Education. Brussels, European Union.
Piacentini, T. (2014): Missing from the Picture? Migrant and Refugee Community Organizations' Responses to Poverty and Destitution in Glasgow. In: Community Development Journal.
Scarry, E. (2010): Rule of Law, Misrule of Men. Boston: MIT Press.
Sontag, S. (2004): Regarding the Pain of Others. New York: Picador.
Turner, V. (1995): The Ritual Process: Structure and Anti-Structure. New York: De Gruyter.

Yahya Al-Abdullah

De-integration of young Syrian activists in Paris

Abstract: The brutality of Syrian's governing regime since the start of the conflict and the widespread culture of surveillance that has emerged as a consequence has succeeded in pushing most of the country's young activists out. Most of those who left in the early years went to neighbouring countries, believing that they could work more effectively from these places and return easily upon the conflict's conclusion. There was a widespread belief that the conflict would not last long. This was not the case and as the situation worsened, the dream of temporary displacement started to vanish and more and more activists began leaving and heading west, mainly to Europe, to look for a better place to continue their struggle. Haunted by old memories of their revolution, some could not think about what might be next. Futures were difficult to imagine. Their struggles became hindered by the lack of language to communicate and some began to realise that their voices were changing as a result. Many are now trying to reconnect with themselves and rediscover their voices, but the process is difficult because in their new surroundings, things are very different – odours are unusual and the cities move differently. These factors make life tough, and many young Syrian activists find themselves confined to marginal spaces, groups with other Syrians, who may share the same struggle but not the same vision.

This chapter is my reflection on a documentary film project that tries to capture the small repetitive details of the lives of young Syrian activists exiled in Paris. The first stage of the project is in Paris and the second might be in Berlin. Although migration and integration policies are at the core of the discussions and of the debates about the new lives of the young activists, the film project presents them as occupying an important space in the background, a looming and imposing backdrop, rather than as front and centre issues.

1. Introduction

In the summer of 2017, I arrived in Paris for a week of fieldwork research in relation to a higher education access project that I was involved with. During my planning for that week, I came across a post on a Syrian activist's Facebook group that mentioned an interactive street performance in Paris. The idea of the performance was to commemorate the fourth anniversary of the chemical attacks on Ghouta, Dam-

https://doi.org/10.1515/9783110628746-003

ascus, in August 2013 by the Assad regime. The rehearsals were starting the same week that I was supposed to be in Paris, so I contacted the group and I joined them when I arrived. Meeting this Syrian activists' group inspired me to extend my stay in Paris for another week. I was maybe drawn to it because when I lived in Budapest for almost two years, from September 2015 to July 2017, this kind of Syrian community was missing. Although I trained myself to deal with my homesickness, the fact that I was able to join this group brought my home back to me and made me want to stay to make a documentary about the everyday life and experiences of the young Syrian exiled activists.

I left Paris to go to Beirut to continue my fieldwork there, but the idea of returning to Paris for the film project never left me. The changes one experiences in the context of forced displacement are significant and need to be highlighted. Miraftab says, 'Telling the story of migration without its interwoven stories of displacement offers not only an incomplete but also an inaccurate picture. As the saying goes, "half the truth is a lie"' (2014). Being a graduate from the School of Public Policy at Central European University in Budapest with an interest in migration policies made me anchor integration policies in the heart of my film project. My personal choice of the subject is because I believe that most of the young exiled political activists go through distinct migration and exile experiences. These experiences form a large outlier of the subjects of immigration and integration policies, which is why we need to consider them when thinking about immigration and integration policies. If we consider the integration policies for migrants in France, for example, we realise quickly that they are following the 'one size fits all' model.[1] This policy is exclusive when it should be as inclusive and comprehensive as possible to accommodate the needs of refugees and asylum seekers. It is important to keep in mind that comprehensive policies require new creative policy methods that in turn require spending time with the people directly affected by the policies so that understanding of the background of their migration may be expanded and incorporated. A reconsideration of the approach to designing and implementing migration and integration policies is needed urgently.

This paper is based on my experience of six months of filming in Paris as part of a longer documentary film project covering the everyday lives and experiences of a group of young Syrian political activists who were granted political refugee status in France due to their active engagement in the Syrian uprising in March 2011. The film is an ethnographic work documenting the impact of the conflict and exile on how people interact with the administrative system and

1 See Algan/Landais/Senik (2012).

their administrative statuses as asylum seeker, refugee, or person under temporary protection. This chapter is about the specific experiences of the activists who are part of the film project and includes my observations and reflections on my active participation. I discuss three important aspects that are often excluded from the considerations of policy makers: voice, language, and memory.

It is also important to mention my position in this project as a filmmaker, a young exiled Syrian activist, and above all a friend to all the participants in the project. This means that my contribution goes beyond the limits of ethnographic methodological tools but definitely keeps me aware of and alert to the different roles I am performing.

2. Voice

> In exile, I had to reinvent and re-encounter my voice. Sometimes, I just do not recognise it. It is completely different to me. Once I made my decision to leave Syria for the second time after my short stay in Turkey and return to Syria, I knew that my voice was left behind. (Informant A, January 2018)

If we have a quick look at the definition of voice in the *Oxford English Dictionary*, two main aspects are highlighted: the sounds produced by our vocal organs but, more importantly, the meaning of voice to one's identity. This notion of treating the sonic aspect of the voice as secondary importance compared to the identity aspect is assumed by Locke and Rousseau who focus on the voice as presence, authenticity, agency, rationality, will, and self (Weidman 2016). In this regard, I would like to add two other dimensions to the meaning of voice as a part of who we are. The first is related to the socio-linguistic understanding of what people receive of the voice as a metaphor in Arabic in general and in the Syrian context in particular. The second is the impact of exile on voice, especially for political refugees.

Voice in Arabic has many metaphorical uses. 'We have not heard your voice' is an expression used to say that someone was present only in the physical sense and lacked a strong and influential opinion. 'Who did you give your voice to?' is a very political expression that means who you voted for. And one last expression to mention here is 'I want to give him/her my voice', which means I want this person to represent me. In this expression voice stands clearly for what one believes in and the person who I want to be my representative because she/he echoes my beliefs. The list of expressions can go on, but I would like to narrow it down to focus on the Syrian context.

In March 2011, many Syrians broke the silence that had been imposed on them by a dictator regime for more than forty years. The Syrian regime was following dictatorship 101 in Syria since Hafez al-Assad took over the country in a military coup in 1971. Assad managed to slowly push out the other significant members of the Ba'ath Party and introduce the official rhetoric of the political sphere in the country (Wedeen 1999). In addition, to strengthen its base and secure its rule, the regime followed a strict policy of surveilling and silencing the prominent voices in the country.

In 1979, the Assad regime crushed a movement that was led by the workers' union and syndicates, which constituted the middle-class intellect in the country, a movement that is considered by Michel Seurat to be the climax of the civic mobilisation in Syria (Seurat 2012). This barbarian act paralysed the political civic opposition in the country. Also, in 1982, after crushing the Muslim Brotherhood uprising, the Assad regime started an era of emergency law that legitimised its brutal practice of arresting people and executing opponents without consequence or fear of being accountable for its deeds. In other words, for almost thirty years, Assad senior managed to establish a culture of political silence and silencing that made everyone fearful of having any kind of voice, even in the company of close friends and relatives. People hushed each other when someone mentioned politics and 'the walls have ears' became a standard warning expression used to avoid voicing one's political opinion. In fact, one of the informants I have been working with describes it this way:

> In more than thirty years, what Assad regime managed to do steal our voices, or the voice of our consciousness if you like. It left us either voiceless or as people who are not in eternal harmony with their own voices. When we managed to free our voices from their imprisonment in 2011, we simply felt alive again! (Informant B, March 2018)

One of the main intrigues that led me to work on the project is that the informants I have been working with insist that what has been happening in Syria since March 2011 is still a revolution. The main argument they use is the regaining of a lost voice. The metaphor of 'breaking the shackles of silence', which is used by young Syrian activists, is an explicit reference to the liberation of the voice. Voice that has stood, bravely facing the machine guns, the tanks, the arrests and torture of the dictator and his criminal regime. When people took to the streets in peaceful demonstrations, the most notable thing about them was that people never stopped chanting. The demonstrations were not silent with banners that had demands. The demands of the protesters were mainly shouted out loud. The call to topple a dictator and for the opportunity to live dignified lives under a political system that respects personal freedom and democratic principles kept circulating and was sung by those young activists:

Ash-sha'ab Yureed Isqat an-nizam (People want to topple the regime).
Yallah Irhal Ya Bashar (Come on, leave now Bashar).
Suriya Badda Huriya (Syria wants freedom).

It is important to highlight that most of those young activists did not experience the brutality of Assad's father first-hand. The barbarian practices the father carried out in the 1970s and 1980s were never mentioned in public nor were they widely documented. Only a few young Syrians had access to primary sources that documented the crimes. However, the politics of silencing was present and emphasised in the reign of the father and his son. When young activists started organising and leading public protests, there was a thrilling moment of meeting with their voices. They used their voices to sing for freedom and to chant for universal and basic human rights. I argue that the feeling of empowerment went beyond the border of their homeland because of the revolutionary attitude that everyone was embodying. Making a statement against French police brutality and participating in demonstrations to support the workers' struggle in France has always been explained by many Syrian activists by saying, 'We have not started a revolution in Syria to accept seeing these corrupted practices anywhere in the world'. Unfortunately, the cathartic feeling of owning a voice in Syria did not last long and was disrupted by the deafening noise of shelling, all kinds of explosives, and barrel bombs.

The imagined liberal west as a defender of human rights and civil liberties stood as the perfect place for these activists to continue their struggle. Most of them managed to find a way to Europe. While Berlin attracted many activists, the French authorities were giving visas to many artists and activists in Lebanon, Jordan, and Turkey. A significant number of those ended up in Paris – the symbolic heart of arts, revolution, and liberty. Some of those activists continued embracing the voice they met in their revolution and took to the Parisian streets and public squares. However, their voices started to fade slowly, and they came face to face with two elephants in the small room. The first was the complicated administrative system that follows the Napoleonic logic of fairness, which is 'one rule fits all'. The second was the language. Most of the activists did not speak French fluently, and given their struggle learning this new language was an additional burden.

In October 2016, I wrote the following lines to describe the slow process of losing the voice and becoming 'voiceless':

Voice tripped in the rise's carter.
It elevated to the bottom of the well.
The well is behind the mountain.
The mountain is in the middle of the desert.

The desert is ascended by the storm's pollen.
In a brutal weather of winter.

3. Language

> To learn how to speak a language to be able to communicate with others might take you a year or so, but to have to learn a language because you are dealing with a new identity in a new place puts a lot of pressure on you. I have been unable to concentrate about learning the language because I just wanted to be able to explain myself and tell the story of our revolution right away! (Informant C, March 2018)

Language courses are the main component of the integration contract refugees sign with the country that grants them official asylum in Europe. There is a special governmental institution known as the l'Office français de l'immigration et de l'intégration (OFII) in France. This office is responsible for the free language courses. I had the chance to take some of these classes, and this was my experience.

I was assigned to a class that meets once a week for eight hours. The number of the students was around twenty. They all came from different age groups and literacy backgrounds. The teacher of the class was using a literacy course book and a very strict formal form of French. The teacher used the imperative most of the time, when addressing the students, and she rejected responses from the students if they made even the slightest pronunciation mistake by saying non-directly to them. I was unluckily misplaced in this class because I already finished my A1 course while waiting for my assignment from the OFII. While sitting there in the class, I noticed that the students were unable to follow the French instructions and had developed some sort of classroom anxiety because they were not able to understand or produce sentences in French. Having a background in foreign language teaching, I thought I would talk to the teacher about the methodology she is using in the class. When I tried to tell her how the students were unable to follow, she kept correcting my pronunciation mistakes and pointing out that I could not speak French.

Several times the teacher spent more than half an hour to get the students to learn how to say 'What is your name?' and by the end of the activity only three or four would be able to understand what the task was and perform it. One of the most frequent responses the teacher used was 'This is France and you should speak French. The old times are over. You have to have all your papers and speak French or just leave'. What I found ironic was the fact that she was saying this in a language course designed to integrate refugees. The other shocking aspect is that even with the language courses, a 'one size fits all' approach is applied but is clearly inefficient. To give you an idea of the bigger picture, I started telling all my Syrian friends and other refugees that I was starting the OFII language course and asking them how their experiences were. The response I most often received was, 'Good luck!'

In fact, the OFII language courses are designed mainly to integrate refugees with the administrative system. The teacher's main argument for being strict on having us perfect the language was that once we started our new life in France, we needed to take care of our documents and get the required papers from the different governmental institutions. Given this responsibility, we should be able to say things in the perfect way to get our papers done. The first institution refugees have to deal with is the local prefecture of the police, so there is a need to adjust to the language used there.

The focus was on understanding the language of the civil servants. Normally, it is very formal and includes a lot of administrative jargon that can be difficult even for French people. We know this because it is a common response from the French people we know who are willing to help us fill in forms or file documents. There are no available translators in the prefecture of the police or immigration department, which makes things even more complicated for the new arrivals. In fact, there is a 'second-class' French that is used by the functionaries when addressing the refugees and the asylum seekers (Al-Zahre 2016). It seems to resemble the broken form of English that Robinson Crusoe describes his slave Friday as having used: half sentences, fragmented sentences without a verb, and sometimes replacing 'who' by 'what'. Here are some of the examples in French:

> « Et tenez vos enfants ! Asseyez-vous ! Pas de bruit ! Éteignez vos téléphones ! » Une sorte de sabir fragmenté commence à se propager dans la salle et aux guichets : « Vous... Enfants... Pays ? » Combien d'interpres chôment en ce moment ? « Ami parler français ? » (Al-Zahre 2016)

In fact, speaking of language is not to be taken as a complementary need. Taking care with language is essential in the context of political exile. Most of the exiled Syrian activists I have been talking to expressed frustration that they have not been able to feel satisfied with the level of French they have achieved. This feeling is twinned with pressure linked to the duty they feel they have to continue talking and explaining their struggle and giving voices to the voiceless. The danger is that they are mainly becoming wordless or do not have enough words on top of survivor's guilt. It was demonstrated perfectly during one of the conversations I had with a group of friends at a French dinner party with Syrian food:

> We came here to complete what we started in Syria. We wanted to tell everyone about our revolution. What we ended up with so far is trying to convince the employee at the Revenu de Solidarité Active (RSA) office that we cannot get a birth certificate from the Syrian political representation office in Paris. Of course the employee is not interested in the 'why' as his/her main interest is the 'what'. And look at us now, we are in a dinner party with a group of French friends. They have their corner and we have ours. Language is absolutely missing. (Informant D, February 2018)

4. Memory

> People are the children of their own memories. As one cannot imagine that the children will be able to overcome the destruction of their homes and the experience of living in a tent or taking a boat to come to Europe, we will not be able to overcome the moments we lived in the revolution, the struggles we had, and the comrades we lost. This is the memory we cling to the most. (Informant E, November 2017)

The Syrian conflict is extremely well documented because of the numerous photos, reports, and videos that are available online since it started as a popular revolution in March 2011 (Roca 2017). This raises some interesting questions about the kind of collective memory an exiled group takes and cherishes. Many Syrians switched to social media to find solitude or a place to be with friends, family, and the selective memories they want to activate. The switch to technology in such a context is noted in Wulf Kansteiner's work: 'as "memory experts" we can explore the social impact of rapidly evolving communication technologies and the uncertainties of collective belonging after the end of the Cold War, and the challenges of coming to terms with war and genocide' (2002).

This urge to cling to a specific memory comes with questions that may be related to the Durkheimian concept of 'collective memory' and its development to 'materiality of memory' by his student Maurice Halbwachs. These concepts are essential to understanding the meaning of the past in how it has been characterised by instability, disorganisation, and non-specialisation. In the case of my film project, the memory in exile has many connections with the virtual input and the virtual spaces that have been created after fleeing Syria. This virtualised memory, as I call it, offers a very interesting window into how young Syrian activists experience exile. Throughout my fieldwork, and the continuous filming process, I observed that the working memory of my friends has become very selective and very vibrant. Most of the friends I have been filming emphasise and recall many memories from the last seven years of their lives. These memories are taking up the most space in their everyday communications. They are also being reproduced virtually and shared in social networks. It is important to highlight that for most of the young Syrian activists, the revolution has been the milestone of their lives that had made the biggest impact on them both as individuals and as members of a community of like-minded people who crave change.

The continuous toil of one's working memory might lead to side effects in the other parts of one's memory at large. That is to say, the work of the instant memory and the long-term memory could be impacted. I observed that the attention span of most of my friends is short and most of them have developed a short temper. When things take a long time, they can lose their patience or their concentration. I think that more questions need to be asked about this and that research is needed on the impact that exiled working memory has on concentration and on the long-term memory. What gets blocked and what gets activated? As I am not a collective memory scholar, I would rather share the experience of two young exiled Syrian painters in France and their work on memory. These two painters are Reem Yassouf, a friend and a participant in the film, and Najah al-Bukai, a friend who has a strong first-hand experience in the political prison in Syria.

4.1. Doing the small part

Speaking about living in memories and how 'our' memories have shifted in a way that Reem Yassouf would describe as moving 'from the individual to the collective' were the first topics I discussed with Reem during one of our projects together in Paris. She started her project 'Pre-Bedtime Stories' in 2016 to capture the very delicate memories people wanted to share with her in her paintings. Reem said that in her project she wanted to put the questions out there because they are not only her questions anymore. The work she was experimenting with while in Syria involved treating herself as the main subject of wonder but this is not viable for her to do now. Her work became a collective quest full of questions and memories of people who wanted to share their specific memories with her. Being the artist, she then mixes all these memories together in an attempt to create a story. These stories are mostly about people who are doing several lively and detailed daily activities, mainly in the nude. Most of them look similar to each other as they do not have eyes, ears, or mouths. If paintings could be translated into words, they would likely take us back to the previous point made about the language in which people lose as much of themselves when they find themselves exiled in a new place and where the creation of a common space and use of a collective memory become a necessity. As for nudity, it could be an explicit reference to vulnerability in exile.

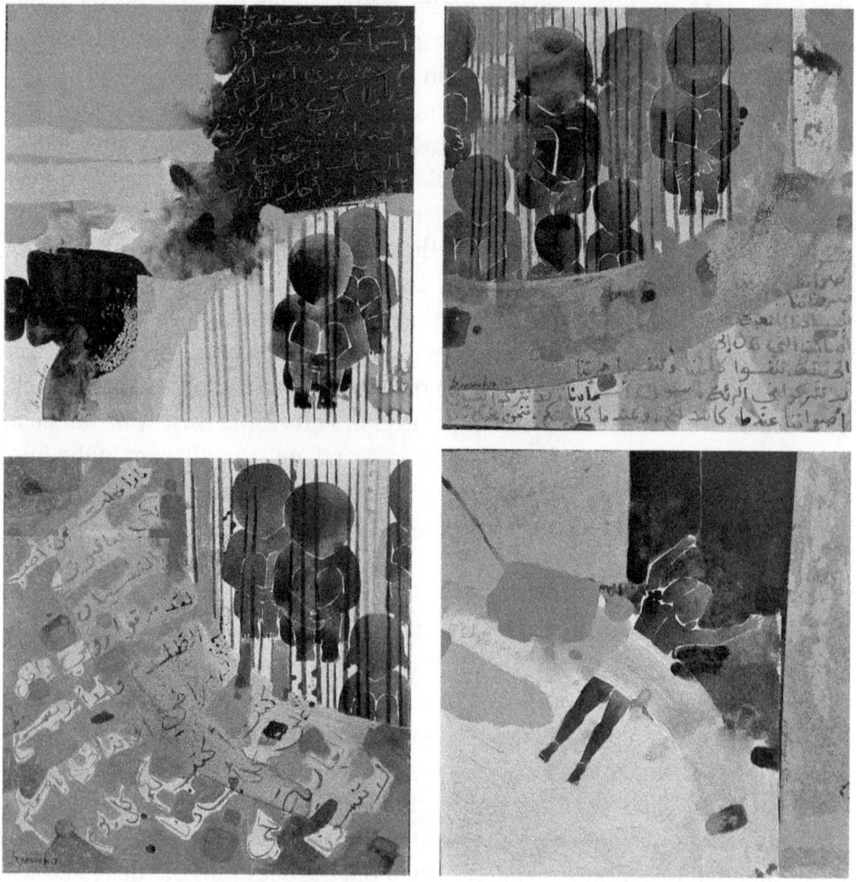

Figures 1–4: 'Siege'. Images included by permission of the artist, Reem Yassouf

The stories that started to have life in them would not really hold and continue in the expected 'normal' direction – people having everyday life activities and starting a new life. Memory led the lines in the paintings in the direction of the survivor's guilt. One can quickly notice that the people in the paintings are not enjoying the daily 'normal' activities they are involved in. The artist could not change the theme of her work on memory right away but switched into another project about memory with a different conduct. The memory work shifted to talk about the memories that some people were struggling to forget, and the artwork that emerged serves as a reminder for everyone, not only for the exiled Syrians, to remember the detainees and their daily struggle. The example of 'Siege', Reem's second project about memory, brings to light just how complicated the work of memory in exile is and how interrelated it is with the psychological status not only of the artist but also of the exiled community. The artist was able to depict survivor's guilt through image and text with the ones who made it to France and gives us a glimpse of the experiences that some of those exiled had lived through in prison back in Syria. Reem also urges 'Us', as humans, not to forget 'Them' and to keep them in our memory because they deserve to be free and they deserve to live just like 'Us'. In this narrative, 'Us' refers both to the survivors and other humans everywhere.

When I asked her about 'Siege' in one of her exhibitions, she explained that she was haunted by the images of the detainees and prisoners in Syria, and that, like most exiled Syrians, she still has friends who are imprisoned for their political views. The idea that people might forget about them is disturbing for her. When asked about how she chose the text, she responded, 'It was an improvised text. I wrote it while I was painting and the next day I needed someone to help me read what I wrote. I remember writing it but I have no memory of what I was writing'.

The original text is in Arabic but this is my personal translation:

1 – "What did I do to the ones I love to punish me with forgetting!
They shattered my soul inside the obscure darkness
And nobody can hear neither my screams nor my appeals.
I was writing your name on our naked bodies every day we pass here
So, you do not forget us.
2 – Breathe our voices and breathe our screams.
Breathe our exhausted bodies, our fingers that points to the truth.
Breathe our dignity and breathe our freedom.
Do not leave in the lungs other than our names and
Do not leave but our voices in your lungs because once it was yours,
Once we were amongst you because we love you.
3 – I have hidden the shapes that construct your names under my skin
And I planted the first letter of the echoes of your voices in my memory
And in the memory of the walls of the prison of my freedom.
The wolves are chasing me, chasing all my days and
Chasing all my dreams.
4 – I won't be afraid anymore, neither of myself
nor from your desertion.
I won't be afraid of my own death because my body will die
But my soul is remaining,
Remaining to protect my children of your evil and your fear.

4.2. Art as therapy for a wounded memory

I want to talk about the experience of a Syrian artist who survived imprisonment by the Assad regime and managed to be smuggled to Lebanon before finally getting asylum in France. Najah al-Bukai is a Syrian artist with a vivid photographic memory. In his second arrest for participating in the Syrian revolution against the regime, Mr. al-Bukai was tortured and forced to see the torture of others. Once inside the prison, or hell as he calls it, he 'forced himself to not see nightmare. Instead, [he] forced [himself] to see beautiful dreams.' (Alami 2018). As difficult as it seems, Mr. al-Bukai became an 'exemplary witness' who has had a 'transformative experience' (Foucault 1978–1979) and who has changed all the physical and mental torture he went through into activist art.

In his work after he left Syria, the artist committed himself to drawing all of the pictures he saw during his time in prison. He considers this 'personal therapy'. Also, his main fight now is to raise awareness about the political prisoners in Syria and how important it is not to forget about them. Here is a sample of his recent work:

Figures 5–8: Images included by permission of the artist, Najah al-Bukai

This unique experience sheds light on a very important and sensitive point about the psychological scars caused by political violence and torture, or as Derrida puts it, 'the crisis of globalisation for psychoanalysis' (Derrida 2000). The artist also shifted in his work from experimenting with self-portraits before the Syrian revolution to powerful images of torture and humiliation through fading features and blurred huddling bodies. This brings us back to the main theme of the book, global and individual responsibility.

The artist here feels an urge, or rather a duty, by the memories that haunt him and images that he experienced and lived. This urge comes mainly from his feeling as an individual who belongs to his individual humanity in the first place and to Humanity at large. Unfortunately, however, they keep coming back because they are part of who he is and what he does – an artist with a duty to reflect and an urge to share. In this regard, it is difficult to imagine that this is a case study and other people who went through torture and political violence will not go through a similar path, especially when we know that most of the Syrian exiled activists went through imprisonment, detention, or at least besiegement. The importance of dealing with these kinds of memory wounds and scars because of how sensitive they are is emphasised through the work of a very small number of centres in France (Sandlarz 2014).

5. Conclusion and Recommendations

Looking at the current situation for a significant number of Syrian refugees in France, especially the political activists, one can see that the integration policies have some problems and do not meet the needs of the exiled. The question of whether there is a problem with the policies and with the beneficiaries is unhelpful because we cannot expect policies that were designed to correspond to the Second World War migration influx to be compatible with the new migration narratives. It is also important to highlight the diversity of the Syrian migrants who arrive in Europe in general and in France in particular.

It is clear that the change of the voice among the activists is not being considered, especially after being granted a special visa by the French authorities to come to France and seek asylum in the land of revolution and liberty. This shift in the voice coupled with the lack of proper language programs led to many of the activists becoming almost voiceless and unable to communicate their own personal stories. In other words, the exile is playing a double role of stripping the exiled of recognition of what they went through and leaving people trapped with a very selective kind of memory that is not easy to deal with and, again, is not accommodated within the integration policies. With this vicious enclosed cycle, the potentiality of excluding a young active generation and pushing it to the margins, leaving it voiceless, is inevitable and requires a serious and sincere set of integration policies.

The exemplary integration practices came as local or NGOed initiatives. Some associations and start-ups, along with some universities in France, began programs to integrate refugees and exiled people in France. Examples such as Je veux parler français (JRS, France), Wintegreat (start-up), and Étudiants exilés (EHESS) have been far more helpful than the official integration public policies of the state. The need for policies to adapt and go beyond the classical realm of policy making is important. I would like to share some of the policy recommendations that are based on my fieldwork and filming experience in the process of making the documentary. It is important to emphasise that there is a need for creative policies, both in terms of crafting and implementing them.

- The need for reception centres to give space to the young activists to tell their stories and listen to the stories of other young people in exile is very important. This could play the role of assessing their personal voice, giving recognition to their personal history, and above all, documenting a toxic period of time in places that have either been destroyed in the conflict or have experienced a dramatic demographic change.
- Specialised language courses that correspond to the diverse levels and backgrounds of the exiled are needed. The courses of OFII are inefficient. There are plenty of local initiatives led by a number of organisations that can be used as successful examples.
- Psychological support is needed for those who have been imprisoned, experienced torture, and/or have had people they know go through these things. The issue is delicate and requires working with specialists. Centres like Primo Levi in Paris are important but they are not enough.
- Political integration courses that explain European politics in general and the French politics in particular would help to bridge language learning gaps, motivate the exiled to reactivate their political work for Syria, and help prevent social and political exclusion from French society.

Bibliography

Alami, Aida (2018): Haunted by Memories of Syrian Torture, Saved by Art. In The New Yorker. February 2. https://nyti.ms/2BQbg8W.

Algan, Yann/Landais, Camilla/Senik, Clauida (2012): Cultural integration in France. In: Yann Algan et al. (eds.): Cultural Integration of Immigrants in Europe. Oxford: Oxford University Press.

Al-Zahre, Nisrine (2016): Tu nu, la tête haut. In: Esprit July–August(7), 112–115.

Derrida, Jacques (2000): États d'âme de la psychanalyse: Adresse aux états généraux de la psychanalyse. Paris: Galilée.

Foucault, Michel (1978–79): Naissance du biopolitique. Cours au collège de France. Paris: EHESS, Gallimard, Le Seuil, 2004.

Halbwachs, Maurice (1925): Les Cadres sociaux de la memoire. Paris: Alcan.

Kansteiner, Wulf (2002): Finding Meaning in Memory: A Methodological Critique of Collective Memory Studies. Middletown: Wesleyan University.

Locke, John (1959 [1690]): An Essay Concerning Human Understanding. 2 vols. New York: Dover.

Miraftab, Faranak (2014): Framing the Global: Entry Points for the Search. In: Hilary Kahn (ed.): Displacement: Framing the Global Relationality. Bloomington: Indiana University Press.

Roca, Christina (2017): Long Read: How the Syrian War Changed How War Crimes Are Documented. In: NewsDeeply, June 1. https://bit.ly/2sGUPYy (last accessed August 2018).

Rousseau, Jean-Jacques. (1990 [1781]): Essay on the Origin of Languages and Writings Related to Music. In: Roger Masters and Christopher Kelly (eds.): The Collected Writings of Rousseau, vol. 7. Hanover: University Press of New England.

Sandlarz, Eric (2014): Le Psychanalyste Face à la Cruauté. La Douleur Dans la Peau. La Clinique Lacanienne 1(25), 189–208.

Seurat, Michel (2017): Syrie: L'Etat De Barbarie. Proche Orient. Paris: Presses Universitaires de France.

Wedeen, Lisa. (1999): Ambiguities of Domination. Chicago: University of Chicago Press.

Weidman, Amanda (2016): Echo and Anthem: Representing Sound, Music, and Difference in Two Colonial Modern Novels. In: Ronald Radano and Tejumola Olaniyan (eds.): Audible Empire: Music, Global Politics, Critique. Durham: Duke University Press.

Debora B. F. Kayembe

Understanding the challenges of integration from the refugee perspective

Abstract: The challenges associated with refugee and asylum seeker resettlement are complex and multifaceted. This chapter offers case reports and insights regarding the complexities of integration by exploring how some of the policies directed at facilitating this actually fall short because of basic communication barriers. More attention needs to be paid to how well refugees understand the cultures of the new societies in which they are expected to settle. Drawing upon the first-hand experiences of an interpreter for Congolese refugees in Britain and the United States, this chapter identifies some of the major issues that confront people during the first year of their resettlement.

The United Nations 1951 Refugee Convention, Article 1.A.2, adopted the following definition of 'refugee' to apply to any person who,

> owing to well-founded fear of being persecuted for reasons of race, religion, nationality, membership of a particular social group or political opinion, is outside the country of his nationality and is unable or, owing to such fear, is unwilling to avail himself of the protection of that country; or who, not having a nationality and being outside the country of his former habitual residence as a result of such events, is unable or, owing to such fear, is unwilling to return to it.

Since the Arab Spring – widely considered the Arab revolution, which was a wave of both violent and non-violent demonstrations, protests, riots, coups, foreign interventions, and civil wars in North Africa and the Middle East that began on December 18, 2010, in Tunisia with the Tunisian Revolution – the world has witnessed an unprecedented movement of refugees to Europe that has resulted in a reception crisis. Thousands of refugees cross the Mediterranean Sea and attempt to settle in more secure places.

Arrival in a host country does not always mean a warm welcome. From refugees' perspectives, a great deal is expected from newcomers. Ideally, settlement is the time to rest, recover, and make choices. Some refugees manage to make it to the place of their choice, some do not, and those most unfortunate end up in detention centres or face deportation to their homeland, depending on the host country's immigration policies.

https://doi.org/10.1515/9783110628746-004

Barriers and practicalities confront any individual who chooses to move from one country to another. Often, asylum seekers and refugees leave their own countries in panicked situations and have to leave everything behind, without an opportunity to plan ahead. Many of them do not know where their journey will take them. When they arrive in a new country, they encounter numerous obstacles that make understanding the integration process difficult. Migration within the Global North seems to be less challenging for people than it does for those arriving in the north from Global South countries. Since there are usually gaps in the living standards, work opportunities, and educational levels between citizens of different countries, resettlement comes with challenges. The process is further complicated by the immigration policies of the host country that are applied upon arrival. The immigration authorities of the country of asylum determine whether or not the asylum seeker will be granted protection and become an officially recognised resident. If asylum is refused, the person will become an illegal immigrant who may face deportation.

For the purposes of this discussion, I want to highlight some of the barriers and practicalities to refugees' lives once they are allowed to settle in the country of their reception. For many years, I have worked as an interpreter for refugees from East Africa in the United States and in the United Kingdom. Most of the refugees from this region who arrive in the United States, for example, through organised programmes are selected from refugee camps. Many who end up in Europe tend to find their own way there.

Consider the civil war in Syria. Ongoing since 2011, this conflict has caused a significant outpouring of refugees, both within the country and into neighbouring ones. In the states of first arrival – mainly Turkey, Lebanon, and Jordan – refugees are confronted with an extremely difficult situation and a lack of prospects. They are usually not granted regular status or work permits and have little access to educational institutions for their children. Although integration is a process of intermixing, which, in an ideal world, should support a society where there is a shared socio-economic and cultural life, from a refugee's perspective, integration with a host country requires great mental and/or physical effort and is a major test of a person's ability. In this context, it becomes important for members of the host society to recognise that all persons need to have something to do in order to strive forward.

Every country has its own policies on refugees and asylum seekers that govern settlement and these have a significant impact on how socio-economic integration and cultural integration occurs. Yet, there is also the question of responsibility that both the host countries and the refugees (including asylum seekers) take for ensuring that the policies work as they should. A new life in a host country places many expectations on refugees and often little thought is given to how much or how well refugees understand the society that they have been called upon to integrate with. While each country has its own systems, they all have some barriers in common such as discrimination, inequity, and segregation. Contributing to these common barriers is a lack of communication arising from refugees not understanding the local languages and the new systems. An inability to communicate segregates people and prevents integration. In most cases, it is difficult for a newcomer in a host county to adapt, even though some structures have been put in place to support them in their earliest days in the new country.

To illustrate this communication barrier, I want to share an experience from my book of interpretation cases (case reference 02/08 – 11.22 – 11.47, Mr Saidi, settled refugee in Washington DC). Mr Saidi, a male refugee born in the Democratic Republic of the Congo, aged seventy-four, was married to his second wife, aged thirty-four, with fourteen children from the two marriages. Originally a farmer in a small village in Kivu, he survived two Congolese civil wars and massacres following the Rwandan genocide, but lost his first wife. He had eight surviving children of marriage and with his second wife had another six children. Mr Saidi suffered from hypertension and diabetes. Having been a farmer, and because of his poor health, Mr Saidi was unable to secure a steady job in Washington, and what he could get was mostly short-term factory packing work.

I was present as an interpreter during his first medical assessment, Mr Saidi was not happy to be asked by a female nurse to put on a gown. He essentially said to me, 'Why do I need to be naked in front of my child?' Coming from a different culture, some of the questions the nurse asked of Mr Saidi were difficult for him to understand; some others came as a shock, such as 'Have you ever had sex with a man?' Later on, he was given a long list of medications that he needed to have filled at a pharmacy with no communication support. During my work with the hospital, it eventually came to light that Mr Saidi could not provide for his family, partly because of regular hospitalization arising from his inability to read his prescriptions and, as a result, to have them refilled. Also, Mr Saidi struggled with side effects consistent with allergies to the medication when he did take it, and he often ended up in crisis in the Emergency ward, where doctors would manage to save him. He was fortunate to be cared for by a former Doctors Without Borders physician who had good knowledge of administering modern medicine to people from countries where medical care was not as good as in the USA. For four months, Mr Saidi benefitted from the care of one experienced doctor and by me, the interpreter, who followed his medical appointments closely.

As an interpreter, I knew about the struggles that Mr Saidi faced because of his lack of understanding of modern medicine, his lack of English, and general culture shock. I was not aware of the financial difficulties he faced in taking care of his large family until the day I received a phone call to say that he had been admitted to hospital and was unconscious, probably suffering from misuse of his medications. At the time, and after being unable to locate Mr Saidi for months, I held an interpreting session with his wife, Mrs Saidi, to try to get the history. Unfortunately, it was not long until he was pronounced dead.

From the information I gathered from Mrs Saidi, I came to understand that because Mr Saidi had struggled to support his family, when he had heard from a fellow refugee that work was available in South Carolina, he moved there without his family. His medical records did not follow him, even though he suffered from chronic illness. Consequently, he was unable to take prescribed medications and was unable to refill his medications when they ran out. Furthermore, he could no longer benefit from being followed by a single physician or by an interpreter who knew his case. He must have struggled from a lack of familiar medical and social care in South Carolina.

There are important lessons to take away from this case. Mr Saidi spent most of his life working as a farmer. His wealth resided in being father to several children, who eventually would take care of his lands and properties that he had in eastern Congo. Mr Saidi had never attended school, and illiteracy was a barrier to understanding English in the host country. He was unaware of the difference in living standards in the US. He could not understand why he was getting payment from the US government to help his family buy food. During our interview, the state advisor and I spent a great deal of time trying to help him understand that he was not stealing from anyone and that it was his right to receive support from the state. The gaps in education and living standards between refugees and residents in the host countries are so great that newcomers are very sceptical about the unfamiliar aspects of the new life.

Mr Saidi and his family suffered greatly from the fact that he was unable to find suitable work and could not earn enough to provide for his family. To make matters worse, his health difficulties always resulted in being let go from any job he managed to find. After his eight months of free healthcare from the resettlement program expired, Mr Saidi was technically able to receive more free care through social security, but I did not know that and so could not tell him. His caseworker left him when his first free healthcare term expired, so he had to rely on the doctor who was taking care of him and who was very familiar with his symptoms. The doctor managed to teach Mr Saidi to contact the interpreting company and ask for one particular translator on the phone. All these arrangements were intended to make Mr Saidi's care run more smoothly. Yet, his financial and family situations were getting worse, unbeknownst to the rest of resettlement his team. It is clear that Mr Saidi's journey to America was not easy.

Indeed, it was probably one of the most challenging periods of his seventy-four years. I believe he might have fared better if he had been sent to a rural area in the southern United States rather than being sent to Washington D.C., where settlement in a modern industrial environment was difficult.

To make matters worse, he could not understand how to administer his own medication, and there was a lack of medical support and outreach services available when he moved to South Carolina. Within eight months, Mr Saidi had died as a result of mixing up his medications as well as being unable to refill his prescriptions at the pharmacy. I have worked as an interpreter in both the United States and the United Kingdom and there are refugee resettlement programs in both countries. In my experience, refugees who are settling in new countries are expected to make a contribution to the new country in one way or another. It feels like resettlement has more to do with how these individuals can contribute directly to the needs of the new country rather than allowing them to come to terms with their status as survivors of wars or violence, who need to find ways to physically and mentally recover. Very few of their needs are addressed. In some parts of the UK, refugees do not have to be treated by a fully qualified doctor. During my decade of work as a linguist there, I witnessed many interpreting sessions where refugees were seen by a nurse practitioner who admited to not understanding the symptoms that patients described. Prescriptions were always free, but only are for the cheapest drugs, which affects recovery times.

In the United States, refugees have free healthcare for eight months. Medicare and Medicaid are designed to help new refugees settle in and receive treatment if needed. During a food stamp and Medicaid interview, applicants are advised to have their medical needs evaluated and treated during these eight months. In practice, it is challenging for those who do not speak English or who have never had to deal with a healthcare system before.

Here is another case related to a pregnant woman (case reference 27/11–19.11–11.44, Feza, settled refugee in the UK, living in Bolton, northern England). Feza was a forty year old woman with six children. She had previously lived in the Congo, and she was in her seventh pregnancy while settling under the United Kingdom's refugee resettlement program. Her level of education was low; she could read and write in Swahili but did not understand any English. Her experience reveals how people's ways of life in other countries can often clash with what is 'normal' in a host country, and how refugees' understanding of a new environment can hinder settlement. Although the UK is known around the world for its free healthcare system, the National Health Service, and for dedicated midwives, Feza was unaware of any of this.

During her life in the Congo, she had managed to look after herself during all six of her pregnancies. Although she had had some stillborn children, she was quite confident that she would be capable of carrying out her seventh pregnancy without prenatal care. In the Democratic Republic of the Congo, healthcare is not expensive but many women choose to have their husband keep the money for other needs, such as paying children's school fees or saving to buy a home instead of prenatal care. Feza had never dealt with midwives during any of her previous pregnancies and so in the UK, she waited at home until she was ready to give birth before she presented herself to the midwives. I was called to assist as an interpreter during this first visit to help get a history of her family. Her first appointment with the midwife was likely to be the last, as she was due to give birth within six days. The midwife indicated that this was one of the most challenging cases of her career. Yet, Feza believed she had made the right decision and had prevented her family from spending money unnecessarily. She was unaware that maternity care is free in the UK and that it is considered unimaginable to give birth in the UK hospital without a midwife's care for a period of at least six weeks prior to the birth. In cases where this does not happen, the pregnancy is classed as high risk, which is more expensive to the National Health Service. The barriers to settlement in this case included lack of English and a lack of awareness of how the United Kingdom's health services operate. The process was very new and quite overwhelming, especially for Feza considering the number of midwife appointments and consults that there would be during a pregnancy. The Congolese cultures encourage women to hide their pregnancy, particularly when the family struggles financially. This is very different from the UK, where people share and often celebrate news of a pregnancy. From Feza's previous six pregnancies, she had never benefitted from carefully screened prenatal care. Although Feza could read and write in her own language, she did not receive much education to learn about the lives of others in other places.

In practice, it would be helpful to make sure that newcomers understand their health evaluation, the available services, and about how they need to interact with institutions or organisations that can support them. For refugees, there are often no equivalent programs where they come from. Informing them of what is available may offer a sense of inclusion and provide people with a sense of being welcome in a host country.

Another issue involves the need to understand the serious gaps that exist in levels of education because illiteracy, compounded with not knowing the dominant language of a host country, can hinder settlement greatly. It is important that the literacy and language levels of refugees are assessed and, where required, that those who need it are given the opportunity to learn the language of the host country to allow them to understand their new environment and the policies that regulate it.

People are led to believe that the world is working towards less racist policies at local levels, but in the context of refugees (and asylum seekers) this has not been my experience. While we need to recognise that a refugee's way of seeing the world after enduring tremendous trauma might be very different from perceptions in a host country, it is reasonable for them to expect compassion. Refugees need opportunities to participate in a dialogue and they need to be open-minded about how they might be perceived. There is a fundamental need for open and inclusive societies that offer refugees opportunities to be introduced to new cultures through non-judgemental inclusion.

Being a refugee in a host country is rather like finding refuge in your neighbour's home. Your neighbour will give you a bed and will probably provide food for you in the earliest days of your arrival but will soon expect you to contribute to their home as long as you stay. But it is also true that the refugee will settle much better if his or her host offers all the necessary help to become self-sufficient. Are there ways that a host country can help refugees overcome the challenges they will certainly face? Has teaching the new ways of living been provided to minimise additional tensions on refugees' lives?

These questions are important to answer, as migration, familiar to my own family, continues to be challenging. My grandmother married an immigrant from Namibia who settled in Zambia, and from that marriage my mother was born. Later on, for educational reasons, my mother moved to the Congo and married my father (a Congolese national). My grandmother used to say in Swahili – one of the elders' oldest proverbs – '*Dunia Duara*'. It means, 'Go wherever you go, you will still return to the same old place'. I thank you for reading this chapter, in peace.

Bibliography

Betts, Alexander (2018): What Europe Could Learn from the Way Africa Treats Refugees. In: *Guardian*. June 26, 2018. https://www.theguardian.com/commentisfree/2018/jun/26/europe-learn-africa-refugees-solutions.

Engler, Dr Marcus (2016): Germany in the Refugee Crisis: Backgrounds, Reactions and Challenges. Heinrich Böll Stiftung. https://pl.boell.org/en/2016/04/22/germany-refugee-crisis-background-reactions-and-challenges.

Barriers and challenges

Nasar Meer

The legacies of race and postcolonialism: Taking responsibility for migration

Abstract: Migration has long been a feature of human societies, in all their variety, even while migration acquires a qualitatively novel status in modernity amidst the organisation of populations according to nation-states. This chapter, consistent with the overall aim of the volume, discusses refugee integration in a way that can shed significant light on the potential and the limits of individual responsibility. It argues that what is key to understanding contemporary debates in Europe is how matters of race and the postcolonial legacies cast a long shadow, and that refugee receiving societies need to take responsibility for these issues rather than ignore them.

'It is hard to find a democratic or democratizing society these days that is not the site of some significant controversy over whether and how its institutions should better recognise the identities of cultural and disadvantaged minorities'. So declared Amy Gutmann (1994, 3) a quarter of a century ago. In the intervening period this trend has continued in debates concerning the separation of public and private spheres (Parekh 2000), the way in which a country's self-image is configured (Uberoi/Modood 2013), as well as in what either could be characterised as mundane or highly political questions of dietary or uniform changes in places of school and work. What all of these debates have in common is that majority groups need to recognise that expressions of common membership (e. g., citizenship or national identity) cannot ignore the internal plurality of societies that play host to 'difference'. As Benhabib (2002, vii) summarises,

> our contemporary condition is marked by the emergence of new forms of identity politics around the globe. The new forms complicate and increase centuries-old tensions between the universalistic principles ushered in by the American and French Revolutions and the particularities of nationality, ethnicity, gender, "race", and language.

Yet migration has always been a feature of human societies, in all their variety, even while migration acquires a qualitatively novel status in modernity amidst the reconfiguration of populations according to nation-states. This chapter, consistent with the overall aim of the volume, seeks to help understand refugee integration in a way that can shed significant light on the potential and the limits of individual responsibility. What is key to understanding contemporary debates

https://doi.org/10.1515/9783110628746-005

in Europe is how matters of race and the postcolonial legacies cast a long shadow, and that receiving societies need to take responsibility for these issues rather than ignore them. Indeed, an uneasy tension between the objectives of race equality and migration control often remains a characteristic of European approaches, including in the societies that we can broadly call 'postcolonial' (e.g., the UK, France, Germany, Belgium, Portugal, and Spain). It is an unsettled tension that periodically reveals itself, as most recently illustrated by the UK's recent 'Windrush scandal'. In this instance, a number of the children of black people who came to Britain from the Caribbean between 1948 and 1973, and who were legally entitled to live there, had their right to stay challenged. Many of those affected moved to the UK as Commonwealth Citizens before their birth countries became independent, and so for any number of reasons may not have applied for a British passport. Other European countries, with comparable colonial histories, face their own challenges. Since it has experience of significant postcolonial settlement, France has pursued a robust assimilationist strategy towards its former subjects from North Africa, wherein equality was understood as uniformity, and, until the beginning of this millennium after unification, post-war Germany maintained a 'returnist' approach, which categorised labour migrants as guest-workers (*Gastarbeiter*) who were expected to return to their country of origin. In this respect, the nature of social and political relations after colonialism continues to have implications long after their formal systems might have been discontinued. The idea of race, and the role of the postcolonial, thus continue to bear enormous relevance across contemporary societies witnessing migrant and refugee arrivals.

1. The role of race – past or present?

The developments described above occur in societies despite the general acceptance that race as an objective or 'real' category is fiction. Instead it is widely accepted that race is a social construction that nonetheless has very real implications and outcomes. In this respect race is a dynamic category. That is to say, racial categories change in response to the social and political contexts in which they are found, neither is permanently fixed across any given society or throughout a society's history. For example, in his study of what the idea of race means in America, Omi (2001, 244) concludes that its expression 'has been and probably always will be fluid and subject to multiple determinations. Race cannot be seen simply as an objective fact, nor treated as an independent variable.' This is one reason why the idea of race as objectively real is frequently derided today as a myth like the title of Montagu's 1942 book, *Man's Most Dan-*

gerous Myth, implies. Many academics therefore refer to it by presenting it in inverted commas in order to indicate that we are referring to a socially constructed category, based upon a problematic idea, instead of something that is self-evidently real in the world. Even those who do not repeat this practice agree with the thrust of the argument. This critical consensus, however, is relatively recent because for much of modernity race was deemed to be very real indeed.

Of course, race has an older pedigree than its modern usage may imply. In pre-modern societies, for example, Christian symbolism portrayed 'white' as synonymous with purity, which in turn was contrasted with 'black' impurity (Meer 2014). Yet a precise content to race was at best ambiguous, and was certainly distinct to how it later became known (Banton 1977). Among others, Michael Biddis (1979, 11) has charted the change in the meaning of race and observes that:

> Before 1800 race was used generally as a rough synonym for 'lineage'. But over the first half of the 19th century race assumed an additional sense that seemed, initially, tighter and more scientific. This usage was evident, at its simplest, in the growing conviction that there were a finite number of basic human types, each embodying a package of fixed and mental traits whose permanence could only be eroded by mixture with other stocks.

So there is here a historical evolution that needs to be understood; namely, how and in what ways in the periods following colonial encounters between the European and non-European populations, say from the late fifteenth and sixteenth centuries onwards, did race began to assume a powerful categorising role? This is an important context because the category was ascendant during a period in which an unprecedented number of entirely new populations entered the European consciousness (Gilroy 1993). The way this difference was understood and explained varied. For example, as well as making recourse to science, by the time the Atlantic slave trade was well under way, Christian theologians were seeking religious justification from the Bible for hierarchies between whiteness and blackness as a way of differentiating coloniser from colonised. This they did by pointing to the story of Canaan (Son of Ham) in the Book of Genesis (9:18–27), which told of a punishment to Canaan of servitude and blackness. This was important, as Garner (2011, 13) reminds us, because

> the frame of reference for educated Europeans until the Enlightenment was one in which: (i) the dominant idea about origins was that everyone was descended from Adam and Eve (*monogenesis*), and signs on the body were read as judgements of God, (ii) the idea of separate origins (*polygenesis*) was a minority one among biblical scholars, and responded to the obvious physical diversity of the human race.

Historically, therefore, racial classifications have been a reflection of prevailing power relations; and just as with theology, so it was the case with science. Walton and Caliendo (2011, 3) remind us of how, in 1684, French scientist François Bernier identified four groups of humans as 'Far Easterners', 'Europeans', 'blacks', and 'Lapps'. Developments in modes of classification were further coupled to what was understood as advancements in scientific inquiry, and so in 1775 five types of races were put forward by the German 'physiologist' Johann Friedrich Blumenbach. These comprised 'Caucasians' (Whites), 'Mongolians' (East Asians), 'Malayans' (South Asians), 'Negroids' (Black Africans), and 'Americans' (First Nations). Indeed, 'by the nineteenth century, there were dedicated searches for a universal definition of race that would be applicable across time and geographic location. Scientists went to work measuring bones and craniums in an attempt to justify racial distinctions on the basis of biology' (Walton/Caliendo 2011, 4). The consensus was that physical appearance was an indication of something deeper, including character and intelligence.

Some of the best known work from this period sought to give the idea of race more authority by mixing science with a revisionist theology, and this mixture was expressed in the work of Robert Knox's (1850) *Races of Men* and Comte Arthur de Gobineau's (1853) *Essay on the Inequality of Human Races*. Others from this period, such as Pieter Camper and Franz Joseph Gall, measured facial angles as indications of what they perceived to be 'stature', 'beauty', and 'intelligence'. Such works reflected and contributed to a mid-nineteenth-century concept of race that made four interrelated truth claims. First, both the physical appearance and social behaviour of individuals was an unalterable expression of biological type. So your race combined two categories, which might describe both your appearance and your character, to serve as your social identity. Second, cultural variation was determined by differences in biological type, the former reducible to the latter. Third, that biological variation was the origin of conflict between individuals and nations. Fourth, races were endowed with different capacities according to a hierarchy, which meant some such were inherently superior to others.

While comical from contemporary perspectives, this racial science was far from benign and affected individuals at intimate levels. Racial engineering in the eugenics movement, for example, was the selective 'breeding' of some humans and 'out-breeding' of others. The most obvious example of this was the Nazi aspiration for a 'Master Race' and the mass exterminations of human populations that did not correspond to an idealised 'Aryan' vision. At the time, racial science went hand in hand with nineteenth-century social Darwinism, especially that advanced in the work of Herbert Spencer, who insisted that 'lesser' races ought to be dominated by their more advanced European masters. Much of this discourse informed and provided intellectual justification for the scramble for Africa and other acts of colonial domination and exploitation by European powers. Indeed, some of the horrors of the Nazi death camps had been trialled earlier in Germany's African colonies with little outcry from other European powers. Germany was not unique in this regard. At the apex of its colonial power, before the First World War, Britain exercised a claim over a quarter of the planet's population. How could a small island in the North Sea have sustained such an expansive reign? The answer requires more than an audit of its military, especially its naval, capacities.

A better explanation rests in how the British Empire administered its rule through 'varying constitutional and political arrangements' across a range of territories, and which were 'connected by a diverse set of strategic, cultural or historical links, rather than by allegiance to Crown or mother country' alone (Krieger 2009, 590). One outcome of this was that even after decolonisation the implications of these 'interconnections lived on and in some ways intensified' (ibid., 191). The concept of postcolonialism thus takes in a number of debates but principally turns on the interaction between the political and cultural relationships forged, first, during colonialism and observed, second, in the aftermath of decolonisation. This is why the appellation 'post' can be misleading, for the challenge that postcolonial inquiry presents is not anchored in what happened *after* decolonisation, but instead on the form and content of colonialism, and its subsequent (indeed contemporary) implications.

Ashcroft et al. (1995, 2) maintain that 'all post-colonial societies are still subject in one way or another to overt or subtle forms of neocolonial domination, and independence has not solved this problem'. In support of this view they point to the repositories of elites that were created or elevated under colonialism, and that have renewed and reproduced themselves following independence. This is alongside how social cleavages and hierarchies constructed during colonialism have blossomed instead of being deconstructed. Each of these examples relate to the internal legacies of given colonial relations, to which we can add the external legacies of political and economic exploitation that continue to hinder opportunities for development. As a concept, therefore, there is a continuing dialogue between colonialism and postcolonialism, one that foregrounds

> issues of power and significance, and even of timing [e.g., why did some Western powers come to prominence at certain times] ... technologies of production and social control, of centres and margins: of metropolitan hubs like London and Paris, and peripheries and margins – like the colonies. (Hawley 2011, 195)

Knowing how one feature connects to the other, however, rests on understanding the relationship between knowledge, representation, and politics. Some scholars, for example, have argued that we should think in terms of the 'post-racial' nature of social and political conventions (cf. Parks/Hughey 2011; Kaplan 2011), something perhaps symbolised in the election of a black US president. In this respect, 'the wish for a post-racial politics is a powerful force, and rewards those that seem to carry its promise' (Vickerman 2013, 8). As Goldberg (2013, 17) describes, this concept has an older pedigree than is presently stated:

> The notion of the 'the postracial' can be traced genealogically and interactively to conceptions of 'colourblindedness' and the US civil rights movement, to anti-apartheid's 'nonracialism' (as articulated most clearly, for example, in the mid-1950s Freedom charter), and broadly to the post World War II romance with racelessness.

Nonetheless, because of the history we have discussed, and despite the lack of a biological basis for the conception of distinct human races, race still wields enormous power as a social category. In many societies then the idea of race as a biological category remains a fixture in the popular discussion, or a basis for social action, a foundation of government policy and often a justification for distinctive treatment of one group over another. Some societies do take racial categories seriously, but equally some do for anti-racist reasons. In these cases it is widely known that races are not established natural forces but products of human perception and classification – they are social constructs. Recent migrants are often among the groups' most commonly attributed racial categories. We invent categories of persons marked by certain characteristics, but these characteristics have no intrinsic meaning in or of themselves – on the contrary, we invest or give them meaning, and so in the process we create races.

To redress the traction of race, however, we sometimes encounter a paradox of race. That is to say, while race is a social construct it has real social and economic consequences. If we therefore choose to ignore race in public policy, we also ignore how racial categories are embedded in the routine practices of societies. So the paradox is that we need to recognise race to challenge it. In a number of countries this recognition has led to policies promoting equal access in such arenas as the labour market, education system, and political participation through state-level sponsorship of race equality agendas. These have often comprised a broad remit spanning public and private institutions; recognition of *indirect* discrimination; imposition of public duties to monitor racial discrimination; and the creation of public bodies to promote these objectives. What this means is that while race has often been a means to deny equal dignity to those deemed as less developed, racial categories exist as social phenomena and are important because the assumption of race exists and has social implications. The researcher's task then is to remain vigilant to the social meanings attributed to such categories.

This is the inherent paradox in the use of race that researchers constantly grapple with, and it was probably first expressed by Huxley and Haddon (1935, 220), who argued against the use of race as a normative concept, though Du Bois (1939, 1) also argued 'that no scientific definition of race is possible'. In his words, 'Race would seem to be a dynamic and not a static conception'. This has long been expressed in how many tend to utilise the term under erasure by, again, presenting it in inverted commas so as to indicate that we are referring to a socially constructed category, based upon a problematic idea, instead of something that is self-evidently real in the world (Nayak 2006). Even those who do not repeat this practice agree with the thrust of the argument (Modood 2005). Perhaps the simplest way to frame this is to say that social scientists tend to be interested in the dynamic and relational properties of race *as both a historical idea and social category.* Either way, what we are left with is a socio-historical understanding of race, something that is described by Omi and Winant (1986, 68–69) as a 'cluster concept' or a way of referring to a group of persons who share, and are thereby distinguished by, several properties.

2. Migration in a broader context

'Give me your tired, your poor, Your huddled masses yearning to breathe free, The wretched refuse of your teeming shore. Send these, the homeless, tempest-tost to me, I lift my lamp beside the golden door!' So begins the inscription at the foot of the Statue of Liberty. Taken from a poem entitled "The New Colossus" (Lazarus 1883), it speaks of the millions of migrants who flocked to the United States through Ellis Island, and then the Lower East Side of New York, between the mid-eighteenth and early twentieth century. While migration has become a more complicated phenomenon than the sentiments betrayed in this poem, the core impulses (e.g., to seek out and create a better life for oneself and family), and the questions that these aspirations may raise (e.g., how to reconcile unity with perhaps novel diversity) remain, in many, respects the same.

The important point for scholars is that the phenomenon of migration cannot be explained as isolated from the choices of people. Instead, migration occurs in tandem with wider economic and social forces that can draw or push movement, such as labour recruitment or social conflict, or group networks that facilitate the process, such as established communities which support migrants, as well as political climates that may be hostile to some kinds of migration but favourable to others (e.g., unskilled and skilled) – despite 'the line between preferences and discrimination' being 'a morally thin one that is easily crossed' (Weiner 1996, 178).

The prevailing context for contemporary migration is that the majority of the world's population resides in 175 poorer countries relative to the wealth that is disproportionately concentrated in around twenty (Pécoud/de Guchteneire 2007, 5). In this context, and with levels of migration increasingly fluctuating and anxieties widespread, it is common to hear governments and other agencies favour 'managed migration' which, though meaning different things in different places, registers migration as an intractable feature of contemporary societies the world over. As Pécoud and de Guchteneire argue (2007, 5), 'migration is now structurally embedded in the economies and societies of most countries: once both sending and receiving countries become dependent upon migration, migration is almost impossible to stop'.

According to the International Labour Organization (ILO) (2010), there are around 214 million international migrants (deemed as people living outside their country of origin or birth for twelve months). This makes up about 3 per cent of the global population but has implications that are far greater than the lives of these migrants. An important outcome, as Martin et al. (2006, 3) observe, is that 'the financial contributions of migrants to developing countries far exceeds official development assistance'. This is to the extent that 'many governments of emigration countries have recognised the development potential of their diasporas abroad and have taken steps to facilitate remittances' (ibid.), something that can include dual citizenship, absentee electoral voting, and other 'special' non-resident status (e.g., the category of 'Non-Resident Indian' or 'NRI'). Migration therefore sits at the intersection of a series of questions concerning the relationship between societies and their citizenry, and challenges states to honour their responsibility to new arrivals.

In their widely cited discussion, Castles and Miller (1998, 8–9) identify five 'general tendencies' shaping current experiences. Firstly, they point to the ways in which the *globalisation* of the scale and complexity of migration have increased (with respect to place of origin, destination, and indeed frequency of migration). Secondly, there has been an acceleration in terms of quantitative 'volume in all major regions at the present time' (ibid., 8). Thirdly, societies are witnessing increasing *differentiation*, with respect to the 'type' of migration, spanning labour seeking, refugee, and settlement. Moreover, 'migratory chains which start with one type of movement often continue with others forms, despite (or often just because of) governments['] efforts to stop or control the movement' (ibid., 9). Fourthly, there is a *feminisation* of migration that marks a contrast with what had previously tended to be male-led patterns of labour migration and subsequent reunification, such that 'today women workers form the majority of movements' (ibid., 9). Finally, there has been a *politicisation* of migration, not simply in a discursive sense with respect to popular opposition, but in terms of how 'domestic politics, bilateral and regional relationships and national security policies of states around the world are increasingly affected' (ibid.).

What, however, are the sources of these tendencies, and how do they contrast with what has proceeded them? A large part of human history reflects the implications of coming to terms with this diversity throughout cycles of migration and patterns of settlement, where upon the intermingling of diverse cultural, religious, and ethnic mores renews and/or unsettles established social and political configurations. However, Martin et al. (2006, 9–11) point to three 'ages' of *mass* migration that they understand as qualitatively different from previously smaller-scale patterns in human history. Their first age of mass migration was touched upon at the outset, and saw roughly sixty million people travel from Europe to the Americas between the middle of the nineteenth and the early twentieth centuries. As they summarise:

> Even though many of the migrants were birds of passage seeking higher wages to finance upward mobility at home, most settled in the New World, and a combination of rapid population growth and displacement from agriculture in Europe as well as a need for labour in the New World and the evolution of networks linking settled immigrants abroad to their communities of origin facilitated transatlantic migration. (ibid.)

During this period, the sources of migration fluctuated in moving between, initially, northern and Western Europe, before the large-scale movement of migrants from the Mediterranean (an internal shift that was deemed as regressive in the then portrayal of southern Europeans as less civilised). Tightening of migration legislation, and then the Second World War, interrupted these flows before a second age of migration commenced in the post-war period. Instead of Europeans being catalogued at Ellis Island, however, this age is characterised, first, by guest-workers in Europe (expected to return with their families to their countries of origin on completion of the employment), and whose recruitment reflected the ways in which 'the Iron Curtain limited migration from the east' in post-war Europe (ibid.). Much of the contemporary discussion around post-migrant integration and citizenship in Germany, Belgium, and, to a lesser extent, France is informed by the legacy of this approach.

Outside of what became the European Union in the post-war period, large population movements and forced migrations, often associated with the end of European Empires, were evident too (e.g., in Palestine, North Africa, Sub-Saharan African, and Southern Asia). Perhaps the largest example came with the partition of India in 1947 and the creation of West and East Pakistan, the latter becoming Bangladesh in 1971 after a sustained period of genocidal violence. The third age is more recent and global with many more countries becoming sites of origin, transit, or destination, such that 'between 1975 and 2000, the number of international migrants doubled with the fastest growth between 1985 and 1995 when the stock of migrants rose by about six million a year in response to, among other things, the fall of Communism, wars and persecution in the ex-Yugoslavia' (Martin et al. 2006, 11).

The important point to remember is that 'pull' (as well as 'push') migratory trajectories are not reflections of choice and/or culture alone, but are instead shaped profoundly by individuals' responses to institutional dynamics too. For example, the North American Free Trade Agreement (NAFTA) linking some Latin and North American economies, Asia-Pacific Economic Cooperation (APEC), and the European Union (especially the Schengen Agreement) all contain procedures and mechanisms to facilitate migration. Yet it still remains the case, as Castles and Miller (1998, xi) observe, that 'the UN's main initiative on migration – the 1990 Convention on the Rights of All Migrant Workers and their families – has been ratified by only a handful of countries'. Hence the US and Mexico, while members of a common free trade agreement, are subject to a highly policed border to prevent people flows.

So why do contemporary migration policies fail? asked Stephen Castles (2004) in a well-known article some years ago. Among the reasons he and others settled upon was more than those routinely mentioned by researchers interested in the 'policy cycle'. This refers to a series of distinct but interrelated stages of problem identification, agenda setting, consideration of potential actions, implementation of agreed action, and policy evaluation. Instead, migration policies often fail because they are poorly designed and delivered, and because their success may be so politically unpalatable that national-level governments are unwilling to expend the necessary political capital in pursuing them. This is, of course, assuming that such actors see and value the importance of migration as a fundamental good that is worth defending, the opposite of which is true in many 'transit' and 'end destination' countries in contemporary Europe.

As the findings from the Prospects for International Migration Governance (MIGPROSP) project have shown, in national-level migration policy 'not only is change seen as difficult to deliver, but change itself is viewed as problematic because of the possibility of unforeseen consequences in an unstable and highly politicised policy field' (Geddes 2016). These are useful findings when we seek to understand how and in what ways the Mediterranean 'migration crisis' has unfolded in recent years. While reason dictates that the reference to a 'crisis' might better describe the circumstance of 'those feeling devastation, or to those trapped in it', as Gurminder Bhambra (2017, 395) has put it, at the national level the portrayal is that receiving EU countries are overwhelmed by the social and political implications of inward migration. In this regard receiving societies at the national levels are often failing in their responsibilities.

What is at risk of being overlooked are ways in which national-level intransigence has been thrown into sharp relief by municipal, local, or city-level initiatives aimed more specifically at supporting individuals. This has an older pedigree in the International Cities of Refuge Network, the City of Sanctuary, the Save Me Campaign, and the EUROCITIES network, each of which elevates the role of the local. Inverting philosopher Giorgio Agamben's (2005) discussion of a 'State of Exception', and so switching from how national-level governments can respond to crises by diminishing and denying rights, to how local level governments have responded to the migration crises by opening up, we might characterise one of the features of the responses to the migration crises as the rise of 'local states of exception'.

Focusing on Germany, but in ways that have much broader implications, Margit Mayer (2016, 5) has observed the ways in which city-level 'concern and support led to a novel form of activism around migrant rights: a sudden surge of non-traditional civic engagement that arose next to, and only partially out of, existing human rights, refugee, anti-racist and urban movements.' Perhaps as much for reasons of race and identity, as well as contingency, local innovation is therefore a profoundly important space.

This is not of course to overlook how cities are also sites in which global exclusions and inequalities are enacted, such that while the city may provide a site for non-traditional civic engagement, it has also become a site where global movements (and their infrastructures) are realised locally. The relationship between civil society and governance is key here, including a focus on the development of new modes of governance that are characterised by two striking features. The first is that local and city-level migrant and refugee reception are sometimes diverging significantly from national-level policy and rhetoric. Possibly an illustration of 'decoupling' across geographies of policy delivery (Pope/Meyer 2016, 290), this variation is patterned by ground-level politics, local strategic incentives, and pre-existing economic resources in a manner that invites further scientific investigation through live cases.

The second is that local and city-level approaches to reception are leading to patterns of successful early integration. These include those cultivated by associations from the third sector, which have assumed a key role in what Anna Elia (2013, 36) has termed 'bottom up welfare' including the ways that 'the slow reactions of national authorities has often left cities at the forefront, forcing them to play a role without having a legal mandate nor any specific budget to do so' (Mayer 2017, 3; EUROCITIES 2016, 13). An emblematic example is the town of Riace in the southern Italian region of Calabria that has led pioneering schemes to welcome migrants. The 'Riace model' has been exported to other nearby towns that are successfully incorporating displaced migrants into the local labour market and allowing them to occupy and regenerate previously abandoned homes.

This includes thinking about 'integration' as something more than that which has animated the so-called 'muscular liberalism' of a number of commentators perhaps best characterised as white supremacists. Giving more emphasis to civic participation and perhaps other forms of 'integration' that are not picked up in narrow and exclusionary integration criteria (especially in the often overlooked terms of political mobilisation, cultural production, and aesthetic engagement). In this respect, and as Maurizio Ambrosini (2017, 579) has put it, 'whatever the national framework of immigrant incorporation policies, the urban level needs to be appreciated as a policy-making field in itself'. It is here that greater responsibility is evident, in communities and localities responding to pressing needs.

Returning then to our opening question, it is also worth bearing in mind that not all migration policies are bound to 'fail'. Some are very successful, including those described by Bridget Anderson (2017, 1529) as ensuring 'vast amounts of state money are poured into mobility controls, technology and policing of borders, the maintenance and expansion of the detention estate, and the funding of in-country enforcement, checks and raids'. These facilitate strategies of everyday bordering and the devolution of the politics of closure. If local states of exception are to live up to their initial promise, they will need to counter and build outward a politics of openness, in a way that turns local exceptions, where individual responsibility is exemplified in a range of services, networks, and reactions, into national norms.

Bibliography

Agamben, G. (2005): State of Exception. Kevin Attell (tr.). Chicago: University of Chicago Press.

Ambrosini, M. (2017): Superdiversity, Multiculturalism and Local Policies: A Study on European Cities. In: Policy and Politics 454, 585–603.

Anderson, B. (2017): Towards a New Politics of Migration. In: Ethnic and Racial Studies 40(9), 1527–1537.

Ashcroft, B./Griffith, G./Tiffin, H. (eds.) (1995): The Postcolonial Studies Reader. London: Routledge.

Banton, M. (1977): The Idea of Race. Boulder: Westview Press.

Benhabib, S. (2002): The Claims of Culture: Equality and Diversity in a Global Era. Princeton: Princeton University Press.

Bhambra, G. K. (2017): The Current Crisis of Europe: Refugees, Colonialism, and the Limits of Cosmopolitanism. In: European Law Journal 23, 395–405.

Biddis, M. (ed.) (1979): Images of Race. New York: Holmes & Meier.

Castles, S. (2004): Why Migration Policies Fail. In: Ethnic and Racial Studies 272, 205–227.
Castles, S./Miller, M. J. (1998): The Age of Migration: International Population Movements in a Modern World. Basingstoke: Palgrave.
Du Bois, W. E. B. (1939): Black Folk Then and Now. New York: Henry Holt.
Elia, A. (2013): The Arrival of North African Migrants in the South of Italy: Practices of Sustainable Welfare within a Non-Welcoming System. In: E. Januszewska /S. Rullac (eds.): Social Problems in Europe: Dilemmas and Possible Solutions. Paris: L'Harmattan.
EUROCITIES (2016): EUROCITIES Social Affairs Refugee Reception and Integration in Cities Report. Brussels: EUROCITIES.
Garner, S. (2011): Racisms. London: Sage.
Geddes, A. (2016): Emerging Themes from MIGPROSP Research. http://migrationgovernance.org/index.php/2016/06/29/emerging-themes-from-migprosp-research/.
Gilroy, P. (1993): The Black Atlantic. London: Verso.
Gobineau, A. (Count Joseph Arthur de Gobineau) (1853): In: A Collins. (tr.): The Inequality of Human Races. London: William Heinemann.
Goldberg, D. T. (2013): The post racial contemporary. In: N. Kappoor/V. Kalra/J. Rhodes (eds.): The State of Race. Basingstoke: Palgrave.
Gutmann, A. (1994): Introduction. In: A. Gutmann (ed.): Multiculturalism: Examining the Politics of Recognition. Princeton: Princeton University Press.
Hawley, J. C. (2011): The bittersweet taste of exile, as muse. In: M. David/J. Munoz-Basols (eds.): Defining and Re-Defining Diaspora. Oxford: Interdisciplinary Press.
Huxley, J./Haddon, A. C. (1935): We Europeans: A Survey of 'Racial' Problems. London: Jonathan Cape.
Kaplan, H. Roy (2011): The Myth of Post-Racial America: Searching for Equality in the Age of Materialism. Lanham: Rowman & Littlefield.
Knox, J. (1850): The Races of Men: A Fragment. London: Renshaw.
Krieger, J. (2009): After empire. In: M. Fliners et al. (eds.): The Oxford Handbook of British Politics. New York: Oxford University Press.
Lazarus, E. (1883): The New Colossus. Washington, DC: Library of Congress.
Martin, P./Martin, S./Weil, P. (2006): Managing Migration: the Promise of Cooperation. Oxford: Lexington Books.
Mayer, M. (2017): Cities as Sites of Refuge and Resistance. In: European Urban and Regional Studies, 1–18.
Meer, Nasar (2104): Key Concepts in Race and Ethnicity. Thousand Oaks: Sage.
Modood, T. (2005): Multicultural Politics: Racism, Ethnicity and Muslims in Britain. Edinburgh: Edinburgh University Press.
Montagu, A. (1942): Man's Most Dangerous Myth: the Fallacy of Race. New York: Columbia University Press.
Nayak, A. (2006): After Race: Ethnography, Race and Post-Race Theory. In: Ethnic and Racial Studies 29(3), 411–430.
Omi. M. (2001): The changing meaning of race. In N. Smelser/W. J. Wilson/F. Mitchell (eds.): America Becoming: Racial Trends and Their Consequences. Washington, DC: National Academy Press.
Omi, M./Winant, H. (1986): Racial Formation in the United States. New York: Routledge & Kegan Paul.

Parekh, B. (2000): Rethinking Multiculturalism. Basingstoke: Palgrave
Parks, G./Hughey, M. (2011): The Obamas and a (Post) Racial America? Oxford: Oxford University Press.
Pécoud, A./de Guchteneire, P. (2007): Introduction: the Migration Without Border Scenario. In A. Pecou/P. de Guchteneire (eds.): Migration without Borders: Essays on the Free Movement of People. Paris: UNESCO Publishing.
Pope, S./Meyer, J. W. (2016): Local Variation in World Society: Six Characteristics of Global Diffusion. In: European Journal of Cultural and Political Sociology 3(2–3), 280–305.
Slemon, S. (1995): 'Unsettling the Empire: resistance theory for the Second World War. In: B. Ashcroft/G. Griffith/H. Tiffin (eds.): The Postcolonial Studies Reader. London: Routledge.
Uberoi, Varun/Modood, Tariq (2013): Has Multiculturalism in Britain Retreated? In: Soundings 53, 129–142.
Vertovec, S. (1999): Conceiving and Researching Transnationalism. In: Ethnic and Racial Studies 22(2): 447–462.
Vickerman, M. (2013): The Problem of Post-Racialism. Basingstoke: Palgrave.
Walton, C. F./Caliendo, S. M. (2011): Origins of the Concept of Race. In S. M. Caliendo/C. D. McIlwain (eds.): The Routledge Companion to Race and Ethnicity. London: Routledge.
Weiner, M. (1996): Ethics, National Sovereignty and the Control of Immigration. In: International Migration Review 30(1), 171–197.

S. Karly Kehoe

Historical perspectives on migrant integration in Atlantic Canada, 1812 – 1825

Abstract: The legacy of British colonialism looms large in many places and has played a major role in the management of ethnic diversity right up to the present day. This chapter explores how racist attitudes inhibited the settlement of formerly enslaved people in two colonies of northeastern British North America. It uses a historical case study to consider the extent to which a culture of social and economic exclusion influenced individual responsibility and agency among approximately 2,500 former enslaved migrants of African descent in the early nineteenth century. In the process it considers the applicability of the term 'refugee' to historical movements of people across borders. While there is no call to stop using the term refugee, it argues that more care must be taken when applying it and that historians need to engage, in more meaningful and honest ways, with the source material that contains migrant and minority voices.

Whether we are able to recognise it or not, the tangible and intangible structures that govern how we interact with each other are historic constructions weighed down by a lot of imperial baggage. In the places that had once been European colonies, the 'institutional rules and interactive routines', which Iris Marion Young sees as being intrinsic components of the structures that surround us, evolved over centuries and in ways that gave power to certain groups and withdrew it from others (Young 2006, 111). Calls from various Indigenous and persons of colour groups for current governments to atone for the wrongs of the colonial past shine a light on how the historic power imbalance has played out and the influence it has had on access to resources, services, and justice. The purpose of Canada's landmark Truth and Reconciliation Commission, which was established in 2008 and ran until 2015, was to enable Aboriginal survivors of the residential school system to speak their truths about what had happened to them in the government- and church-run boarding schools, where any expression of their cultures was forbidden (Truth and Reconciliation Commission 2015). Declared a 'cultural genocide' by both the Commission's Chair, Justice Murray Sinclair, and Canada's then Supreme Court Chief Justice, Beverly McLachlin, these state-sanctioned institutions are a stark reminder of the British colonial legacy (Eisler 2015). In the Caribbean, CARICOM's reparations project is seeking redress for the widespread impact that four centuries of slavery have had on regional de-

https://doi.org/10.1515/9783110628746-006

velopment and progress. In addition to monetary compensation, the Reparations Task Force Chair, Pedro Welch, has called for a deeper engagement with the 'psychological impact which is transferred in the culture of the people' (CARICOM 2018). Hilary Beckles, a highly respected historian, agrees and wants the British government to acknowledge the role that its people played in perpetrating crimes against humanity and to recognise the 'open wounds' that persist today because of slavery (Beckles 2013, 1). It is incumbent upon historians of empires to broaden understandings of just how far the arm of colonialism extended and how its processes shaped and continue to shape the management of ethnic diversity in our societies (Bleich 2005, 171).

Colonialism's effects continue to shape integration processes and in a country like Canada, which has depended upon immigration to grow its population, they have been profound. Unlike the various islands of the Caribbean, many of which were first acquired through war and then transformed into slave societies, Britain's northern colonies (British North America) were earmarked for White settlement. While slavery certainly existed there, it was not on the industrial scale of the southern colonies, meaning only that the slaves in these colonies were, as Ira Berlin asserts, 'marginal to the central production processes'; it does not mean that the enslaved were treated with any less brutality (1998, 8). During Britain's late eighteenth- and early nineteenth-century conflicts with France and the United States, thousands of African-descended migrants, many of whom were slaves running away from their American owners, moved north. The following discussion explores how racist attitudes inhibited the settlement of formerly enslaved people in northeastern British North America and uses a historical case study to consider the extent to which a culture of social and economic exclusion influenced individual responsibility and agency among approximately 2,500 former enslaved people of African descent in the second decade of the nineteenth century. Sometimes referred to as 'refugees', these escapees arrived during and immediately following the War of 1812, a three-year conflict between Britain and the United States that coincided with the tail end of the Napoleonic Wars.[1]

The British super state that emerged over the course of the eighteenth and nineteenth centuries was an amalgam of four constituent 'home' nations (England, Wales, Scotland, and Ireland), and it governed a growing collection of colonies and territories around the world. For free people, movement around this 'British' world was largely unrestricted and a myriad of economic, religious, security, and political factors influenced the constant flow of migrants from the

1 I do not always place the word refugee in quotations in the pages that follow, but I intend them as such throughout this chapter.

home nations to the various colonies. Former enslaved people and free people of colour were among those on the move, and while many were already British subjects a number were not. All of them, however, encountered an entrenched culture of racial antagonism propagated by the White settler class. Thus, the 1812 migrants were not the first people of colour to attempt settlement in the north-eastern Atlantic colonies of British North America but represented one movement in a series of many spurred by the plans of colonial officials, who encouraged or forced groups to move from one place to another depending on security and/or economic needs. In 1796, when 549 Jamaican Maroons arrived in Nova Scotia, one of the Atlantic colonies, as part of a scheme introduced to bolster the colony's defence capabilities in the event of a French attack, they had joined approximately 3,000 free people of colour (mostly loyalists – i.e., those who remained loyal to Britain during the American Revolution) already there. Their experience was largely negative and so, like the 1,000 who had already deserted the colony in favour of Sierra Leone, it was not long before almost all of the new Maroons left for West Africa (Chopra 2017, 5, 6, 10 – 11; Whitfield 2006, 22). Unsurprisingly, non-English-speaking migrants and people of colour faced numerous obstacles in Britain's White settler colonies that impeded or prevented their integration into an emerging 'mainstream' society. Labelled subversives and accused of undermining colonial progress, they confronted the persistent threat of removal if colonial officials felt that they could not be 'reformed' (Kehoe 2018). This precariousness contrasts sharply with the imagined narrative of Canada as a safe haven for escaped slaves and of Britain as the bastion of abolition.

When wading into this difficult and emotional terrain, historians need to be mindful of how they tell stories of migration and movements, and when exploring the archival record, they must take care to seek out and include a range of voices. When Canada's former Parliamentary Poet Laureate, George Elliott Clarke, coined the term 'Africadian' to describe part of the legacy of the African Diaspora in Nova Scotia, he flagged an important voice that challenged people to rethink what Nova Scotia was all about (Clarke 1991; Samson 1994). Those of us who consider migration will encounter issues related to integration and may be tempted to categorise people as refugees, but we need to be cautious when applying this term. During the second half of the twentieth century, the term was formalised by the United Nations as a way of coping with the post–Second World War migrant crisis and in the process became subject to legal obligations and international protocols. In the discussion that follows, I am not proposing that we stop using the term refugee, when interrogating cases of historical movement, but rather that we take much more care with its use and pursue more meaningful engagements with the source material (evidence) that contains migrant and minority voices. As I explain below, historians' reticence does not always sit well with colleagues in other disciplines, but how we engage with historical migrations, by being more aware of the agency of those on the move as exhibited in the evidence has much to offer a field such as refugee studies.

1. Historicising the 'Refugee'

In an article on the place of refugees in historical research, Peter Gatrell, a historian of migration, advocates using 'an emerging history of displacement across space and time' to consider the life paths of refugees and classifies displacement as 'history from below' (Gatrell 2016, 172). Considering the life paths of refugees is a valuable way forward, but categorising this as 'history from below' with no explanation of how race fits within a methodological approach that emerged to examine class is restrictive and has the potential to do serious harm. In addition to presupposing a socio-economic category that may or may not be accurate for people on the move, it risks oversimplifying an inherently complex experience and sidesteps an engagement with what was happening on the ground in the country or region of origin that prompted the migration in the first place. One need only consider the migrations of clergy and women religious from Revolutionary France during 1793–4, of Highlanders from Scotland before the 1810s, and of British loyalists from the United States following the American Revolution. These historical migrations have features in common with those happening today from Syria, Turkey, and Iran in that they were a result of war and conflict, persecution, cultural attack, and/or dramatic socio-economic upheaval, and because they include people from diverse backgrounds and class levels. Yet, perhaps the chief issue with categorising displacement as 'history from below' is that it instantly restricts understandings of how and when the term refugee was applied in historical settings and limits discussion of when applying it to historical groups is appropriate. Usually, it was assigned to people whose movement corresponded with a specific and catastrophic event such as a war or a natural disaster. The French émigrés of the mid-1790s, briefly mentioned above, had faced violent religious and class persecution in Revolutionary France. In Scotland, dramatic and widespread socio-economic upheaval saw people abandon or be cleared from the settlements that they and their families had occupied for centuries. In the United States, thousands of Black people made the decision to reject their enslavement during the window of opportunity that the War of 1812 provided. In each of these cases, the term refugee was used, but not all the time and less so by those actually on the move.

Philip Marfleet, a sociologist working on migration and refugee studies, is deeply critical of what he sees as historians' amnesia about the topic of refugees and mass displacements. He may have a point. Located within his criticism is an awareness of the necessity of historical enquiry in extending understandings of the migrant experience and the role it has played in shaping the national narratives that surround us. 'Understanding the circumstances in which displacements take place and the ways they have been experienced over time', he posits, 'should be integral to our analysis of contemporary issues' (Marfleet 2013, 15). Of course, he is correct and they should be incorporated. As someone who works on religious minority and migrant integration in Britain and its North Atlantic colonies, it is this point that forced me to pause and to reflect on why I tend not to categorise the people I study as having been refugees even though some of them at certain points could be (and were) classified as such. It makes me wonder if historians, because of how we approach and describe migration, have actually normalised mass movement in our work by considering it as simply one element of a protracted process. After all, the stories of empires include voluntary and forced migration as a matter of course and yet even though we encounter it regularly and see it as a relatively common feature of imperialism and colonization, we should still have significant reservations about the appropriateness of applying the term refugee to historical mass movements. Specifically, how, when, and by whom the term refugee was used in the past needs to be assessed sensibly. If we proclaim migrants as having been refugees, when there is no evidence to suggest that this is how they were perceived or, more importantly, how they perceived themselves, then we risk breaking the number one rule: be true to the past by being true to the evidence.

How the Black people, who arrived in Nova Scotia and New Brunswick during and immediately following the War of 1812, described themselves depended very much on the situation. Harvey Amani Whitfield, the expert on this, has found that these escaped slaves were discerning in their self-identification and that while official colonial records designate them as 'black refugees', 'negro refugees', 'people of colour', and 'black people', they referred to themselves as 'inhabitants of colour', 'people of colour', and 'refugees' depending on need and circumstance (Whitfield 2002, 32).[2] Given this difference in perception, there is a need to be mindful of the agency that their choice of designation denoted. Thinking in terms of agency and seeing it as an intrinsic part of a person's or of a people's movement enables us to build nuanced and more informed under-

2 For an example, see CO 217/145.f.211. Copy of letter from Sir James Kempt, Lieutenant Governor of Nova Scotia, to George Harrison, Treasury, January 20, 1821.

standings of how migrants participated in host societies and how they advocated for their own integration. In her work on African American migration in the early nineteenth century, Bronwen Everill declines to describe escaped or manumitted slaves as refugees but rather refers to them as migrants and emigrants who demonstrated agency in the decisions they took to move to places like Liberia on the West African coast. While acknowledging that there were American Whites, for example, who saw the establishment of the Liberian colony as a way to remove Black people from the United States, Everill points out that the decision to leave happened because people took responsibility for shaping their own futures (Everill 2012). Kit Candlin shares this view and emphasises the influence that the French Revolution had on how slaves and free people of colour began to think about themselves and their future as part of emerging colonial societies (Candlin 2018).

There is value in pairing the words migration and participation because of the recognition it offers to migrants as co-creators of the larger empire-building process. After all, the main point of Paul Gilroy's ground-breaking book *The Black Atlantic* is that free people of colour, slaves, and former slaves played active roles in the creation of new societies through their enterprise, networks, labour (stolen and not), and resistance, and that they need to be factored in to our analyses (Gilroy 1993). The historical record is replete with evidence of their activity and in viewing them as participants, we are able to ask *how* migrants integrated and achieved autonomy rather than questioning *whether they were* integrated. This tweak to a fundamental question compels us to rethink who gets to label someone a refugee and to begin our enquiries from a different position. Unearthing archival sources that give a clear picture of how migrants labelled themselves and under what circumstances such labels changed requires a new approach to analysing their movement and a recognition of the fact that they charted their own courses in how they chose to respond to their circumstances.

In a pioneering article on English humanitarianism in early nineteenth-century Nova Scotia, Judith Fingard linked the emergence of associational culture and voluntarism with the paternalistic desire of Whites to 'improve' the circumstances of disadvantaged groups such as the Indigenous Mi'kmaq and the newly arrived migrants of African descent (Fingard 1973, 136–38). Unfortunately, her analysis excludes any consideration of the independence and agency that these groups possessed, which enabled them to advocate on their own behalves. Whitfield, argues, rightly, that if historians look beyond the traditional (and often government-created) sources, then there is a much better chance of locating the missing voices and improving our research and analyses. In the case of the formerly enslaved people, he points to the petitions they made to government requesting changes to land allocation as one such cache (Whitfield

2002, 30–31). Literature, including poetry and songs, is also illuminating. Kit Candlin, who concentrates on the agency of the enslaved in the Caribbean, agrees. He is an advocate of the use of agency as an analytical tool, but is justified in questioning the extent to which it fits and may be of use if researchers habitually overlook or deliberately ignore the voices of the enslaved by failing to engage with a broader source base (Candlin 2018).

In the context of the British Empire, considerations of migration and integration from the perspective of individual and/or group agency immediately shift the analysis to a deeper level by permitting a more critical and precise consideration of citizenship (often understood as active, earned, or agreed status) and subjecthood (often seen as assigned and passive status). In an imperial setting, any examination of migrant integration needs to be considered as having been connected with these two categories of belonging. While subject status is often thought of as the precursor to citizenship, it was much more complicated than this, and Hannah Weiss Muller suggests that a starting point is to explore how historical actors understood their status in relation to each category. Citizen and subject are inherently complex terms and usually viewed as opposites despite their interchangeable use in the early modern era (Muller 2017, 3–6). Being aware of the distinctions that emerged between the two terms from the late eighteenth century, as serious debates about parliamentary reform, Catholic relief, and the emancipation of slaves took place, raises important new questions. Specifically, to what extent did refugee or migrant integration challenge people's thinking about what it meant to be a citizen and/or a subject? Predictably, major distinctions between the two emerged during Britain's war with revolutionary America. In his work on the connections between naval impressment and perceptions of subject and citizen, Denver Brunsman argues that the American belief in consensual citizenship, for example, stood in stark contrast to the British Crown's perception of citizenship being obligatory and based on place of birth (Brunsman 2010, 559, 570, and 585). This was the case in British territories beyond North America. In Australia, for example, the Indigenous population, although classed as British subjects, did not receive the rights of citizens (Chesterman 2005, 31, 32 and 36). Nasar Meer's point that 'the citizenship of certain types of people implies the non-citizenship of others' is easily confirmed (2018, 1168).

In the colonies and territories of the British Empire, whiteness determined citizenship but there were varying categories of White. In the United Kingdom, Scottish Highlanders and the Irish, for example, were Celts and perceived as less White than their Anglo-Saxon neighbours (Craig 2018, 103–144). A number of them were also Catholics (Britain's largest religious minority) and so confronted a kind of double discrimination, but their whiteness enabled them to use the opportunities that the British Empire provided to extend the boundaries of their citizenship in ways that free people of colour and slaves could not (Kehoe 2017; Brannigan 2009; Beatty 2016). Thus, out in the empire both Scottish Highlanders and Irish Catholics became 'whiter' as they encountered Indigenous populations, free people of colour, and slaves. While there was a willingness to use people of colour to boost the imperial economy and Britain's defence capacity, their inclusion fell far short of equality and significant barriers relating to land access, education, and more general support were put in place to cement their lower status. Race and perceptions of race played a fundamental role in migrant integration, and historians of the British Empire encounter references to both on a regular basis. Yet an important question is what would integration look like at a time when race functioned as an immediate (dis)qualifier? Enlightenment theories about social hierarchy and race, advanced by influential contemporaries such as John Millar, David Hume, Thomas Macaulay, and, more controversially, James Mill, whose views were considered by many to have been extreme, shaped ideas in colonial society (Bayly 1999, 34–37). This kind of thinking resonated with colonial administrators, traders, sojourners, settlers, and others, who believed that the natural and human resources surrounding them were theirs for the taking, and was used to justify aspects of Britain's imperialism. Notwithstanding the devastating effects that this mindset had on local Indigenous groups, it also meant that the free people of colour and former slaves, when they tried to compete with White settlers for land, stood almost no chance. Given agriculture's importance as an imperial tool, restricting or delaying access to land or allocating good land to one group and poor land to another, even withholding seeds and tools, confirmed social, racial, and economic hierarchies in colonial societies that remain in place today (Reid 2004, 675).[3]

Gatrell's point that today's integration policies are continuations of those developed for past empires is entirely appropriate and supports the supposition that understanding post colonialism or colonialism's impact on the maturation of former colonies requires a broader awareness of what the process entailed and who was included (Gatrell 2016, 187). Moreover, it necessitates an awareness of who gets to label someone else a refugee and why. The need to delve deeper into this becomes immediately apparent when one considers the low status and persistent exclusion of various groups. The following section provides an overview of the northward migration and settlement of one group of migrants of African descent during the second decade of the nineteenth century. What is irrefutable is that the deck was stacked against them for all of the reasons discussed above.

3 For an interesting commentary, see Bouie, 2018.

2. Black people in Nova Scotia and New Brunswick

Britain's acquisition of numerous French colonies during the eighteenth century, coupled with its own persistent connections with slavery and the Atlantic slave trade meant that unfree people were ubiquitous across its imperial landscapes. Ironically, during the American Revolution, the French Revolutionary Wars, and the War of 1812, the British government offered freedom to slaves in exchange for loyalty through military service. A consequence of 'contrasting visions of citizenship' between Britain and the American public, approximately 3,500 slaves from Georgia, Maryland, and Virginia sought freedom in British territories (Brunsman 2010, 570). Some went west and south, boarding British vessels that took them to Bermuda or further afield to one of a number of Caribbean islands, but many more went north to Nova Scotia and New Brunswick (Whitfield 2002, 33). A proclamation, issued on 2 April 1814, by Royal Navy admiral and former governor of Guadeloupe, Sir Alexander Cochrane, gave notice that:

> all persons who may be disposed to emigrate from the United States with their families be rec'd on board His Majesty's ships or vessels of war, or at the military ports that may be established on or near the coasts of the United States, where they will have their choice of either entering His Majesty's sea or land forces or of being sent as free settlers to the British possessions in North America or the West Indies, where they will meet with all due encouragement. (*Ad*miral Cochrane's Proclamation, 1814)

This statement merely sanctioned what many slaves had already been doing – obtaining their freedom by going to British ports or by boarding British vessels. The previous September, for example, six slaves aged between twenty-two and thirty were 'picked up in an open boat' (they were joined by another two days later) by the Royal Navy and transported to Nova Scotia's capital, Halifax (*American Slaves, Deserted from the Enemy... 1813)*. More arrived the following year; it was a journey that carried many risks as evidenced when a ship arrived in Halifax on 1 September 1814, and it was reported by a local newspaper that it carried 'a *few* hundred negroes (dead and alive)' (*Acadian Recorder* 1814). The decision by these slaves and many others to free themselves by seeking out a British ship is indicative of the agency each exercised on his or her own behalf. Historians need to pay more attention to this point and recognise that the decision to seek refuge elsewhere (which may or may not include an acceptance of the designation refugee) was an assertion of personal agency. Not content to wait for a representative of the British government to give them permission to seek freedom, they had capitalised on the fact that the war between the two countries had opened a window of opportunity for freedom. Britain ended its Atlantic slave trade in 1807, but an extremely powerful pro-slavery lobby and the intimidating prospect of managing hundreds of thousands of freed slaves throughout its numerous colonies meant that the government did not abolish slavery until 1833, when the British parliament passed the Act for the Abolition of Slavery throughout the British Colonies.[4] Until that year, the position of all formerly enslaved people (escaped or even manumitted) remained precarious. In fact, when this particular migration of escaped slaves to Nova Scotia and New Brunswick occurred, legislative provision recognising slavery's existence was in place in neighbouring Prince Edward Island and large-scale plantation slavery was ongoing in all of Britain's Caribbean colonies (Whitfield & Cahill 2009; Riddell 1921). Nova Scotia and New Brunswick stood out because local courts and elected assemblies resisted pressure from slave owners living in both colonies to validate its existence, but they were an anomaly. Yet, in opting for these two colonies, places willing though reluctant to receive them, the migrants showed themselves as having been very aware of their vulnerability and of the need to minimise their risk of being re-enslaved.

Those who went to New Brunswick faced major struggles. Established as a separate colony in 1784, New Brunswick's government was dominated by White loyalists, who had migrated north into British territory after their defeat by the Americans in 1783 (Mancke 1997, 23). Many had been slave owners themselves or were sympathetic to slave ownership and so had little desire to support their fellow loyalists and were even less interested in helping the escaped slaves who arrived during the 1812 war. They accepted them because they were under pressure to do so from neighbouring Nova Scotia, whose legislators feared a backlash from local Whites if more settled there (Humble Address of the House of Representation… 1815, 107). New Brunswick agreed to accept a small number; it was with the proviso that it would not have to assume any responsibility for their physical needs (Spray 1977, 64). Although the migrants received permission to go to New Brunswick, they were essentially on their own and had little if any access to the support systems that the Irish, Scottish, English, and Welsh (White people) settlers took for granted from their growing diaspora communities. Having their attempts to make a successful settlement in New Brunswick all but blocked throws into sharp relief the differences faced by Black and White settlers. White settlers were prioritised for land allocation and had access to a wider range of 'agricultural and emigrant societies, church organizations and other charitable groups' (Spray 1977, 74), whereas the Black

4 For an overall account of this era, see Draper 2010; and Hall et al. 2014.

people struggled to acquire even the smallest tracts of land. Moreover, they had only tentative access to a handful of support systems that were almost always predicated upon the benevolence of the White settlers who ran them. In the context of this volume and in connection with the broader theme of individual responsibility, there is a need to be cognisant of the legacies of charitable activism and how it was often directed towards certain groups and away from others. The lack of a diaspora community for these newcomers put them at a significant disadvantage. They had no access to pre-existing networks established by the friends and relatives, who arrived before them, that would ease their transition. The nature of slave ownership meant that deliberate efforts were undertaken to erode the potential of diaspora community formation; plantation owners and managers purposely purchased slaves from different regions and language groups to minimise the risk of revolt (Everill 2012). Those escaping enslavement had little in common apart from their experience as slaves.

Another major challenge revolved around land and from the outset, the colonial government imposed significant restrictions on these settlers' access to it. The decision by New Brunswick's assembly to offer 'licenses of occupation for three years', which was only the first step towards holding title to land, undermined their ability to integrate as a permanent population in colonial society (Spray 1977, 71).[5] To make matters worse, migrants from Scotland and Wales petitioned the government for (and were granted) free title to large tracts of land which, in some cases, had already been promised to the Black settlers (Spray 1977, 69). Given these circumstances, it is hardly surprising that the small community of 400 to 500 individuals dispersed with many deciding to leave and move to neighbouring Nova Scotia. Those who went there were marginally more successful but even though many did eventually receive land, what they got had been rejected by White settlers because it was of such poor quality. The promises made to the Black settlers, which included land grants, shelters, tools, and seeds, were either broken or delivered only in part. In spite of the hardships they encountered on a regular basis, they continued to demonstrate agency in numerous ways. Perhaps the most impressive example was in the refusal of those in Nova Scotia to relocate to Trinidad when strongly encouraged to do so by the local governor. In 1821, the Nova Scotia lieutenant governor, James Kempt, wrote to an official in the London Treasury, George Harrison, that they had refused to board a ship bound for Trinidad.[6] The reason for this, he relayed,

---

5 Thank you to Shirley Tillotson for helping me to clarify this point of law.

6 The National Archives (Kew, England) (TNA) CO 217/145.f.211. Copy of Letter from Sir James Kempt to George Harrison, 20 January 1821.

was a fear of re-enslavement and it was one that persisted as another statement from Kempt, this time to Henry, 3rd Earl Bathurst, Secretary of State for War and the Colonies, the following year, reveals:

> I have to acquaint your Lordship that I have in vain used every influence in my power to accomplish so desirable an object but these people entertain so great a fear of slavery that no persuasions can induce them to remove to any place where slavery exists. It would afford me great satisfaction could I effect the removal of this population from this Province on which it is a very expensive burden.[7]

Two years later, Kempt was still trying to convince 'many of these miserable beings to join their friends in Trinidad', but was having little luck – even after he had agreed a transportation price of '£5.15 for each grown person and £3 for each child'.[8] It is telling that out of the 2,500 who had settled in Nova Scotia as part of the 1812–1815 migration, only 95 (81 adults and 14 children) agreed to go to Trinidad.[9] There was a clear determination to remain in Nova Scotia and to continue the job of living their lives and building up their communities and this included integrating with the maturing colony. A petition of 11 November 1820, signed by James Bell, a prospective schoolmaster, and supported by at least '30 householders', to the governor for school and a schoolmaster so that 'people of colour' could learn 'at least ___ to read and to write', is evidence of this and of their belief that their integration and transition to freedom would be easier if they were literate:

> At the request of the undermentioned inhabitants of colour of Preston, who wish to have their children instructed and being in a state of great indigence are incapable of supporting a school master. Your Excellency's humble petitioner is therefore induced to make application for the salary that is allowed from government and hopes by a steady application to the improvement of those intrusted to his charge to meet your Excellency's approbation. (Bell 1820)

As Whitfield explains, one legacy of this migration and settlement was the rise of a culture of 'racism and bitterness' against these settlers and their descendants (Whitfield 2012, 17). Anti-Black sentiment pre-dated their arrival and had been informed by a dominant perception that former slaves, despite many having

7 TNA. CO 217/145. Letter from Sir James Kempt to Henry, 3rd Earl Bathurst, 16 October 1823.
8 TNA. CO 217/144. Letter from Sir James Kempt to Henry, 3rd Earl Bathurst, 7 June 1825; and CO 214/140.f.209. Letter from George Harrison, Treasury, to Henry Goulburn, Colonial Office, 4 April 1821.
9 TNA. CO 214/140.f.211. Copy of letter from Sir James Kempt to George Harrison, 20 January 1821.

been loyalists and people who had served alongside Whites in the British Army and Royal Navy, were public nuisances and unable to adjust to life as free people (Chopra 2017, 10 and 23; Whitfield 2006, 20). As the notion that they would fill the labour gap evaporated as the post–Napoleonic War economic slump hit, resentment towards them mounted which resulted in the rejection of their petition.

3. Conclusion

Mary Hickman, a sociologist working in the field of Irish studies, highlights the value of historical perspectives to expanding our understandings of integration by noting that people's ideas of how it was, meaning specifically a place and/or a way of life, shapes how they see it as being now (Hickman 2012, 141). It is incumbent upon historians to ensure that past representations are corrected in light of new evidence and that we move our analyses beyond the traditional narratives and power dynamics. We must interrogate the use of terms, such as refugee, and consider how it fits (or does not) within the context of people's lives. Classification, specifically how we think about, order, or group people together, has a place in historical enquiry, but it needs to be done carefully. When it comes to people on the move, by force, by choice, or by a mix of both, the term migrant, as opposed to refugee, is probably more suitable since it assigns power to those normally perceived as having had less power than those who remained in the country or nation of origin and those of the host country.

When considering movements that were the result of specific events such as a war or a famine, it is imperative that care is taken over when and how the term refugee is (or is not) to be applied. It is the responsibility of the historian to explore a range of collections to determine whether an archival source base exists to merit the application of the term. We must also bear in mind how designating someone a refugee, which often happens without their consent, undermines or compromises the agency of the individuals who took action by first making the decision to leave and then by going to a new place. As argued above, the incorporation of agency as a fundamental component of any migration story frames the experience of migrants and minorities in this way and elevates the power and responsibility of individuals on the move to a level where it mattered. The significance of this in relation to the British Empire, for example, is that it prompts new understandings of what it actually was, how it grew, and how it acquired more and more authority. In the context of migrant and/or refugee integration in a given historical period, the imperial backdrop must be considered and used to inform our thinking about this topic today. Migrants have had a profound influence on colonial development via settlement patterns, economic opportunities, and social hierarchies. In the development of Nova Scotia, the contribution made by these settlers is rarely, if ever, mentioned.

Bibliography

Acadian Recorder (1814): In: Nova Scotia Archives. September 3, 1814. https://novascotia.ca/archives/africanns/archives.asp?ID=71 (last accessed September 25, 2018).

Admiral Cochrane's Proclamation (1814): In: Nova Scotia Archives (NSA). RG 1 vol. 111. 99–100. April 2, 1814. https://novascotia.ca/archives/africanns/archives.asp?ID=70&Page=200402137&Language= (last accessed June 4, 2018).

American Slaves, Deserted from the Enemy on Board His Majesty's Sloop Rifleman (1813): In: Nova Scotia Archives. RG 1 vol. 240, no. 1. List of 7. September 28, 1813.

Beatty, Aidan (2016): Masculinity and Power in Irish Nationalism, 1884–1938. London: Palgrave Macmillan.

Beckles, Hilary (2013): Britain's Black Debt: Reparations for Caribbean Slavery and Native Genocide. Jamaica: University of the West Indies Press.

Bell, James (1820): Preston Schoolmaster's Petition for a Salary. In Nova Scotia Archives. RG 1. Vol. 422, no. 22. November 11, 1820. https://novascotia.ca/archives/africanns/archives.asp?ID=87 (last accessed September 26, 2018).

Berlin, Ira (1998): Many Thousands Gone: The First Two Centuries of Slavery in North America. Cambridge: Harvard University Press.

Brannigan, John (2009): Race in Modern Irish Literature and Culture. Edinburgh: Edinburgh University Press.

Brunsman, Denver (2010): Subjects vs. Citizens: Impressment and Identity in the Anglo-American Atlantic. In: Journal of the Early Republic 30, 557–586

Candlin, Kit (2018): The Role of the Enslaved in the 'Fedon Rebellion' of 1795. In: Slavery & Abolition 39(4), 685–707.

CARICOM (2018): Culture Minister Receives Reparations Report. In: January 31, 2018. https://caricom.org/media-center/communications/news-from-the-community/culture-minister-receives-reparations-report (last accessed July 18, 2018).

Chesterman, John (2005): Natural-Born Subjects? Race and British Subjecthood in Australia. In: Australian Journal of Politics and History 51(1), 30–39

Chopra, Ruma (2017): Maroons and Mi'kmaq in Nova Scotia, 1796–1900. In: Acadiensis 46(1), 5–23.

Clarke, George Elliot (ed.) (1991): Fire on the Water: An Anthology of Black Nova Scotian Writing. Volume One. Lawrencetown Beach: Pottersfield Press.

Craig, Cairns (2018): The Wealth of the Nation: Scotland, Culture and Independence. Edinburgh: Edinburgh University Press.

Draper, Nicholas (2010): The Price of Emancipation: Slave-ownership, Compensation and British Society at the End of Slavery. Cambridge: Cambridge University Press.

Eisler, Dale (2015): First Nations and Public Policy: A Legacy of Failure with Blame All Around. In: Policy Magazine 3(4), 28–30.

Everill, Bronwen (2012): Destiny Seems to Point Me to that Country: Early Nineteenth-Century African American Migration, Emigration and Expansion. In: Journal of Global History 7, 53–77.

Fingard, Judith (1973): English Humanitarianism and the Colonial Mind: Walter Bromley in Nova Scotia, 1813 – 2. In: The Canadian Historical Review 54(2), 123 – 151
Gatrell, Peter (2016): Refugees: What's Wrong with History?. In: Journal of Refugee Studies 30(2), 170 – 189.
Gilroy, Paul (1993): The Black Atlantic: Modernity and Double Consciousness. Cambridge: Harvard University Press.
Hall, Catherine/ Draper, Nicholas/ McClelland, Keith/ Donington, Katie/Lang, Rachel (2014): Legacies of British Slave-ownership: Colonial slavery and the Formation of Victorian Britain. Cambridge: Cambridge University Press.
Hickman, Mary (2012): Past Migrations, Contemporary Representations and Complex Multicultures in London. In: Irial Glynn and J. Olaf Kleist (eds.): History, Memory and Migration: Perceptions of the Past and the Politics of Incorporation. Basingstoke: Palgrave Macmillan, 138 – 153.
Humble Address of the House of Representation, in General Assembly (1815): In Journal of the House of Assembly Nova Scotia Archives. April 1, 1815. 107. https://novascotia.ca/archives/africanns/archives.asp?ID=76 (last accessed September 26, 2018).
Kehoe, S. Karly (2017): Catholic Relief and the Political Awakening of Irish Catholics in Nova Scotia, 1780 – 1830. In: Journal of Imperial and Commonwealth History 46(1), 1 – 20.
Kehoe, S. Karly (2018): Colonial Collaborators: Britain and the Catholic Church in Trinidad, c. 1820 – 1840. In: *Slavery & Abolition.*
Mancke, Elizabeth (1997): Another British America: A Canadian Model for the Early Modern British Empire. In: Journal of Imperial and Commonwealth History 25(1), 1 – 36.
Marfleet, Philip (2013): Explorations in a Foreign Land: States, Refugees and the Problem of History. In: Refugee Survey Quarterly 32(2), 14 – 34.
Meer, Nasar (2018): 'Race' and 'Post-Colonialism': Should One Come Before the Other? In: Ethnic and Racial Studies 46(1), 1163 – 1181.
Muller, Hannah Weiss (2017): Subjects and Sovereign: Bonds of Belonging in the Eighteenth-Century British Empire Oxford: Oxford University Press.
Samson, Daniel (1994): George Elliott Clarke's Songs of Love and Pain from Africadia: An Introduction to The Apocrypha of Whylah Falls. In: Left History 2(1), 67 – 91.
Reid, John (2004): *Pax Britannica* or *Pax Indigena?* Planter Nova Scotia (1760 – 1782) and Competing Strategies of Pacification. In: Canadian Historical Review 85(4), 669 – 692.
Sher, Richard B. (2015): Church and University in the Scottish Enlightenment: The Moderate Literati of Edinburgh, Second Edition. Edinburgh: Edinburgh University Press.
Riddell, William Renwick (1921): The Baptism of Slaves in Prince Edward Island. In: The Journal of Negro History 6(3), 307 – 309.
Spray, William (1977): The Settlement of the Black Refugees in New Brunswick. In: Acadiensis 6(2), 64 – 79.
Truth and Reconciliation Commission of Canada (n.d.): http://www.trc.ca/websites/trcinstitution/index.php?p=890.
Whitfield, Harvey Amani (2002): 'We Can Do as We Like Here': An Analysis of Self Assertion and Agency of Black Refugees in Halifax, Nova Scotia, 1813 – 1821. In: Acadiensis 32(1), 29 – 49.
Whitfield, Harvey Amani (2006): Blacks on the Border: The Black Refugees in British North America, 1815 – 1860. Hanover: Vermont University Press.

Whitfield, Harvey Amani (2002): 'We Can Do as We Like Here': An Analysis of Self Assertion and Agency of Black Refugees in Halifax, Nova Scotia, 1813–1821. In: Acadiensis 32(1), 29–49.

Young, Iris Marion. (2006): Responsibility and Global Justice: A Social Connection Model. In: Social Philosophy and Policy 23(1), 102–130.

Yves Frenette

National minorities, immigration, and responsibility: French Canada as a case study, 1840–1960

Abstract: In some host countries and regions where national minorities coexist, the latter's relative weight and relations to each other and to the majority may be the most decisive factors in influencing representations of and policies towards immigrants and refugees. This has been the case for French Canadians who generally perceived immigration – especially non-Catholic and non-francophone immigration – as strengthening the anglophone majority, and thus weakening the French Canadians and threatening their very cultural survival in a hostile continent. Up to 1960, French Canadians opposed immigration and categorized immigrants as those who were ideal, i.e., Franco-Catholic immigrants; those who were tolerated, i.e., non-francophone Catholic immigrants; and those who were undesirable, i.e., non-Catholic immigrants, especially Jews.

As millions of migrants and refugees transform the twenty-first-century world, it is imperative to look back into the past, not to draw lessons but to acquire a historical perspective that is often lacking but can be helpful in understanding and informing current debates about immigration and the integration of newcomers.

In some host countries and regions, the existence of national, religious, and linguistic minorities – often themselves the products of earlier migrations – complicate both interactions with immigrants and refugees and the *problématique* of responsibility. Seeing themselves as dominated and, more often than not, as persecuted by majorities, national, religious, and linguistic minorities often feel acutely threatened by the mass arrival of newcomers who do not share with them a common language, religion, and/or ethnicity. In these situations, each immigrant group is assessed according to its capacity to reinforce or weaken a given minority in its struggle for survival within a nation or a region. At the same time, members of national minorities are not isolated from larger currents of thought, notably those that marginalize or demonize other groups.

French Canada is a good example of this.[1] There, French migrants first settled in the St. Lawrence Valley (Quebec) in the seventeenth century, where they

1 This chapter deals only with French Canada, i.e. Quebec and its diaspora. It does not take into

https://doi.org/10.1515/9783110628746-007

displaced Indigenous people and created a colonial society, which was then conquered by Britain between 1760 and 1763. From then on, largely for economic reasons, French Canadians migrated throughout the North American continent and expressed their distinctiveness through their Catholicism, which has important cultural associations, their French language, and a collective memory of struggle for cultural survival.[2] Given this background, my chapter's primary focus is to understand how this historical experience shaped French Canadians' relationship with later immigrants and to explore the responsibility they felt or did not feel towards them between 1840 and 1960.

I have chosen 1840 as a starting point because it was in the wake of a failed Liberal rebellion against British rule in 1837–1838 that clerical and lay Catholic elites developed a coherent vision of the group to which they belonged and began to express it with the creation and the dissemination of the name 'French Canadians'. As a bookend, 1960 is important because it marks the symbolic end of French Canada as a cultural entity and the beginning of its mental fragmentation into groups that were confined within Canada's various provincial boundaries: Québécois, Franco-Ontarians, Franco-Manitobans, etc. (Martel 1997; Juteau-Lee 1999; Laniel/Thériault, eds., 2016). In the United States, the acculturation process had been more rapid. There, as early as the first decade of the twentieth century, francophone leaders had started to refer to the group as Franco-Americans (Roby 2004, 562).

Dispersed throughout Canada and the United States, francophones were a minority in Anglo-American North America. Only in Quebec did they control state institutions. But even there the state was relatively weak and other social actors, mainly the Catholic Church, oversaw and took charge of education, health, and social services (Linteau/Durocher/Robert 1989). As this volume focusses on the role of individuals in the integration of refugees, it is appropriate to look at French Canada prior to the advent of a strong state, when immigration was largely the concern of civil society.

In the first section of the chapter, I briefly discuss some sociological characteristics of French Canadians. It is followed by a consideration of their attitudes towards immigration before and after the Second World War. It then moves on to show how different immigrant groups were perceived and treated in French Can-

account Acadia, the French-speaking area of the Maritimes, or Louisiana. Originally settled by the French, Louisiana received African slaves and two groups of political refugees in the eighteenth and early nineteenth centuries: Acadians following a massive deportation, and refugees from Saint-Domingue (Haiti). On Acadia see Griffiths 2004; and Farragher 2005. On Louisiana see Hall 1992; Brasseaux 2005; Dessens 2010; and Vidal 2013.

2 For an introduction to the history of French Canada, see Frenette 1999, 538–586.

ada as 'ideal', 'undesirable', or tolerated according to their potential for reinforcing or weakening French-Canadian identity. The three groups highlighted here are respectively the Franco-Europeans, the Jews, and the Italians.[3]

1. French Canadians: between a nation and an ethnic group

According to some scholars, between 1840 and 1960 French Canadians and, to some extent, Franco-Americans were a *groupe nationalitaire* whose self-representation in history was weaker than a nation but stronger than an ethnic group (Juteau-Lee 1999; Thériault 1995). In Canada and in parts of the United States, they saw themselves as the legitimate successors of the first European inhabitants of the continent. In their view, their history was much longer and richer than that of later groups who joined the American melting pot or the Canadian mosaic. Indeed, they considered themselves to be a community of history and destiny, whose members, wherever they lived, spoke a common language, practised a common religion, and shared cultural traits that centred on family and kin. According to French Canada's self-appointed spokespeople, such as Henri Bourassa and André Laurendeau, both of whom were politicians and journalists, Canada's founding in 1867 was a pact between two equal nations and for many of them, the resulting biculturalism became a tool for cultural survival (Bock 2004; Lamarre 2016). Perhaps paradoxically, it was in the province of Quebec, with its French-speaking majority, that feelings of persecution and socio-economic domination by *les Anglais* were the most intense (Cook 1982; Trofimenkoff 1982).

3 Attitudes toward these three groups did not vary much in different regions of French-Canada. On the other hand, French-Canadian relations with Irish immigrants were more complex. At the time of Irish mass migration in the middle decades of the nineteenth century, French Canadians shared with Protestant North Americans negative stereotypes toward Irish immigrants, which were tempered by the Catholicism of the newcomers. With time, in Quebec, the children of the immigrants developed close relations with the French-Canadian majority, which did not perceive them as a threat. In addition, French-Canadian nationalist leaders felt great sympathy for Irish nationalist leaders who shared with them a common enemy. Outside of Quebec, in Canada as in the United States, members of the two minorities competed for jobs and for power within the Catholic Church and in the political sphere. Irish immigrants and their children had a linguistic advantage and joined Protestant anglophones in restricting the use of the French language. On these issues, see Frenette 1999; McQuillan 1999, 133–164; Jolivet, 2011; Perin/Sanfilippo 2012, 199–206; and Cardinal/Jolivet/Matte (eds.) 2014.

Despite French Canadians' high degree of geographic mobility, French Canada was perceived by French Canadians and outsiders alike as a sedentary, almost immobile society in which families stayed in the same place for generations and social change occurred at a very slow pace.[4] This perception expressed itself in the language of rootedness, which essentially captured the migration from France to New France in the seventeenth and eighteenth centuries, the settlement of Quebec's hinterland in the nineteenth century, the urbanization that French Canadians experienced over the course of the nineteenth and twentieth centuries, and the migration of more than one million of them from Canada to the United States between 1840 and 1930 (Frenette 2015, 21–37).

Before I start to analyse the relationship between French Canadians and immigrants, it is important to draw attention to two points. First, prior to 1951, the term 'refugee' applies rather broadly to anyone leaving an environment where his or her human security is threatened (Epp 2017).[5] Second, this chapter cannot be taken as an exhaustive study since I have not been able to show the full complexity of the relationship between French Canadians and immigrants. It should rather be seen as a brief overview, but one that sheds important light on how in-migration can affect pre-existing minority identity. What is presented here are the dominant discourses as they were expressed by intellectuals and politicians, but we need to appreciate that more marginal voices also existed. Moreover, it is very difficult to assess the impact of these discourses surrounding immigration on the representations of the population. While they surely had an impact, what this impact actually was is not always clear.

2. French-Canadian representations of immigration, 1900–1940

The French-Canadian intelligentsia was conservative and yet was not isolated from Western currents of thought. For instance, starting in the second half of the nineteenth century, it became influenced by theories borrowed from the natural sciences, including the idea that communities, societies, and nations were 'organic' and thus were living organisms in which each individual had a place, a

4 See, for instance, the influential monograph by member of the Chicago School of Sociology Horace Miner (1939).

5 Although the 1951 Refugee Convention marked an international watershed, Canada refused to sign it until 1969. However, the country did participate in some international initiatives in the years after the introduction of the Convention.

function, duties, and responsibilities (Pâquet 2005). Thus, in their opinion, immigrants were 'foreign bodies' who had the potential to destabilize the French-Canadian social organism and threaten its very survival. In this context, some believed that it was 'natural' to categorize immigrants by ethnic origin. There were other categories of inclusion, including their contribution to economic prosperity, their utility and their willingness to assimilate, and exclusion, such as the desire to keep order, a perception of a threat to public health, and concerns about ethnic origin. Moreover, in the context of tensions that existed between French Canadians and English Canadians, the fear that immigrants strengthened the linguistic majority always loomed large (Harvey 1987).

In the first half of the twentieth century, almost every French-Canadian nationalist organization, every nationalist leader, and every nationalist newspaper opposed immigration. Furthermore, the great majority of French-Canadian associations denied membership to immigrants (Behiels 1991). In a bi-confessional education system, where both Catholics and Protestants had rights, the Commission des écoles catholiques de Montréal (CECM) became the seat of French-Canadian culture and Catholicism. It showed little interest in the assimilation of immigrants and instead encouraged them to retain their mother tongues. After the CECM created an English-speaking sector in 1928, Catholic immigrants who realized early on the importance of learning English in Montreal, left the francophone sector with little fuss, and the leaders of the CECM were indifferent to their departure. The attitude of French-Canadian school authorities was in stark contrast to that of the Anglo-Protestant elites who, as early as 1867, had created a school system where all non-Catholics were welcomed, so long as there was no attempt to undermine their authority. Indeed Anglo-Protestant elites instrumentalised immigrants as tools for constructing a country where they would assimilate into the dominant British colonial culture. Essentially, they resented their demographic minority status in Montreal and wanted more bodies in their schools, which meant that immigrant children became an important way of boosting numbers (Croteau 2016).

French-Canadian clerics were not favourably disposed towards immigration, but they had to follow the lead of Catholic authorities in Rome who thought that Catholic migrants around the world required oversight from the point of departure from their country of origin to their point of arrival in a new one to avoid conversion to another church or apostasy. Thus, the Œuvre protectrice des immigrants catholiques was founded in 1912 and set up bureaus near the government immigration offices in the port cities of Halifax (Nova Scotia), Saint John (New Brunswick), and Quebec City (Quebec). The Œuvre provided basic information, practical materials, and 'moral' assistance, which was of the utmost importance to the Church. It was assisted by the Ligue des femmes catholiques, which was present in 28 Canadian dioceses and 432 parishes. Catholic service associations, such as the Knights of Columbus and the St. Vincent de Paul Society, were also involved. The Œuvre des immigrants catholiques was constantly raising funds to cover its costs, but when the Great Depression hit in 1930 and migratory flows slowed considerably, its activities ceased (Pâquet 2002).

3. French-Canadian attitudes towards immigration and immigrants, 1940–1960

During the provincial electoral campaign of 1943–1944, the Opposition leader and populist politician Maurice Duplessis declared that he had proof of a plot fomented by the Canadian government and by Jews to bring to Quebec 10,000 Jewish refugees. Duplessis's speech, which was anti-Semitic and false, ignited a province-wide campaign to prevent European immigration. Hundreds of thousands of people signed petitions, somewhere between 300 and 400 cities and towns passed resolutions against immigration, and many unions followed suit (Rajotte 2007; Chevalier-Caron 2017).

Vicious and xenophobic, this campaign also marked the last of its kind in Quebec because the Second World War represented a turning point in French-Canadian attitudes towards immigration. Even the outspoken traditionalist intellectual François-Albert Angers had started to alter his views on immigration and immigrants and began to advocate for assimilating 'some of the more compatible ethnic groups into the French-Canadian milieu' (quoted in Behiels 1991, 11). After the war, as the pace of urbanization increased, as reports surfaced of French Canadians outside Quebec assimilating into anglophone society, and as younger nationalist leaders began to emerge, concerns grew over French Canada's demographic future. The realities shifted the discourse on immigration because it became obvious that French Canadians' past indifference or hostility towards immigration had benefitted English Canada and had impoverished French Canada. In Canada, immigration is a shared responsibility between the federal and provincial governments, and in Quebec, provincial officials came under pressure from several quarters to develop a selective and rational immigration policy (Pâquet 1997).[6] Yet, it was not until the 1960s that the Quebec government became proactive in attempting to attract immigrants. Duplessis, who served as the province's premier between 1944 and his death in 1959, remained staunchly opposed

6 In neighbouring Ontario, some French-Canadian leaders were also starting to change their attitudes toward immigration. See Martel 1995.

to newcomers, believing that they undermined Quebec's identity: 'pour progresser, un pays a besoin d'une population saine, animée d'un même esprit, possédant les mêmes aspirations patriotiques' (quoted in Dubé 2015, 101). In this opinion, he was supported by a small number of politicians and intellectuals, such as Dominique Beaudin, who continued to denounce immigration as an 'invasion of the hordes from Northern Europe and the Eastern Mediterranean' (quoted in Pâquet 1997, 7).

Calls for a change to this line of thinking were growing louder, and one of the most vociferous was from the Catholic Church because Catholics were among the multitudes of displaced persons from the Second World War and from the rise of Communism in Eastern Europe, which pushed them out of this region and towards countries like Canada.[7] The Vatican established an Emigration Bureau in 1946, and the following year Pope Pius XII implored all Christian countries to share responsibility for the hundreds of thousands of refugees and to meet their spiritual and social needs. Concern for Catholic refugees continued to grow, and in 1951 Rome established the International Catholic Migration Commission. In response, French-Canadian archbishops and bishops created the Société catholique d'aide aux immigrants. The Diocese of Quebec also established the Société du bien-être des immigrants and the Diocese of Montreal encouraged the creation of a welcoming centre for immigrants and opened the Société d'assistance aux immigrants (Harvey 1993). Until then, with a few exceptions including the Œuvre des immigrants catholiques discussed above, finding support had been left to immigrant groups themselves and, sometimes, to foreign governments who were expected to provide support and settlement services.[8]

For editors at the influential daily *Le Devoir*, the indifference and hostility of the population towards immigration were not only deplorable in 'national' terms, but they were also morally reprehensible. For one, André Laurendeau wrote, 'Cet homme déraciné, inquiet, souvent malheureux, nous devons apprendre à l'accueillir fraternellement' (quoted in Anctil 2015, 179). The CECM also reversed its policies and began facilitating assimilation within its French-speaking sector and created the Service des Néo-Canadiens in 1948 as a response (Croteau 2016).

New attitudes and policies towards immigration were put to the test in 1956, when 37,000 Hungarian refugees settled in Canada after a failed uprising against

---

7 On the refugee crisis of the post-war years, see Gatrell 2015.

8 For the French case, see Linteau/Frenette/Le Jeune 2017. For Jewish charitable organisations, see Anctil 2017.

Soviet rule; a few thousand of them went to Montreal. Cardinal Paul-Émile Léger called for solidarity and founded l'Œuvre des réfugiés hongrois, which worked with the City of Montreal Immigration Service, to provide temporary shelter, clothes, and food, and to help the newcomers find jobs. In January 1958, after a request from Léger, Quebec's legislative assembly passed a law that created the Provincial Committee to Aid Hungarian Refugees. As elsewhere in the 'Free World', French Canadians showed an eagerness to help the Hungarian 'Freedom Fighters' (Patrias 1999).

4. 'Ideal immigrants': the French and the Belgians

In the nineteenth and twentieth centuries, the "ideal immigrants" were those who shared with French Canadians their religion and their language (Pâquet 1997).[9] These were the French and the francophone Belgians and Swiss. Not only would they become part of the French-Canadian organic community, but it was felt that they would also counterbalance the growing expansion of Anglo-Protestant Canadians, especially in the new territories of the West that became open to white settlement (Painchaud 1987). Between 1880 and 1914, the Catholic Church, as well as the Quebec and Canadian governments (the latter put under pressure by French-Canadian politicians) sent recruiters to French-speaking Europe. These agents could rely on a vast network of sympathisers who were rooted in Catholic circles. In France, they concentrated on regions that were experiencing economic problems and where Catholics felt persecuted by the Third Republic's successive governments, which were becoming increasingly anticlerical (Linteau/Frenette/Le Jeune 2017).

Although these efforts did not give the hoped-for results, about 50,000 French and an undetermined number of francophone Belgians and Swiss migrated to Canada before the First World War. In the case of the French, half of them stayed and their relationship with the French Canadians was complex. In Montreal and in Ottawa, members of the two groups were neighbours, and in Western Canada, they shared the same churches and schools. In that part of the country, though, they were at a significant geographic distance from Quebec, and a number of immigrant leaders born in France emerged and defended vigorously the religious and linguistic rights of francophone minorities.[10] Furthermore, French

---

9 See also Pâquet 1999.

10 For an example, see Champagne 2003.

journalists founded newspapers and played key editorial roles, and in the 1940s and 1950s French Canadians, French, and Franco-Belgian immigrants campaigned together for the creation of francophone radio stations in Western Canada (Linteau/Frenette/Le Jeune 2017).

Even if Franco-Europeans were 'ideal immigrants', their relations with French Canadians were not always amicable. For instance, members of the two groups rarely intermarried, and those who did often had to fight their parents. It was only with the coming of age of the second and third generations that intermarriages became more common. In religious congregations, which were composed of French-Canadian and French members, mutual hostility prevailed due to constant power struggles between the two groups and because the French Canadians were frustrated by perceived notions of linguistic and cultural superiority on the part of the French. Indeed the language question was a central feature of the French/French-Canadian relationship as French immigrants were generally more desirous than French Canadians of acquiring English and of integrating into the anglophone mainstream. In France, they had learned to resist attacks on their religious freedom, but fighting for their language was new to them. In addition, like other immigrants, they realized that their future and the future of their children was linked to the acquisition of the English language (Linteau/Frenette/Le Jeune 2017).

Immigration from France to Canada declined in the 1920s and almost stopped completely during the Great Depression and the Second World War. But at the end of the conflict, it reached new peaks. In the 1950s the number of France-born individuals living in Canada increased by 131 per cent, reaching 36,000. The numbers would have been much greater if the Canadian Embassy in Paris and the Royal Canadian Mounted Police had been able to manage the flow of applications more effectively. France was trying to reconstruct following the damage sustained during the war and in 1948 the Canadian government finally recognized the French as preferred immigrants, which put them on the same footing as British and American immigrants, though in reality, British immigrants were still favoured (Linteau 2008; Frenette 2012).

Post-war French immigrants tended to settle in Quebec and this inspired historian Paul-André Linteau to cast this as a love story between the French and the province (Linteau 2008, 179). French immigrants mostly lived in Montreal where, as in other Canadian cities, they did not form an ethnic neighbourhood on their own. While they had close contacts with the French-Canadian population, their integration was hampered by the negative perceptions that many of them had of the French-Canadian 'dialect' and culture. For their part, French Canadians developed the stereotype of the 'maudit Français' who felt superior and who constantly complained about Quebec and Canada (Frenette 2012).[11]

5. 'Undesirable' immigrants: the Jews

At the opposite end of the spectrum from Franco-European immigrants were those declared to be 'undesirable' and according to historian Pierre Anctil, the Jews represented the 'total others'.[12] The fact that they were not Christian, let alone Catholic, was a major issue for many French Canadians. Coming mostly from Eastern Europe, they also spoke an unfamiliar language, Yiddish, and some of them were members of revolutionary groups. By being concentrated in Montreal, they embodied both an urbanity and a modernity that contrasted sharply with Quebec conservatives' world view and because of all of these factors, it was felt that they could never assimilate.[13]

Yet, Jews had been part of the landscape of French Canada since the seventeenth century and had built a synagogue in Montreal as early as 1768. Numbering a mere 409 in this city in 1871, their numbers grew steadily in the following decades: from 2,473 in 1891 to 28,540 in 1911 and then to 57,772 in 1931. By then, Jewish immigrants had built Montreal's largest non-French and non-British community. Their numerical importance, their residential concentration, and their community's institutional completeness allowed them to minimise their daily encounters with people from outside of the community, including the city's French-Canadian majority. The situation was different in Quebec's small towns and in the countryside, where about 12,000 Jewish immigrants lived. There, Jewish peddlers and merchants were, by the nature of their work, in close contact with the local population. In these parts of the province, and as service providers, who were so few in number, they needed to learn at least some French. Importantly, in these more rural areas, they did not seem to be considered a threat to the survival of the French-Canadian community.

---

11 Unfortunately, we know far less about Belgian and Swiss immigrants. For instance, it is almost impossible to determine the numbers and the percentages of francophones among them. On the Belgians see Jaenen 1991; Jaumain 1999; Ghislain 2015. On Swiss immigrants see Khalid 2009.

12 As Larochelle (2018) has recently shown, Arabs, Asians, Blacks, and Indigenous people also acted as 'total others' for French Canadians. But as few members of these groups were present on the streets of Montreal, they were not considered an immigrant threat.

13 This section relies heavily on the work of Anctil: 1988a; 1988b; 2014; 2015a; 2015b; 2017.

In Montreal, Jewish people like other non-Catholic immigrants could not send their children to CECM's schools, but they were welcome in the schools that were under the jurisdiction of the Protestant School Board. This arrangement suited them because their social mobility was linked to the acquisition of the English language and not the French. In 1903, the provincial Education Act formalized their presence in Protestant schools, but it precluded them, as non-Christians, from holding seats on the Protestant School Board. Two decades later, when members of the Jewish community agitated for the creation of a Jewish School Board, the Catholic hierarchy opposed it, arguing that it would set a dangerous precedent (Croteau 2016, 249-250).

Anti-Semitic discourse was present and at times thriving in French Canada, largely among the intelligentsia. This discourse was rooted in a centuries-old Catholic tradition, and as the size of the Jewish community expanded, many priests launched verbal and written attacks against it. Their superiors issued no reprimand beyond a warning to them that they be prudent (Dumas 2015). On the other hand, in the 1930s the Church condemned the Nazi-inspired violent anti-Semitism of the journalist-politician Adrien Arcand, who, in spite of his bluster, was never able to gather more than a few followers. At a fundamental level, the Church was deeply opposed to Judaism, but it did not believe that its adherents should be persecuted and physically threatened.[14]

In the first half of the twentieth century, there were four outbursts of violent anti-Semitism in French Canada. The first occurred in 1910 in Quebec City after real estate lawyer Jacques-Édouard Plamondon gave a vitriolic speech against Judaism and called for a boycott of Jewish businesses. Members of the city's tiny Jewish community were assaulted and their synagogue vandalized (Normand 2005). Some twenty-five years later, Université de Montréal's students broke shop windows in the heart of the city's Jewish neighbourhood. Their actions were condemned by *Le Devoir* and by the Catholic Church hierarchy. In the same period, medical interns at the Notre-Dame Hospital, the most important Catholic hospital in Montreal, went on strike to protest the appointment of a Jewish colleague. They were joined by interns from other Catholic hospitals and altogether about seventy-five medics participated in the protest movement. The strikers had the support of all the French-Canadian associations which were involved in an 'achat chez nous' campaign targeting Jewish stores.[15] The last violent public anti-Semitic episode took place during the Second World War. On the eve of its inauguration in 1944, the Beth Israël Ohev Sholom in the bourgeois

14 On Arcand and the fascist movement, see Nadeau 2010; Théorêt 2012.

15 On the Notre-Dame Hospital interns' strike, see Robinson 2015.

upper town of Quebec City was set on fire. It was an act of terror that corresponded with the anti-Jewish immigration campaign that had been raging for months.

Yet, there were dissenting voices, and in the 1930s, liberal newspapers condemned the anti-Semitic campaigns and some Catholic clerics engaged in dialogue with rabbis. But it was not until after the Second World War that the situation truly improved as the horrors of the Shoah became widely known and the state of Israel was established. In 1958, *Le Devoir*'s director, Gérard Filion, went to Israel and lauded its citizens, declaring them a model: 'La solidarité des Juifs doit nous servir de leçon [...]. Il n'y a pas de peuple plus divisé en surface que les Israéliens, et cependant ils savent poser les gestes qui assurent leur statut collectif [...]. Il faudrait que plus de Canadiens français aillent en Israel' (quoted in Anctil 2017, 318). Ten years earlier, the Canadian Jewish Congress had launched the Cercle juif de langue française to facilitate relations between Jews and French Canadians. The Cercle really took off in 1954 after the involvement of Naïm Kattan, a young Jewish man from Baghdad, who had learned French and who had sojourned in Paris. Kattan organized a series of activities, where members of the two groups met for a lecture or a round table, held in the French language. The *rapprochement* would take time and would be painful but it had started.

6. Italian immigrants

Between the two extremes of the 'ideal' Franco-European immigrants and the 'undesirable' Jews, were the non-francophone and non-anglophone Catholic immigrants. Although not encouraged to immigrate by French-Canadian elites, they were tolerated, and one group of particular interest is the Italians, the fourth largest linguistic group in Montreal.[16] Before the end of the nineteenth century, a few dozen Italians resided in Montreal. Coming mostly from northern Italy, they were musicians, artisans, and small business owners who integrated rapidly into French-Canadian society, especially through bonds of marriage. But from the 1890s, the level of Italian immigration took new proportions: in 1901, the Italian community numbered 2,000 people, by 1914 it was 10,000, and on the eve of the Second World War, it has doubled to 20,000. At the same time, the geographic origin of Italian immigrants and their occupational profile shifted, with the majority being unskilled workers from the south, notably the Molise region. Most of

16 The best introduction to Italian immigrants is Ramirez 1989. On Montreal's Italians, see Boissevain 1970; Ramirez and Del Balso 1980; Ramirez 1984; Painchaud and Poulin 1988.

them settled around two 'national' parishes served by Italian priests but located in the midst of working-class French-Canadian Montreal. Their children attended French-language Catholic schools.

This pattern began to change during the 1930s and 1940s, a consequence of the Great Depression, which saw a dramatic rise in ethnic conflict as people struggled for work. During these years, destitute Italian families learned about the reality of the severe financial limitations of the Catholic Church's charitable institutions. Consequently, many families were forced to turn to Protestant social welfare agencies to survive, but getting access to these services required them to enrol their children in Anglo-Protestant schools. More importantly, though, was the fact that a growing number of Italian families began to feel that their children needed to learn English in a city where economic power was concentrated in the hands of Anglo-Protestants. Acquiring English was impossible in the French-language sector of the CECM, where the teaching of English only started in grade five. Moreover, Quebec did not have a fully developed public French-language high school system, and many Italians transferred their children to the English-language sector of the CECM. This meant that by 1945, half of the school board's Italian students were enrolled in the English sector; that percentage increased to 75 per cent by 1957. In the following decade, Québécois nationalists began to denounce vehemently this situation, and as a result tensions between them and the Italian community exploded.

7. Conclusion

The historian's job is not to make policy or to teach lessons about today based on what has been learned from the past because no two situations in time and place are alike. What the historian can do, however, is shed light on contemporary events and phenomena based on what has happened in the past. Regarding immigration, the historian can point to factors that have eased or hindered immigrants' acceptance and integration. And in those countries or territories where there are pre-existing national minorities, such as in Canada and Quebec, these minorities' relative weight and relations to each other and to the majority may be the most decisive factors in influencing how immigrants and refugees are perceived and the kinds of policies that are adopted to manage their integration.

Quebec is an example of this. Although cultural and religious diversity and the federal policy of multiculturalism[17] are debated everywhere in Canada, it is

17 A brief introduction to Canadian multiculturalism is provided by Troper (1999). The concept

in Quebec that the most acrimonious discussions are taking place in the public sphere. Exploring this example from the perspective of a historian helps understand why this is so. Francophone Quebeckers have resisted assimilation into the anglophone mainstream for more than 250 years. Many of them, likely a majority, are sceptical of the very notion of diversity since it has the potential to undermine their language and culture. Although few Québécois actually think that there is a plot to assimilate them through immigration, many of them continue to see immigrants as people who will weaken their nation (Quebec).

However, and somewhat paradoxically, francophone immigrants may also be seen as linguistic instruments in the survival and the promotion of both French Quebec and francophone minorities throughout Canada.[18] But at the time of writing, this perspective is not at the forefront of public debate. What is being discussed at the moment is the notion that Quebec is receiving too many immigrants and refugees who cannot integrate into the francophone mainstream. It would seem that Muslims are the focus of current attention and seem to be perceived as the new 'undesirable' immigrant group.

Bibliography

Anctil, Pierre (1988a): Le Devoir, les Juifs et l'immigration: De Bourassa à Laurendeau. Québec: Institut québécois de recherche sur la culture.

Anctil, Pierre (1988b): Le rendez-vous manqué: Les Juifs de Montréal face au Québec de l'entre-deux-guerres. Québec: Institut québécois de recherche sur la culture.

Anctil, Pierre (2014): À chacun ses Juifs: 60 éditoriaux du DEVOIR à l'égard des Juifs, 1910–1947. Québec: Septentrion.

Anctil, Pierre (2015a): Complexité et foisonnement d'un rapport oblique: Les Juifs face au monde francophone catholique. In: Études d'histoire religieuse 81(1–2), 141–163.

Anctil, Pierre (2015b): Le Devoir et les Juifs: Complexités d'une relation sans cesse changeante (1910–1963). In: Globe, 18(1), 169–201.

Anctil, Pierre (2017): Histoire des Juifs du Québec. Montréal: Boréal.

Behiels, Michael (1991): Quebec and the Question of Immigration: From Ethnocentrism to Ethnic Pluralism, 1900–1985. Ottawa: Canadian Historical Society.

Bock, Michel (2004): Le sort de la mémoire dans la construction historique de l'identité franco-ontarienne. In: Francophonies d'Amérique 18, 119–126.

Boissevain, Jeremy (1970): The Italians of Montreal: Social Adjustment in a Plural Society. Ottawa: Queen's Printer.

---

and the policy of multiculturalism have had many critics. Quebec public intellectual Gérard Bouchard has proposed instead the notion of interculturalism: see Bouchard 2015.

18 On this perspective see Frenette 2016.

Bouchard, Gérard (2015): Interculturalism: A View from Quebec. Toronto: University of Toronto Press.
Brasseaux, Carl A. (2005): French, Cajun, Creole, Houma: A Primer on Francophone Louisiana. Baton Rouge: Louisiana State University Press.
Cardinal, Linda/Jolivet, Simon/ Matte, Isabelle (eds.) (2014): Le Québec et l'Irlande: Culture, histoire, identité. Québec: Septentrion.
Champagne, Juliette Marthe (2003): De la Bretagne aux plaines de l'Ouest canadien: Lettres d'un défricheur franco-albertain, Alexandre Mahé (1880–1968). Québec: Presses de l'Université Laval.
Chevalier-Caron, Christine (2017): Fausses nouvelles, altérité et manifestations du racisme, In: Histoire Engagée, 28 December. http://histoireengagee.ca/fausses-nouvelles-alterite-et-manifestations-du-racisme/.
Cook, Ramsay (ed.) (1969): French Canadian Nationalism: An Anthology. Toronto: Macmillan.
Croteau, Jean-Philippe (2016): Les commissions scolaires montréalaises et torontoises et les immigrants 1875–1960. Québec: Presses de l'Université Laval.
Dessens, Nathalie (2010): From Saint Domingue to New Orleans: Migration and Influences. Gainesville: University Press of Florida.
Dubé, Sandra (2015): 'Personne n'est antisémite, mais tout le monde est opposé à l'immigration': Les discours des responsables politiques québécois sur les réfugiés juifs, 1938–1945. In: Globe 18(1), 101.
Dumas, Alexandre (2015): L'Église catholique québécoise face à l'antisémitisme des années 1930. In: Globe 18(1), 65–85.
Epp, Marlene (2017): Refugees in Canada: A Brief History. Ottawa: Canadian Historical Society.
Farragher, Jo Mack (2005): A Great and Noble Scheme: The Tragic Story of the Expulsion of the French Acadians from their American Homeland. New York: W.W. Norton.
Frenette, Yves (1999): French Canadians. In: Paul Robert Magocsi (ed.): Encyclopedia of Canada's Peoples. Toronto: University of Toronto Press, 538–586.
Frenette, Yves (2012): Les migrants français au Canada, 1760–1980: Essai de synthèse. In: Didier Poton, Micéala Symington, and Laurent Vidal (eds.): La migration française aux Amériques: Pour un dialogue entre histoire et littérature. Rennes: Presses Universitaires de Rennes, 141–171.
Frenette, Yves (2016): Immigration et francophonie canadienne, 1990–2006. In: Dean Louder and Éric Waddell (eds.): Franco-Amérique, Second Edition. Québec: Septentrion, 367–378.
Frenette, Yves (2015): Bouchard, Faucher, Roby et les autres: les migrations canadiennes-françaises à l'ère industrielle. In: Claude Couture and Srilata Ravi (eds.): Autour de l'œuvre de Gérard Bouchard: Histoire sociale, sociologie historique, imaginaires collectifs et politiques publiques. Québec: Presses de l'Université Laval, 21–37.
Gatrell, Peter (2015): The Making of the Modern Refugee. London and New York: Oxford University Press.
Ghislain, Cédric (2015): Les Belges du Canada: Une minorité qui se découvre de 1881 à 1911. PhD dissertation. Université Laval.
Griffiths, Naomi (2004): From Migrant to Acadian: A North American Border People, 1604–1755. Montreal and Kingston: McGill-Queen's University Press.

Hall, Gwendolyn Midlo (1992): Africans in Colonial Louisiana: The Development of Afro-Creole Culture in the Eighteenth Century. Baton Rouge: Louisiana State University Press.

Harvey, Fernand (1987): La question de l'immigration au Québec: Genèse historique. In: Léo Gagné (ed.): Le Québec français et l'école à clientèle pluriethnique: Contributions à une reflexion. Québec: Éditeur officiel du Québec, 1–55.

Harvey, Julien (1993): L'Église catholique de Montréal et l'accueil des immigrants au XXe siècle. In: Études d'histoire religieuse 59, 92–95.

Jaenen, Cornelius (1991): The Belgians in Canada. Ottawa: Canadian Historical Association.

Jaumain, Serge (1999): Survol historique de l'immigration belge au Canada. In: Serge Jaumain (ed.): Les Immigrants Préférés: Les Belges. Ottawa: University of Ottawa Press, 35–49.

Jolivet, Simon (2011): Le vert et le bleu: Identité québécoise et identité irlandaise au tournant du XXe siècle. Montréal: Presses de l'Université de Montréal.

Juteau-Lee, Danielle (1999): L'ethnicité et ses frontières. Montréal: Presses de l'Université de Montréal.

Khalid, Samy (2009): Les Suisses, révélateurs de l'imaginaire national canadien: Construction identitaire et représentations de la citoyenneté à travers l'expérience des migrants suisses au Canada (XVIIe–XXe siècles). PhD dissertation. University of Ottawa.

Lamarre, Jean (2016): La francophonie nord-américaine: Bilan historiographique et bibliographique. In: Bulletin d'histoire politique, 24(2).

Laniel, Jean-François/Thériault, Joseph Yvon (eds.) (2016): Retour sur les États généraux du Canada français: Continuités et ruptures d'un projet national. Québec: Presses de l'Université du Québec.

Larochelle, Catherine (2018): L'apprentissage des Autres: La construction rhétorique et les usages pédagogiques de l'altérité à l'école québécoise (1830–1915). PhD dissertation. Université de Montréal.

Linteau, Paul-André (2008): Quatre siècles d'immigration française au Canada et au Québec. In: Serge Joyal and Paul-André Linteau (eds.): France-Canada-Québec: 400 ans de relations d'exception. Montréal: Presses de l'Université de Montréal, 165–181.

Linteau, Paul-André/Durocher, René/Robert, Jean-Claude (1989): Histoire du Québec contemporain, 2 vols. Montréal: Boréal.

Linteau, Paul-André/Frenette, Yves/Le Jeune, Françoise (2017): Transposer la France: L'immigration française au Canada (1870–1914). Montréal: Boréal.

Martel, Marcel (1995): Le dialogue avec l'Autre: les dirigeants franco-ontariens et la question de l'immigration, 1927–1968. In: Journal of the CHA, 6, 273–287.

Martel, Marcel (1997): Le deuil d'un pays imaginé. Rêves, lutte et déroute du Canada français: Les rapports entre le Québec et la francophonie canadienne (1867–1975). Ottawa: Centre de recherche en civilisation canadienne-française and Presses de l'Université d'Ottawa.

McQuillan, Aidan (1999): Des chemins divergents: Les Irlandais et les Canadiens français au XIXe siècle. In: Eric Waddell (ed.): Le dialogue avec les cultures minoritaires. Québec: Presses de l'Université Laval.

Miner, Horace (1939): St. Denis: A French-Canadian Parish. Chicago: University of Chicago Press.

Nadeau, Jean-François (2010): Adrien Arcand, führer canadien. Montréal: Lux.

Normand, Sylvio (2005): Plamondon, Jacques-Édouard. In: Dictionary of Canadian Biography 15: (1921–1930). http://www.biographi.ca/en/bio/plamondon_jacques_edouard_15E.html.
Painchaud, Claude/Poulin, Richard (1988): Les Italiens au Québec. Hull: Éditions Asticou.
Painchaud, Robert (1987): Un rêve français dans le peuplement de la Prairie. Saint-Boniface: Éditions des Plaines.
Pâquet, Martin (1997): Towards a Quebec Ministry of Immigration, 1945–1968. Ottawa: Canadian Historical Association.
Pâquet, Martin (1999): Variations sur un même thème: Représentations de l'immigrant belge chez les responsables provinciaux du Canada-Uni et du Québec, 1853–1968. In: Serge Jaumain (ed.): Les immigrants préférés: Les Belges. Ottawa: Presses de l'Université d'Ottawa, 101–136.
Pâquet, Martin (2002): Marquage identitaire et pastorale catholique: L'Œuvre protectrice des immigrants catholiques (1912–1930). In: Jean-Pierre Wallot (ed.): Constructions identitaires et pratiques sociales. Ottawa: Presses de l'Université d'Ottawa, 125–146.
Pâquet, Martin (2005): Tracer les marges de la Cité: Étranger, immigrant et État au Québec, 1627–1981. Montréal: Boréal.
Patrias, Carmela (1999): Hungarians in Canada. Ottawa: Canadian Historical Association.
Perin, Roberto/Sanfilippo, Matteo (2012): Les conflits ecclésiastiques, 1860–1930. In: Yves Frenette, Étienne Rivard, and Marc St-Hilaire (eds.): La francophonie nord-américaine. Québec: Presses de l'Université Laval.
Rajotte, David (2007): Les Québécois, les juifs et l'immigration durant la Seconde Guerre mondiale. In: Bulletin d'histoire politique 16(1), 259–270.
Ramirez, Bruno (1984): Les premiers Italiens de Montréal: L'origine de la Petite Italie du Québec. Montréal: Boréal Express.
Ramirez, Bruno (1989): The Italians in Canada. Ottawa: Canadian Historical Association.
Ramirez, Bruno/Del Balso, Michael (1980): The Italians of Montreal: From Sojourning to Settlement, 1900–1921. Montréal: Éditions du Courant.
Robinson, Ira (2015): 'Maîtres chez eux': La grève des internes de 1934 revisited. In: *Globe* 18(1), 153–168.
Roby, Yves (2004): The Franco-Americans of New England: Dreams and Realities. Montreal and Kingston: McGill-Queen's University Press.
Théorêt, Hugues (2012): Les Chemises bleues: Adrien Arcand, journaliste antisémite canadien-français. Québec: Septentrion.
Thériault, Joseph Yvon (1995): L'identité à l'épreuve de la modernité: Écrits politiques sur l'Acadie et les francophonies canadiennes minoritaires. Moncton: Éditions d'Acadie.
Trofimenkoff, Susan Mann (1982): The Dream of Nation: A Social and Intellectual History of Quebec. Toronto: Macmillan.
Troper, Harold (1999): Multiculturalism. In: Paul Robert Magocsi (ed.): Encyclopedia of Canada's Peoples. Toronto: University of Toronto Press, 997–1006.
Vidal, Cécile (ed.) (2013): Louisiana: Crossroads of the Atlantic World. Philadelphia: University of Pennsylvania Press.

Niamh McLoughlin and Harriet Over

Less "human" than us: dehumanisation as a psychological barrier to the integration of migrants

Abstract: Prejudice and discriminatory behaviour remain significant barriers to positive intergroup relations. In a time in which global migration rates are at their highest (and continue to rise), recent emphasis has been placed on the negative perceptions of certain immigrant and refugee group members in Western media and political discourse. A prominent feature of these debates involves the perceived "humanness" of migrant individuals. The tendency to view culturally dissimilar others as less human compared to one's own cultural group is not a novel social phenomenon however. In this chapter, we draw from the fields of philosophy, social and developmental psychology to examine the nature of dehumanisation in the context of migration. Through understanding the psychological processes by which dehumanising perceptions are acquired and expressed, this research ultimately hopes to inform strategies to foster the inclusion of newcomers within their host countries.

1. Introduction

Concerns over the perception and treatment of immigrant and refugee group members have been recently highlighted in Western public discourse. This particular emphasis in debate has followed a number of significant political and social-cultural shifts – namely, the mass migration of those seeking refuge in Europe from conflicts in Syria and the rise of populism across Western societies. One of the most striking aspects of these debates involves the perceived "humanness" of migrant individuals (Bruneau/Kteily/Laustsen 2017). Their humanity has often been questioned in the public domain of their prospective host nations, whether that be the derogatory language chosen to describe their arrival or the crude visual depictions of their plight (Esses/Medianu/Lawson 2013; Bleiker et al. 2013). As well as potentially contributing to human rights violations (e. g., the separation and detainment of families at the southern US border), the assumption that certain social groups are less human than others in some respect could be a substantial challenge for their successful integration within host communities. The harmful phenomenon of "dehumanisation" has been a topic of im-

https://doi.org/10.1515/9783110628746-008

port to philosophers and social psychologists, and most recently for researchers interested in the origins of prejudice in young children (McLoughlin/Over 2018).

In this chapter, we summarize psychological research on dehumanisation in the context of migration with adults and what this means for their willingness to engage in moral action. We then discuss some of the potential psychological mechanisms (e.g., perceived threat) that could clarify why migrant groups are particularly vulnerable to dehumanising perceptions. Lastly, we argue for the importance of examining the development of dehumanising attitudes towards migrants among children in order to ultimately overcome this intergroup barrier.

2. Dehumanisation and moral responsibility

Early psychological theorists first studied the phenomenon of dehumanisation in an effort to explain extreme intergroup violence witnessed during the twentieth century (Bar-Tal 1989; Kelman 1973; Opotow 1990). In his theory of moral disengagement, Albert Bandura posits that viewing other people not as individuals with 'feelings, hopes, concerns, but as subhuman objects...as mindless "savages", "gooks", "satanic fiends"...and other bestial creatures' is a core psychological process for weakening moral inhibitions against cruel behaviour (Bandura et al. 1996). This explicit denial of humanness is typically seen in the perceptions of outgroup members (persons who have a different social identity to one's own, for example, different race or national affiliation) and is easily recognizable in public rhetoric regarding migrants. Established politicians in Europe have warned local constituents of a 'swarm' or a 'flood' due to rising migration rates (Shah 2015) and have even referred to this demographic as 'wild beasts' and 'human trash' (Bruneau/Kteily/Laustsen 2017). In addition to the very explicit dehumanisation of migrants, it has been further suggested that more implicit dehumanising beliefs play a role in perceived moral responsibility for members of these groups. In this section, we explore the research in social psychology which has investigated the harmful consequences that both blatant and more subtle forms of dehumanisation have for moral engagement among adults. Specifically, this work has focused on adults' endorsements of the cultural inclusion of migrants, their general concern for migrant individuals, and their prosocial intentions towards minorities in need.

Researchers from several different traditions have characterized outgroup dehumanisation in terms of overt references to animals, primates, and other more lowly biological entities (Smith 2012; Goff et al. 2008; O'Brien 2003). In an advance on the study of blatant dehumanisation across contemporary societies, Kteily and colleagues (Kteily et al. 2015) developed a measure that assesses adult perceptions about how "evolved" or civilized social groups appear to be. For these studies, participants were asked to make scalar judgements using the popular graphic of the "Ascent of Man" (i.e., five silhouettes representing important physiological steps in the evolution of humans). They found that participants' ratings of different outgroups on this scale, when compared with ratings of people from their own social group (ingroup), were consistently linked to their endorsement of discriminatory attitudes (especially in the case of persecuted minority outgroups). For example, the perception that Arab ethnic outgroups are 'less evolved' than Americans predicted increased agreement with controlling the migration of Arab individuals and fewer expressions of compassion when an Arab person experienced an injustice. Similarly, these dehumanising beliefs predicted British participants' support for anti-Muslim policies and Hungarian adults' reluctance to provide financial aid for the integration of the Roma community into the larger society.

This measure has also been applied to study the current dynamics of rising migration rates in Europe. The results of a large-scale study conducted in the Czech Republic, Hungary, Greece, and Spain showed that dehumanising perceptions of Muslim refugees (again, that they are less 'evolved' than the ingroup) were uniquely associated with less willingness to engage in affirmative action for asylum seekers (Bruneau/Kteily/Laustsen 2017). This association was stronger in the Eastern European countries which the authors attribute in part to the higher frequency of explicit anti-migrant rhetoric in the political domains of these two nations.

Apart from the research outlined above, social psychologists have tended to focus more on capturing everyday instances of dehumanising thought in their experimental research (Haslam/Loughnan 2014). This body of work has shown that, across various cultural settings, adults attribute fewer traits uniquely linked to 'humanness', including intelligence, openness, and cultural refinement, to social outgroups (Vaes et al. 2012; Haslam et al. 2008). One influential account developed by Leyens et al. (2000) suggests that outgroup members are perceived to be less capable of the complex emotional experiences thought to be uniquely human, like the ability to feel proud or remorseful. This bias in emotion perception has been coined outgroup 'infra-humanisation' in social psychology (Leyens 2009).

Building on this theoretical perspective, researchers have provided experimental evidence that speaks to how implicit attributions of humanness can shape intergroup interactions within the context of migration. For instance, Leyens, Demoulin, Gaunt, Vaes and Paladino (2007) found that the belief Muslim refugees experience fewer complex emotions (infra-humanisation) was associated with the objection of their migration into European territory. In a related study, Portuguese participants demonstrated greater opposition to Turkey joining the European Union after reading a description which implied that people from this culture more readily express basic emotions over uniquely human emotions (Pereira/Vala/Leyens 2009). More generally, other research has revealed that attributing fewer human-like capacities to others can reduce individual contributions to humanitarian aid in the aftermath of natural disasters (Cuddy/Rock/Norton 2007; Andrighetto 2014).

Overall, these studies are compelling evidence that thinking of migrant groups as not entirely human can have a direct negative influence on the host society's understanding of their social and moral obligations towards them. The harmful effects of dehumanisation are observed even when intergroup distinctions are based on more subtle differences in a person's ability to experience and express human feeling. Needless to say, it is not only migrants that experience the effects of dehumanisation. This phenomenon is clearly evident in group relations between and within different societies, for example, amid the historically rooted racial tensions in the United States (Goff et al. 2008). Yet, some of the intergroup and psychological features that characterize periods of mass migration might make immigrants and refugee groups especially vulnerable to dehumanising perceptions.

3. Psychological mechanisms of migrant dehumanisation

Previous research has delineated several psychological processes that contribute to the derogation of migrants: incoming migrant groups are perceived to represent a threat to the host nation; migrants are typically part of a group associated with lower status; and migrants originate from cultural backgrounds that are considered very different, and perhaps impenetrable, to the ingroup (Chavez 2001; Fiske et al. 2002; Haslam et al. 2006).

3.1. Perceived threat

Many of the public representations of migrants in Western countries highlight the potential dangers their arrival can pose to the host nations (Esses/Medianu/Lawson 2013). Analyses of media content have revealed that common descriptions of migrant groups involve claims that they are carriers of contagion or disease, that they aim to 'cheat' the system and become dependent on the state, and that they are likely to commit violent criminal acts (Cisneros 2008; Louis 2006; Vaes 2017). Comparing outgroup members to threatening entities in this way encourages certain inferences about their character traits (Tirrell 2012) and can licence severe behavioural responses – that they must be monitored, detained, or, in the most extreme cases, eliminated for the benefit of the general public (Smith 2012).

Experimental research has revealed that each of these depictions plays a role in facilitating the dehumanising percept. For example, portraying migrants as potential contaminants increased hostile attitudes (via emotive reactions such as disgust and contempt) among US and Canadian participants (Esses/Medianu/Lawson 2013; Utych 2017). Priming the idea that incoming asylum seekers are attempting to undercut host systems was also highly correlated to the belief they inherently lack moral sensibility (Esses et al. 2008) – a belief which has been conceptualized as a more indirect form of dehumanisation (Schwartz/Struch 1989). In addition, reading editorials which imply that certain migrant groups belong to a terrorist organization elicited faster implicit associations between migrants and animalistic concepts (Esses/Medianu/Lawson 2013). Indeed, Kteily et al. (2015) observed a spike in blatant dehumanising ratings of Arab individuals in the aftermath of real-life terrorist situations, such as the Boston Marathon bombing in 2013. Thus it seems that, beyond the harmful impact of messages disseminated by the media, more general states of psychological threat can facilitate dehumanising biases.

3.2. Perceived status

The harsh circumstances in which many migrants find themselves might make them more vulnerable to perceptions of low status in the host society. Philosophers and social psychologists have reasoned that perceived status differences might be integral to the concept of dehumanisation. In his philosophical account of explicit dehumanisation, Smith (2012) notes that targeted minority group members throughout history were not only considered less human than members of the dominant cultural group, but *less than* human. Bruneau et al. (2017) also suggest that status plays an important role in the belief that migrant groups are 'less evolved' than other social groups in Europe. Across their studies, participants tended to think of high-status outgroups (e.g., German or Swedish) as equally human to their own group. Moreover, individual differences in relative support for the hierarchical structure of group relations has been related to dehumanising perceptions of migrants (Costello/Hodson 2011; Esses 2008; Haslam/Loughnan 2014).

The literature investigating the impact of status differences for more subtle attributions of humanity is more mixed (Vaeset al. 2012). While some researchers argue that both high and low status groups assign fewer uniquely human traits to outgroup members (Leyens 2009), others suggest the social groups that are at least judged as less competent (a distinct but closely related construct to status (Fiske et al. 2002)) are more likely to be infra-humanised (Vaes/Paladino 2009).

3.3. Perceived 'fundamental' differences

It is often the case that migrant groups possess myriad cultural characteristics that differ from the population of the host nation, including their first spoken language, their ethnic background, and/or their religious values (Algan et al. 2012). These intercultural differences could highlight the psychological boundaries between groups and, under specific conditions, may foster the perspective that members of migrant groups represent fundamentally different 'kinds' of people (Prentice/Miller 2007; Rhodes/Mandalaywala 2017). A number of prominent theorists have proposed that the belief that outgroup members are inherently different from the ingroup, and that their unfamiliar behaviour and traits are explained by a fixed underlying quality or 'essence', could be involved in dehumanising thought (Smith 2014; Leyens et al. 2001). Simply put, social outgroup members are often denied the innate 'humanness' that is more automatically attributed to perceived similar others.

Social psychological research suggests that less knowledge of and contact with migrant groups contribute to greater perceived intergroup differences and can promote dehumanising beliefs. For instance, Capozza et al. (2013) found that Italian adults' lower reports of interactions with migrants predicted increases in the salience of intergroup boundaries, which was ultimately associated with fewer attributions of human traits. In a similar vein, it was observed that, across several cultural contexts, less awareness and understanding of another group's cultural viewpoint was linked to decreases in their perceived capacity for complex emotion (Rodríguez-Pérez et al. 2011). Bruneau et al. (2017) also implied that the finding that blatant dehumanising Muslim perceptions were less severe among participants in Greece may be because of the increased proximity between host and Muslim refugee communities in this setting.

4. The development of dehumanising perceptions

Given that the current generation is witness to some of the highest migration rates in modern times (International Organization for Migration 2011), it is important to also direct attention to the development of potentially derogatory migrant attitudes in young children. Developmental researchers have illustrated how the psychological features of stereotyping, prejudice, and discrimination are present from a young age (Over/McCall 2018). From about the age of five, children profess explicit liking for members of their own groups and are more concerned with helping and staying loyal to socially similar others (Kinzler/Dupoux/Spelke 2007; Over 2018; Dunham/Degner 2010). Recent efforts have strived to extend this work to measure the social origins of dehumanisation. The research we now outline has not investigated the development of dehumanising migrant perceptions per se, to our knowledge this topic has been unexplored to date, but it rather has measured variations in human-like attributions across parallel social divisions (i.e., racial, ethnic, national).

As in research with adults, previous studies have demonstrated how children may conceive of in- and outgroup members differently with regards to the traits thought to distinguish humans from animals. Costello and Hodson (2014) revealed that six- to ten-year-old White children attributed Black children with fewer uniquely human capacities (e.g., curiosity, guilt) in the United States, and Chas et al. (2018a) found that ten- to thirteen-year-olds were quicker to implicitly associate animalistic words, like 'wild', 'creature' and 'pet', with Arab names than with (ingroup) Spanish names. Other work has examined the development of dehumanising biases on the basis of nationality. Scottish children, aged six to ten, judged members of a national outgroup football team as experiencing less intense second-order emotions than members of their own national team (Martin/Bennett/Murray 2008). Focusing on perceptions of physical humanness, our research has shown that six-year-old British children rated ambiguously animate (doll-human) faces to be less human when they were told they originated from a country far away from their own town (McLoughlin/Tipper/Over 2017).

More broadly related to this harmful phenomenon, Dore and colleagues (Dore et al. 2014; Dore et al. 2017) found that the belief that Black children feel less pain than do other White children gradually emerges between the ages of five and ten among White participants in the US. Chas et al. (2018b) have also explored the effect that group membership has for children's understanding of others' pain. They were interested in judgements of both physical and 'social pain', such as personal distress in response to social rejection. Their results revealed that Spanish children (nine- to thirteen-year-olds) expected peers with typical Arab names to experience a lower level of socially driven negative pain. (They did not find any differences in children's judgements of in- and outgroup members' experiences of physical pain in this culture however.) Our own research has shown that children may reason about the internal experiences of social groups differently: British five- and six-year-olds were less likely to spontaneously refer to the mental states (i.e., thoughts, desires, emotions) of agents who spoke a different language and lived in a different country to them (McLoughlin/Over 2017).

The convergence of this evidence suggests that children can hold dehumanising views of perceived culturally distant others, but also that dehumanisation may be at least partially socially learned. For example, we observed that British five-year-olds perceived equal humanness across in- and outgroup faces, whereas there was a significant decrease in outgroup humanness ratings in the older children (McLoughlin/Tipper/ Over 2017). Furthermore, ten-year-old White children in the United States perceived that racial outgroup members experience less physical pain than their own racial group, whereas this bias in the perception of physical pain was not evident among similarly aged children in Spain. Future studies need to examine how dehumanising beliefs might be culturally transmitted to young observers from parents, the media, and other influential sources and to determine whether this transmission process relies on certain psychological biases (e.g., perceived fundamental distinctions between groups) (McLoughlin/Over 2018).

Another way that developmental research could be useful in the study of this social problem is by providing insight into how dehumanising biases can be overcome before they become deeply entrenched in social interactions and perception. Reducing the tendency to dehumanise outgroup members has received relatively little research attention in work with adults, especially when it comes to improving the perceptions of immigrants and refugees. Individual variations in contact with and knowledge of migrant group members, as well as higher levels of trait empathy (Bruneau/Kteily/Laustsen 2017), are related to increases in human attributions. One strategy that has been successful in increasing the perceived 'humanness' of outgroups in other contexts involves priming a shared social identity beyond that of the current group division. In these experimental studies, reminding adults of the broader national or ethnic identity that different local groups have in common, or emphasizing that outgroup individuals also belong in a superordinate 'human' category, had benefits for humanness perceptions (Gaunt 2009; Albarello/Rubini 2012).

Research in developmental psychology has highlighted some promising routes for combatting dehumanising attitudes towards migrants. Complimentary to findings with adults, exposing children and adolescents to indirect contact with migrants, even just by reading about positive intergroup interactions in a storybook, can lead to increases in social preference for a member of this group (Cameron et al. 2006; Vezzali/Stathi/Giovannini 2012). Looking more specifically at dehumanising biases, Vezzali et al. (2012) have revealed that asking nine-year-olds to imagine interacting with an immigrant peer (over a three-week period and in different environments) had a positive indirect influence on the extent to which they attributed uniquely human emotions to them.

We recently sought to measure whether encouraging children to reflect on the mental lives of migrant group members – an important aspect of folk conceptions of humanity (Waytz/Epley/Cacioppo 2010) – had a positive effect on their moral obligations towards another migrant individual (McLoughlin/Over forthcoming). In this study, five- and six-year-old British participants were either prompted to talk about the thoughts and feelings (e.g., "What are they thinking about?") or the actions (e.g., "What are they doing?") of children who were described as migrants to the UK. We found that the children asked to discuss the mental states of migrant peers in everyday situations were more willing to share resources with another migrant child who was victim to a minor transgression (i.e., one of their belongings were stolen). Hence, thinking more deeply about the behaviour of a migrant group had a significant positive impact on children's prosocial behaviour over and above simply talking about the actions of this group more generally. Future work should continue to build on these experimental approaches in order to identify the optimal intergroup training for improving migrant perceptions at a young age.

To conclude, dehumanisation is a pervasive social problem and is closely connected to the negative treatment and neglect of incoming immigrant and refugee groups. In this chapter, we have outlined research investigating the dehumanising perceptions of migrants from a variety of perspectives in philosophy, social and developmental psychology. This work has often converged to identify some of the psychological factors which may facilitate or impede the tendency to think of perceived culturally dissimilar others as 'less human', but has also highlighted the multifaceted nature of this harmful phenomenon. We hope that this review will ultimately be informative for strategies to enhance the inclusion of newcomers within their host nations.

Bibliography

Albarello, F./Rubini, M. (2012): Reducing Dehumanisation Outcomes Towards Blacks: The Role ofMmultiple Categorisation and of Human Identity. In: European Journal of Social Psychology 42(7), 875–882. doi: 10.1002/ejsp.1902.

Algan, Y./Bisin, A., A./Manning, A./Verdier, T. (2012): Cultural Integration of Immigrants in Europe. Oxford: Oxford University Press.

Andrighetto, L./Baldissarri, C./Lattanzio, S./Loughnan, S./Volpato, C. (2014): Human-itarian Aid? Two Forms of Dehumanization and Willingness to Help after Natural Disasters. In: Br J Soc Psychol 53(3), 573–584. doi: 10.1111/bjso.12066.

Bandura, A./Barbaranelli, C./Caprara, G. V./Pastorelli, C. (1996): Mechanisms of Moral Disengagement in the Exercise of Moral Agency. In: Journal of Personality and Social Psychology 71(2), 364–374. doi: 10.1037/0022–3514.71.2.364.

Bar-Tal, D. (1989): Delegitimization: The extreme case of stereotyping and prejudice. In: Daniel Bar-Tal, et al. (eds.): Stereotyping and Prejudice: Changing Conceptions. New York: Springer New York, 169–182.

Bleiker, R. Campbell, D. Hutchison, E. Nicholson, X. (2013): The Visual Dehumanisation of Refugees. In: Australian Journal of Political Science 48(4), 398–416. doi: 10.1080/10361146.2013.840769.

Bruneau, E./Kteily, N./Laustsen, L. (2017): The Unique Effects of Blatant Dehumanization on Attitudes and Behavior Towards Muslim Refugees during the European 'Refugee Crisis' across Four Countries. In: European Journal of Social Psychology 48(5), 645–662. doi: 10.1002/ejsp.2357.

Cameron, L./Rutland, A./Brown, R./Douch, R. (2006): Changing Children's Intergroup Attitudes toward Refugees: Testing Different Models of Extended Contact. In: Child Development 77(5), 1208–19. doi: 10.1111/j.1467–8624.2006.00929.x.

Capozza, D./Trifiletti, E./Vezzali, L./Favara, I. (2013): Can Intergroup Contact Improve Humanity Attributions? In: International Journal of Psychology 48(4), 527–541. doi: 10.1080/00207594.2012.688132.

Chas, A./Betancor, V./Delgado, N./Rodríguez-Pérez, A. (2018a): Children Consider their Own Groups to be More Human than Other Social Groups: Evidence from Indirect and Direct Measures. In: Social Psychology 49(3), 125–134.

Chas Villar, A./Betancor Rodriguez, V./Delgado Rodriguez, N./Rodriguez-Perez, A. (2018b): They Do Not Suffer Like Us: The Differential Attribution of Social Pain as a Dehumanization Criterion in Children. In: Psicothema 30(2), 207–211. doi: 10.7334/psicothema2017.236.

Chavez, L. R. (2001): Covering Immigration: Popular Images and the Politics of a Nation. Berkeley: University of California Press.

Cisneros, J. D. (2008): Contaminated Communities: The Metaphor of "Immigrant as pollutant' in Media Representations of Immigration. In: Rhetoric and Public Affairs 11(4), 569–601.

Costello, K./Hodson, G. (2011): Social Dominance-Based Threat Reactions to Immigrants in Need of Assistance. European Journal of Social Psychology 41(2), 220–231. doi: 10.1002/ejsp.769.

Costello, K./Hodson, G. (2014): Explaining Dehumanization among Children: The Interspecies Model of Prejudice. In: British Journal of Social Psychology 53(1), 175–197. doi: 10.1111/bjso.12016.

Cuddy, A. J. C./Rock, M. S./Norton, M. I. (2007): Aid in the Aftermath of Hurricane Katrina: Inferences of Secondary Emotions and Intergroup Helping. In: Group Processes & Intergroup Relations 10(1), 107–118. doi: 10.1177/1368430207071344.
Dore, R. A./Hoffman, K. M./Lillard, A. S./Trawalter, S. (2014): Children's Racial Bias in Perceptions of Others' Pain. In: British Journal of Developmental Psychology 32(2), 218–231. doi: 10.1111/bjdp.12038.
Dore, R. A./Hoffman, K. M./Lillard, A. S./Trawalter, S. (2017): Developing Cognitions about Race: White 5- to 10-year-olds' Perceptions of Hardship and Pain. In: European Journal of Social Psychology 48(2), O121–O132. doi: 10.1002/ejsp.2323.
Dunham, Y./Degner, J. (2010): Origins of Intergroup Bias: Developmental and Social Cognitive Research on Intergroup Attitudes. In: European Journal of Social Psychology 40(4), 563–568. doi: 10.1002/ejsp.758.
Esses, V. M./Medianu, S./Lawson, A. S. (2013): Uncertainty, Threat, and the Role of the Media in Promoting the Dehumanization of Immigrants and Refugees. In: Journal of Social Issues 69(3), 518–536. doi: 10.1111/josi.12027.
Esses, V. M./Veenvliet, S./Hodson, G./Mihic, L. (2008): Justice, Morality, and the Dehumanization of Refugees. In: Social Justice Research 21, 4–25.
Fiske, S. T./Cuddy, A. J./Glick, P./Xu, J. (2002): A Model of (often Mixed) Stereotype Content: Competence and Warmth Respectively Follow from Perceived Status and Competition. In: Journal of Personality and Social Psychology 82(6), 878–902.
Gaunt, R. (2009): Superordinate Categorization as a Moderator of Mutual Infrahumanization. In: Group Processes & Intergroup Relations 12(6), 731–746. doi: 10.1177/1368430209343297.
Goff, P. A./Eberhardt, J. L./Williams, M. J./Jackson, M. C. (2008): Not Yet Human: Implicit Knowledge, Historical Dehumanization, and Contemporary Consequences. In: Journal of Personality and Social Psychology 94(2), 292–306. doi: 10.1037/0022–3514.94.2.292.
Haslam, N./Kashima, Y./Loughnan, S./Shi, J./Suitner, C. (2008): Subhuman, Inhuman, and Superhuman: Contrasting Humans with Nonhumans in Three Cultures. In: Social Cognition 26(2), 248–258. doi: 10.1521/soco.2008.26.2.248.
Haslam, N./Loughnan, S. (2014): Dehumanization and Infrahumanization. In: Annual Review of Psychology 65(1), 399–423. doi: 10.1146/annurev-psych-010213–115045.
International Organization for Migration (2011): About Migration. Retrieved from http://www.iom.int/jahia/Jahia/about-migration/lang/en.
Kelman, H. G. (1973): Violence Without Moral Restraint: Reflections on the Dehumanization of Victims and Victimizers. In: Journal of Social Issues 29(4), 25–61. doi: 10.1111/j.1540–4560.1973.tb00102.x.
Kinzler, K. D./Dupoux, E./Spelke, E. S. (2007): The Native Language of Social Cognition. In: Proceedings of the National Academy of Sciences USA 104(30), 12577–80. doi: 10.1073/pnas.0705345104.
Kteily, N./Bruneau, E./Waytz, A./Cotterill, S. (2015): The Ascent of Man: Theoretical and Empirical Evidence for Blatant Dehumanization. In: Journal of Personality and Social Psychology 109(5), 901–931. doi: 10.1037/pspp0000048.
Leyens, J. P. (2009): Retrospective and Prospective Thoughts about Infrahumanization. In: Group Processes & Intergroup Relations 12(6), 807–817. doi: 10.1177/1368430209347330.

Leyens, J. P./Demoulin, S./Vaes, J./Gaunt, R./Paladino, M. P. (2007): Infra-humanization: The wall of group differences. In: Social Issues and Policy Review 1(1), 139–172. doi: 10.1111/j.1751–2409.2007.00006.x.

Leyens, J. P./Paladino, P. M./Rodriguez-Torres, R./Vaes, J./Demoulin, S./Rodriguez-Perez, A./Gaunt, R. (2000): The Emotional Side of Prejudice: The Attribution of Secondary Emotions to Ingroups and Outgroups. In: Personality and Social Psychology Review 4(2), 186–197. doi: 10.1207/s15327957pspr0402_06.

Leyens, J. P./Rodriguez-Perez, A./Rodriguez-Torres, R./Gaunt, R./Paladino, M.-P./Vaes, J./Demoulin, S. (2001): Psychological Essentialism and the Differential Attribution of Uniquely Human Emotions to Ingroups and Outgroups. In: European Journal of Social Psychology 31(4), 395–411. doi: 10.1002/ejsp.50.

Louis, W. R./Duck, J. M./Terry, D. J./Schuller, R. A./Lalonde, R. N. (2006): Why Do Citizens Want to Keep Refugees Out? Threats, Fairness and Hostile Norms in the Treatment of Asylum Seekers. In: European Journal of Social Psychology 37(1), 53–73. doi: 10.1002/ejsp.329.

Martin, J./Bennett, M./Murray, W. S. (2008): A Developmental Study of the Infrahumanization Hypothesis. In: British Journal of Developmental Psychology 26(2), 153–62. doi: 10.1348/026151007X216261.

McLoughlin, N./Over, H. (2017): Young Children Are More Likely to Spontaneously Attribute Mental States to Members of their Own Group. In: Psychological Science 28(10). doi: 10.1177/0956797617710724.

McLoughlin, N/Over, H. (2018): The Developmental Origins of Dehumanization. In: Advances in Child Development and Behavior 54, 153–178. doi: 10.1016/bs.acdb.2017.10.006.

McLoughlin, N./Over, H. (forthcoming): Encouraging Children to Mentalise about a Perceived Outgroup Increases Empathic Helping towards Them. *Developmental Science.*

McLoughlin, N./Tipper, S. P./Over, H. (2017): Young Children Perceive Less Humanness in Outgroup Faces. In: Developmental Science 21(2), e12539. doi: 10.1111/desc.12539.

O'Brien, G. V. (2003): Indigestible Food, Conquering Hordes, and Waste Materials: Metaphors of Immigrants and the Early Immigration Restriction Debate in the United States. In: Metaphor and Symbol 18(1), 33–47. doi: 10.1207/S15327868MS1801_3.

Opotow, S. (1990): Moral Exclusion and Injustice: An Introduction. In: Journal of Social Issues 46(1), 1–20. doi: 10.1111/j.1540–4560.1990.tb00268.x.

Over, H. (2018). The Influence of Group Membership on Young Children's Prosocial Behaviour. In: Current Opinion in Psychology. doi: 10.1016/j.copsyc.2017.08.005.

Over, H./McCall, C. (2018): Becoming Us and Them: Social Learning and Intergroup Bias. In: Social and Personality Psychology Compass 12(4), e12384. doi: 10.1111/spc3.12384.

Pereira, C./Vala, J./Leyens, J. P. (2009): From Infra-humanization to Discrimination: The Mediation of Symbolic Threat Needs Egalitarian Norms. In: Journal of Experimental Social Psychology 45(2), 336–344. doi: 10.1016/j.jesp.2008.10.010.

Prentice, D. A./Miller, D. T. (2007): Psychological Essentialism of Human Categories. In: Current Directions in Psychological Science 16(4), 202–206. doi: 10.1111/j.1467–8721.2007.00504.x.

Rhodes, M./Mandalaywala, T. M. (2017): The Development and Developmental Consequences of Social Essentialism. In: Wiley Interdiscip Reviews: Cognitive Science 8(4), e1437. doi: 10.1002/wcs.1437.

Rodríguez-Pérez, A./Delgado Rodríguez, N./Betancor Rodríguez, V./Leyens, J. P./Vaes, J. (2011): Infra-humanization of Outgroups throughout the World: The Role of Similarity, Intergroup Friendship, Knowledge of the Outgroup, and Status. In: Anales de Psicología/Annals of Psychology 27(3), 9.

Schwartz, S. H./Struch, N. (1989): Values, Stereotypes, and Intergroup Antagonism. In: Daniel Bar-Tal, et al. (eds.): Stereotyping and Prejudice: Changing Conceptions. New York: Springer New York, 151–67.

Shah, V. (2015): Swarms and Marauders: The Dehumanising Language of Migration. In: *Cafébabel*. Retreived from http://www.cafebabel.co.uk/culture/article/swarms-and-marauders-the-dehumanising-language-of-migration.html.

Smith, D. L. (2012): Less than Human: Why We Demean, Enslave, and Exterminate Others. New York: Macmillan.

Smith, D. L. (2014): Dehumanization, Essentialism, and Moral Psychology. In: Philosophy Compass 9(11), 814–824.

Tirrell, L. (2012): Genocidal Language Games. In: I. Maitra and M. K. McGowan (eds.): Speech and Harm: Controversies Over Free Speech. Oxford: Oxford University Press, 174–221.

Utych, S. M. (2017): How Dehumanization Influences Attitudes toward Immigrants. In: Political Research Quarterly 71(2), 440–452. doi: 10.1177/1065912917744897.

Vaes, J./Latrofa, M./Suitner, C./Arcuri, L. (2017): They Are All Armed and Dangerous! In: Journal of Media Psychology 1–12. doi: 10.1027/1864–1105/a000216.

Vaes, J./Leyens, J. P./Paladino, M. P./Miranda, M. P. (2012): We Are Human, They Are Not: Driving Forces behind Outgroup Dehumanisation and the Humanisation of the Ingroup. In: European Review of Social Psychology 23(1), 64–106. doi: 10.1080/10463283.2012.665250.

Vaes, J./Paladino, M. P. (2009):The Uniquely Human Content of Stereotypes. In: Group Processes & Intergroup Relations 13(1), 23–39. doi: 10.1177/1368430209347331.

Vezzali, L./Capozza, D./Stathi, S./Giovannini, D. (2012): Increasing Outgroup Trust, Reducing Infrahumanization, and Enhancing Future Contact Intentions via Imagined Intergroup Contact. In: Journal of Experimental Social Psychology 48(1), 437–440. doi: 10.1016/j.jesp.2011.09.008.

Vezzali, L./Stathi, S./Giovannini, D. (2012): Indirect Contact through Book Reading: Improving Adolescents' Attitudes and Behavioral Intentions toward Immigrants. In: Psychology in the Schools 49(2), 148–62. doi: 10.1002/pits.20621.

Waytz, A./Epley, N./Cacioppo, J. T. (2010): Social Cognition Unbound: Insights into Anthropomorphism and Dehumanization. In: Current Directions in Psychological Science 19(1), 58–62. doi: 10.1177/0963721409359302.

Eva Alisic & Dzenana Kartal

The role of trauma and cultural distance in refugee integration

Abstract: This chapter explores how refugees' exposure to psychological trauma plays a role in integration, how this relationship is influenced by cultural distance between host and refugee communities, and what this means for individuals' responsibility. Although many refugees show high levels of resilience, their capacity to integrate can be affected by exposure to multiple traumatic events and other severe adversity before, during and after their flight. Substantial cultural differences and negative attitudes towards these differences can affect integration efforts, including those related to supporting or improving people's mental health. Trauma and cultural distance affect both refugees and host individuals, and knowledge about them should inform integration expectations as well as how we shape integration initiatives.

When considering the responsibility of individuals in the integration of refugees, we think not only of the responsibility of the 'host' but also of the refugee. Often, the view is that refugees should be grateful and cooperative recipients of integration support. However, the question is whether refugees can be held fully accountable for their integration: traumatic experiences and cultural barriers play a major role, affecting people's mental health and capacity to integrate. At the same time, the medical model that focusses on mental health difficulties and deficiency is countered by rights-based approaches that focus more on refugees' resilience. In this chapter, we provide an overview of what might constitute traumatic experiences in refugees' lives, what cultural distance (the distance between cultures) and the process of 'acculturation' entail, and how both trauma and cultural distance may affect mental health and integration efforts. We argue that, even though resilience is a dominant characteristic, capacity and, therefore, responsibility in the context of refugee integration may be diminished due to trauma, severe adversity, and cultural distance, and that appropriate expectations from both host and newcomer individuals are important. Since we focus on trauma and cultural distance in the context of individual responsibility, our focus will mainly be adults, but it is important to recognize that children constitute over 50 per cent of all refugees (UNHCR 2018), and many of them support their families and communities as if they were adults, and often play a signifi-

https://doi.org/10.1515/9783110628746-009

cant role in families' integration through, for example, their capacity to acquire the host language quickly.

1. Trauma and displacement

Forcibly displaced populations leave their homes to escape conflict, violence, and persecution, and ensure their own and their family's survival. The process itself can be local and temporal, involving internal displacement for the duration of conflict, or distal and more or less permanent, involving transnational resettlement. In this edited volume, the focus is on the latter: long-term settlement in far-away, high-income countries. The process of forced migration is seen as being constituted of phases involving a series of events that are influenced by several push and pull factors over a prolonged period of time (Bhugra 2004). While there is no typical 'refugee journey', often three broad phases are distinguished: pre-flight, peri-flight, and post-flight. The transitions between the phases may be fluid, and the phases may even overlap as they have no specific starting or end point. Traditionally, mental health research, which forms the disciplinary basis of this chapter, focussed on pre-flight traumatic events and their impact. Recently, though, exposure during migration as well as during and after settlement has received greater recognition as severely disturbing and disruptive. People may be exposed to major adverse and traumatic events in each of the three phases.

1.1. What is a traumatic event?

While many experiences may be stressful, for an event to be considered traumatic it needs to satisfy certain criteria. The *Diagnostic and Statistical Manual of Mental Disorders, 5th Edition* (American Psychiatric Association 2013) explains that a potential trauma needs to involve exposure to death, threatened death, actual or threatened serious injury, or actual or threatened sexual violence. This exposure also has to have a specific form. It can be direct, when the person is the victim or when they witness the event first-hand. It can also be indirect, when someone learns that a close relative or close friend was exposed to trauma. In case of the latter, an event involving actual or threatened death must have been violent or accidental. This excludes, for example, the natural death of a grandparent. Finally, exposure can also consist of repeated or extreme indirect exposure to aversive details in the course of professional duty. This refers to, for example, first responders collecting body parts or professionals repeatedly exposed to the details of child abuse. Indirect non-professional exposure through electronic media, television, movies, or pictures is not considered a traumatic event, even though it may be distressing and serve as a reminder of a traumatic event. Refugees are often exposed to multiple and complex traumatic events (Nickerson et al. 2017), as well as to adverse events and circumstances that might not satisfy 'trauma' criteria but certainly add to the burden. In the remainder of the chapter, we will talk about traumatic events as well as severe adversity since both are known to affect refugees' mental health, and they interact with each other.

1.2. Pre-flight trauma and adversity

In the first of the three (fluid) migration phases, future refugees are exposed to a range of potentially traumatic events that are often based on deliberate and targeted persecution because of their ethnic, cultural, religious, or political beliefs and values. Traumatic and highly adverse events may involve experiences of torture and other interpersonal violence, loss of family members, and bombardment as well as deprivation of food, healthcare, and shelter (Schweitzer et al. 2006; Silove et al. 1997). In addition, people may be exposed to traumatic events that have nothing to do with conflict. A large proportion of people in peace time are exposed to serious car crashes, disasters (e. g., floods, earthquakes, bush fires), domestic violence, or community violence (see e. g., Dückers et al. 2016). Furthermore, the experience of one type of exposure can also increase the risk of exposure to another type. For example, in the aftermath of a disaster, domestic violence is known to increase in prevalence (Parkinson 2017). Together, the evidence suggests that many if not most refugees have experienced one or more traumatic events pre-flight. Often, their history includes multiple traumatic experiences.

1.3. Peri-flight trauma and adversity

In the second of the three phases, peri-migration, the transition period begins. It may be as short as a few days or weeks, or last up to several years or even decades. During this period, forced migrants experience the transition from their place of residence as they seek refuge, asylum, and permanent resettlement in a new and, hopefully, safer environment (Bhugra 2004). Recently, it has become clear that the usually long journeys towards high-income countries, the focus of this edited volume, involve major vulnerability to traumatic events. The journey is often highly perilous, with long treks through deserts and over sea. Often, it cannot be made without human traffickers, involving high rates of sexual and physical violence (Kingsley 2017). In addition, daily stressors related to living in refugee camps (Miller/Rasmussen 2010), harm associated with long-term detention during the asylum process (Steel et al. 2004), and losses experienced due to separation from family members, communities, and social networks (Miller et al. 2002) are features of this phase.

1.4. Post-flight trauma and adversity

In the third phase, post-migration, mental health researchers and providers have traditionally been more attentive to (major) adversity and disadvantage among refugees rather than to 'pure' trauma. Forced migrants deal with language difficulties, economic loss of occupational or social status, discrimination, restrictive policies, breakup of social and family ties (Bhugra/Becker 2005; Porter/Haslam 2005), and difficulties related to cultural differences, which we will discuss later in this chapter. However, several of these problems also increase the risk of exposure to traumatic events. For example, limited financial means might lead to living in unsafe neighbourhoods and a higher risk of exposure to community violence. Also, reduced physical health related to prolonged periods of deprivation and trauma in the earlier phases of migration is linked to increased disability and mortality (Mollica et al. 2001), and therefore also increases the risk of losing loved ones or one's own life.

1.5. The mental health consequences of trauma and severe adversity

Although exposure to traumatic events and severe adversity, including the loss of loved ones, is very common among refugees, the majority do not develop mental disorders (Nickerson et al. 2017). Stress reactions after trauma and grief reactions after loss are considered normal reactions (see e.g., Hobfoll et al. 2007), and while most people experience some form of emotional reaction including fear, anxiety, sleep disturbance, guilt, or anger, they naturally recover using their own coping strategies and available social support (ACPMH 2013; Bonanno 2004): most people show high degrees of resilience. Nevertheless, rates of mental health difficulties among refugees are substantially elevated compared to general populations in peacetime conditions.

Most empirical research investigating consequences of trauma exposure among refugees has concentrated on post-traumatic stress disorder (PTSD) and/or depression. PTSD is characterised by symptoms of intrusion (e.g., involuntary distressing memories of the event), avoidance of stimuli related to the trauma (e.g., trying to avoid people, places, or conversations that are reminders of what happened), alterations in mood and cognition (e.g., strong feelings of guilt or shame), and hyperarousal (e.g., being irritable or having trouble concentrating) that exist for at least one month (APA 2013). PTSD rates have varied widely in studies among refugees, with grouped estimates ranging from 15 per cent to 31 per cent for PTSD and from 17 per cent to 31 per cent for depression (Nickerson et al. 2017). Other mental health difficulties are increasingly studied, and include complex or prolonged grief, somatic (physical) symptom disorders, panic disorder, obsessive-compulsive disorder, substance abuse, and psychotic symptoms (see e.g., Nickerson et al. 2017 for an overview).

As is observed in trauma survivors more broadly, refugees may have two or even more mental health conditions at the same time ('comorbidity'). PTSD and depression often co-occur (Bogic/Njoku/Priebe 2015; Fazel/Wheeler/Danesh 2005). There is also evidence of a dose-response relationship, meaning the greater the exposure to traumatic events, the greater the risks and intensity of subsequent mental health problems (Steel et al. 2009). For example, Steel and colleagues (2002) reported that in a sample of long-term resettled Vietnamese refugees exposure to three or more traumatic events had an eight-fold increase in risk of mental health conditions compared to those who did not report any trauma exposure.

1.6. What does this mean for refugees' integration efforts?

Mental health conditions have several effects that do not only directly affect refugees' emotional well-being, personal relationships, and outlook on life. They also have very practical effects on integration efforts that may be interpreted differently if one is not aware of the possible causes. For example, traumatic exposure alters the neural pathways in the brain that are associated with cognitive domains and executive functioning (Etkin/Gyurak/O'Hara 2013), and PTSD symptoms relate to impairment in memory (Kanagaratnam/Asbjørnsen 2007). One of the possible consequences is forgetting appointments. Not showing up for meetings might therefore be an indication of limited capacity rather than lack of interest. Learning a new language is also difficult when one is struggling with reminders of traumatic events and has trouble concentrating (see Al-Abdullah 2019, in this volume). A result of depression can be a lack of enthusiasm for any well-meaning offers of support and a lack of effort to build new social ties.

Mental health difficulties can be addressed effectively via treatment. Multiple psychological treatments targeting PTSD, depressive and anxiety symptoms among refugees have demonstrated efficacy (Lambert/Alhassoon 2015) and are recommended by treatment guidelines (ACPMH 2013). These include, for example, trauma-focussed cognitive behavioural therapy (for both adults and children) and prolonged exposure therapy, narrative exposure therapy and interpersonal therapy (for adults). However, such therapies are not commonly utilised or offered to refugees in need (we discuss further challenges to this below), and instead refugees commonly receive other psychosocial treatments, which have less demonstrable evidence (Tol et al. 2011). Effective psychological treatments are often inaccessible or unfamiliar to refugees (Pirkis et al. 2001) as refugees face a range of access barriers due to social, language, gendered and cultural issues, and potentially even lack of pre-migration education and literacy (Watkins/Razee/Richters 2012). Many people do not have access to specialised mental health care, even in well-resourced contexts. For example, in Switzerland, it takes on average eight years for refugees to access specialised mental health care after they have arrived in the country (Schick et al. 2016).

2. Acculturation: cultures coming into contact

During migration, refugees come into contact with various cultures, including their eventual host-country culture. The process of cultural and psychological change resulting from contact between two different cultures is described as *acculturation* (Berry 1997). During the process, both cultures can be shaped by cross-cultural interactions and can influence acculturative patterns towards the other culture. These patterns are influenced by differences between the cultures in beliefs, values, and religion, but also by host-country policies on migration (Berry 2006a). In addition, these patterns influence the acculturative attitudes of the individuals in both host and ethnic cultures brought into contact.

The concept of acculturation has developed substantially over the past few decades. Early models proposed that acculturation requires the shedding of the culture of origin and adoption of the beliefs and values of the host culture (Gordon 1964). This suggested that there was only one outcome of the acculturation – adoption or assimilation into the host culture. This unidirectional approach has been criticised for ignoring the possibility that the host and origin cultures in contact influence each other (Teske/Nelson 1974; cited in Sam 2006). Therefore, a more bidimensional perspective emerged, arguing that it is possible to acquire the new culture without necessarily losing the original culture.

Currently, acculturation is defined as a complex process driven by the cultural maintenance of the culture of origin and contact and participation with the host culture (Berry 1997). This process is influenced by two components: attitudes or preferences towards the host culture and the culture of origin on the one hand, and behavioural engagement (i.e., actual practices) towards the host culture and culture of origin on the other. This interplay of attitudes and behaviours towards the host and origin cultures is thought to promote the development and persistence of two independent identities: ethnic identity and national identity (Phinney 1989; Phinney/Devitch-Navarro 1997). Ethnic identity refers to the individual's subjective sense of belonging to his or her cultural group, while national identity refers to the membership with one's new culture (Phinney 1989).

2.1. Strategies and preferences when cultures come into contact

The process of acculturation is influenced by factors that exist prior to and during acculturation taking place (Berry 2006b). For refugees, these include the reasons for the flight, personal characteristics such as age, gender, and education, and post-migratory stressors such as discrimination, social isolation, unemployment, and host language difficulties. These factors can act as risks or protective factors depending on their degree and level. In addition to these 'objective' factors, acculturation is influenced by the subjective appraisal of these factors and the degree of stress assigned to them (Berry 2006b). This is referred to as *acculturative stress*. Personal characteristics, resources, strategies, and social support are seen to influence the process of coping with acculturative stress. The degree of acculturative stress itself influences a minority group's cultural orientation and adaptation to the host culture. All these factors together determine which of four acculturation strategies is preferred or adopted: *integration* (orientation towards both ethnic and host culture); *assimilation* (orientation towards host culture); *separation* (orientation towards ethnic culture); or *marginalisation* (orientation towards neither culture) (Berry 1997 and 2006b).

These four acculturation strategies have been criticised because they are based on the assumption that migrant communities can choose which acculturation style they want to adopt, while in reality, their experience depends on conditions in the larger host society. Berry (2006a) identified four different strategies that represent the preferred acculturation attitudes of the host societies – i.e., how they might want the immigrants/refugees to acculturate. *Melting pot* refers to the attitudes of the host society where they seek or even enforce the assimilation of all their non-dominant groups. When separation or marginalisation of the non-dominant groups is sought or enforced by the host society, this is known as *segregation* and *exclusion* respectively. On the other hand, if cultural diversity is valued and even encouraged by the society as whole, it is called *multiculturalism*.

The acculturative model has taken to emphasise aspects of contact between the origin and host cultures and its associated consequences for refugee resettlement. Consequently, host-country attitudes towards minority groups and cultural difference, as well as cultural diversity and social policies (including any potential barriers) play an important role in the extent to which host societies "allow" the refugee experience of acculturation (Allen/Vaage/Hauff 2006). The responses of the host cultures and specific refugee services, such as the status determination process, access to services and social support extended to refugees to assist relocation and resettlement, can function as barriers and lead to less desirable acculturative preferences for the refugee communities. These acculturative factors are argued to interact and influence cultural change in both origin and host cultures, thereby exerting major influences on the psychological and sociocultural adaptation of the individual (Allen/Vaage/Hauff 2006).

2.2. Culture and mental health

Culture is pertinent in understanding mental health because beliefs, values, and languages influence how different cultures express their mental health symptoms, interpret them, seek help for them, and treat them (Crosby 2013; Stuart et al. 1998). Furthermore, individual factors such as cultural identity and stress of adaptation to a new culture constitute risk and resilience factors for mental health problems (Bhugra 2004).

Some research suggests that bicultural identification or integration (i.e., high identification with both ethnic and host cultures) relates to better psychological and sociocultural adaptation (Nguyen/Benet-Martínez 2012). At the same time, studies report that higher levels of assimilation (i.e., association with the host culture at the expense of the ethnic culture) are associated with worse mental health outcomes, including depression, substance use and abuse (Gupta et al. 2013). This phenomenon is named the "immigrant paradox" (for discussion see Berry et al. 2006; Bhugra 2003 and 2004; Schwartz et al. 2010).

Specific acculturative factors present a more consistent relationship with mental health. For example, acculturative stress experienced in response to migratory challenges is regularly identified as a significant risk factor for mental health problems among adults and youth (Berry 2006b; Bogic/ Njoku/Priebe 2012; Ellis et al. 2008; Knipscheer/Kleber 2006). A multitude of factors related to the refugee community, service system, and society more broadly are identified as significant barriers preventing access to and utilisation of mental health services. These include the low priority often placed on the mental health of refugees, high costs of services, lengthy waiting times, service complexity and gaps in the service, low cultural awareness, and lack of cultural competence (De Anstiss et al. 2009). Similarly, refugee-specific factors can act as barriers, including poor mental health itself, limited knowledge of services, distrust of services, difficulties with the host language, lack of coping skills or social support, and cultural beliefs and stigma regarding mental health (Cross/Singh 2012; Lustig et al. 2004). These barriers lead to the underutilisation of, or ineffective encounters with, mental health services (Crosby 2013; Pirkis et al. 2001), with the risk that mental health symptoms and conditions become entrenched. There is indeed evidence that they lead to chronicity and comorbidity of symptoms commonly experienced by refugees and migrants in resettlement (De Anstiss et al. 2009; Mollica/Caridad/Massagli 2007). Given this, refugees become even more vulnerable to an array of psychosocial, economic, security, and health issues flowing from exposure to traumatic events, forced migration, and acculturative barriers.

Particularly salient to the issue of service utilisation and effectiveness is the level of cultural competence, and cultural sensitivity, of service providers. Cultural competence is generally based on the knowledge of cultural beliefs, values, and practices of minority groups and represents an understanding of how culture modifies illness perception, illness behaviour, and acceptability of specific interventions (Bhui et al. 2007). Culture is frequently identified as the most important factor pervading the help-seeking pathway, from identification and diagnosis to help seeking (Cauce et al. 2002). Subsequently, western treatment methods for mental health problems, and their emphasis on psychopathological symptoms, are barriers to effective treatment because they are not acceptable or familiar to culturally and linguistically diverse communities that have their own explanatory models of mental health and illness. They fail to capture and to respond to, or engage with, the variety of culturally shaped post-traumatic stress reactions presented among non-western cultures (e.g., Eisenbruch 1991; Summerfield 1999).

3. No 'model' citizens: Where to from here?

Based on the evidence described above, it is unlikely that refugees who experience moderate to severe mental health difficulties and/or come from communities with a large cultural distance to the host community, can or should be expected to behave as 'model' citizens. So how should host expectations and actions be adjusted to accommodate this realisation? While this edited volume focusses on individuals' responsibility, many of the implications of this chapter's sections on trauma and cultural distance concern collective levels of organisation: volunteer projects, support services, and local or national policies. There is a need to coordinate efforts and reach scale. Nevertheless, these efforts involve many individuals, and the implications described below have elements that are or can be directly relevant to individuals' personal responsibility. These include individuals' responsibility to inform themselves, to engage, and to advocate for better support for others in need. Those roles apply to both refugee and host-society individuals.

3.1. Trauma-informed initiatives and mental health care

It seems crucial, with regard to the impact of trauma on integration, that host as well as refugee individuals are 'trauma-informed' (SAMHSA 2016). For example, for individuals involved in volunteer initiatives, this includes having a solid understanding of the role and impact of trauma, when it is necessary for individuals to seek specialised mental health support, and where services can be found. Two points are of particular note. First, there is a myth that talking about trauma with survivors is 're-traumatising'. While conversations about previous experiences may elicit emotions and while the specific method of 'critical incident stress debriefing' in the immediate aftermath of a trauma has not been shown to be helpful (Rose et al. 2002), talking about a traumatic event in a safe and caring environment is not the same as being in the trauma situation again. Such a conversation needs to have a constructive purpose, be controlled by the survivor rather than the conversation partner, and facilitate referral to mental health care services if needed, but if those conditions are met, it can be a good and important conversation to have, even if it is eliciting unpleasant emotions for one or both conversation partners (see e. g., Becker-Blease/Freyd 2006). Second, while the current chapter focusses on the mental health of refugees, the mental health of host individuals involved in refugee support initiatives needs to be considered as well. The confrontation with traumatic experiences of refugees and the frustration and despair that can be associated with resettlement procedures, injustice, and discrimination, in combination with limited availability of staff care in some initiatives, can be stressful for host individuals. Vicarious trauma, as well as vicarious resilience, has been reported for volunteers and staff working with refugees (see e.g., Guhan/Liebling-Kalifani 2011). It would be helpful for volunteer and professional organisations to have peer support in place for these circumstances.

Another important point that emerges from the evidence regarding the impact of trauma on refugees' mental health and integration efforts is simply the need to provide mental health care. Key barriers, as noted above, include the lack of mental health care services, lack of evidence-based care within these services (e.g., clinicians are reluctant to use trauma-focussed mental health interventions due to lack of training and fear of symptom exacerbation, even though these interventions have the best evidence base; see e.g., van Minnen/Hendriks/Olff 2010), and stigma attached to seeking care. Individuals from both host and refugee communities can play important roles here, advocating for the funding and improvement of services, and supporting stigma reduction efforts. An important new trial in this respect is the STRENGTHS project, funded by the EU, which tests short-term group and individual mental health care programs for people affected by war, focusses on addressing their self-nominated key problems (e.g., relationship difficulties) rather than providing a diagnosis (Sijbrandij et al. 2017). This program may address several of the identified barriers.

3.2. Increasing cultural competency

Any practical or policy recommendations should be aligned with multiculturalism rather than either extreme of assimilation or segregation/separation. In improving cultural competency on the side of both refugees and host citizens, it appears important to expand opportunities for contact and engagement. Part of these opportunities involve providing employment opportunities. Employment has come to the fore as a key driver for successful integration and well-being, since it directly links to a range of outcomes, including financial, social (new connections and network), and psychological (self-worth, being able to provide for the family; Fleay/Hartley/Kenny 2013; Dresen 2019, in this volume).

Part of refugees' responsibility is to learn the dominant language of a country. The lack of language acquisition is a significant contributor to the health inequalities experienced by refugees when compared to the general population; knowledge of the host language is a major factor underpinning the process of acculturation that refugees experience (Berry 1997). The process of segregation based on (a lack of) proficiency in the host language can lead to social exclusion and discrimination (Correa-Velez/Gifford/Barnett 2010), difficulties in daily functioning (Beiser/Hou 2001), and reduced participation in the employment market (Birman et al. 2014). Host citizens can be involved in efforts to improve and tailor language education services, and more broadly in providing/contributing to culturally competent support services. Again, advocacy appears to be a key issue, in which both refugees and host citizens can be involved.

Sometimes, refugees may not fully appreciate the long-term benefits of participation in the host culture. This can be explained and promoted through health education but should avoid pressuring assimilation (De Anstiss et al. 2009). Rather, such health education messages should be based on intercultural exchange emphasising the maintenance and value of the ethnic culture. Furthermore, this message should be reinforced with policies and assistance that support and promote cultural diversity and enable ethnic communities to establish ethnic, religious, and/or spiritual associations and organisations. Overall, in the development of individual and collective efforts it appears important to assess the cultural distance and differences. The larger the distance, the greater the need for cultural competency training on both sides. In this respect, there is great value in appreciating in-depth perspectives and incorporating experience and expertise from the sides of both individual refugees and hosts. In this edited volume, for example, viewpoints from both sides are included for this reason.

Bibliography

Al-Abdullah, Y. (2019): De-integration of Young Syrian Activists in Paris. In: S. K. Kehoe, E. Alisic and J.-C. Heilinger (eds.): Responsibility for Refugee and Migrant Integration. Berlin/Boston: de Gruyter, 25 – 39.

Allen, J./Vaage, A. B./Hauff, E. (2006): Refugees and Asylum Seekers in Societies. In: D. L. Sam & J. W. Berry (eds.): The Cambridge Handbook of Acculturation Psychology. New York: Cambridge University Press, 198 – 217.

Australian Centre for Posttraumatic Mental Health (2013): Australian Guidelines for the Treatment of Acute Stress Disorder and Posttraumatic Stress Disorder. Melbourne: Australian Centre for Posttraumatic Mental Health.

American Psychiatric Association (2013): Diagnostic and Statistical Manual of Mental Disorders, 5th ed. Washington, DC: American Psychiatric Association.

Becker-Blease, K. A./ Freyd, J. J. (2006): Research Participants Telling the Truth about Their Lives: The Ethics of Asking and Not Asking about Abuse. In: American Psychologist 61(3), 218 – 226.

Beiser, M./Hou, F. (2001): Language Acquisition, Unemployment and Depressive Disorder among Southeast Asian Refugees: A 10-Year Study. In: Social Science & Medicine 53(10), 1321–1334.
Berry, J. W. (1997): Immigration, Acculturation, and Adaptation. In: Applied Psychology 46(1), 5–34.
Berry, J. W. (2006a): Contexts of acculturation. In D. L. Sam & J. W. Berry (eds.): The Cambridge Handbook of Acculturation Psychology. New York: Cambridge University Press, 27–42.
Berry, J. W. (ed.) (2006b): Stress Perspectives on Acculturation. New York: Cambridge University Press.
Berry, J. W./Phinney, J. S./Sam, D. L./Vedder, P. E. (2006): Immigrant Youth in Cultural Transition: Acculturation, Identity, and Adaptation across National Contexts. Mahwah: Lawrence Erlbaum Associates.
Bhugra, D. (2003): Migration and Depression. In: Acta Psychiatrica Scandinavica. Supplementum 108, 67.
Bhugra, D. (2004): Migration and Mental Health. In: Acta Psychiatrica Scandinavica 109(4), 243–258.
Bhugra, D.,/Becker, M. A. (2005): Migration, Cultural Bereavement and Cultural Identity. In: World Psychiatry 4(1), 18–24.
Bhui, K./Warfa, N./Edonya, P./McKenzie, K.Bhugra, D. (2007): Cultural Competence in Mental Health Care: A Review of Model Evaluations. In: BMC Health Services Research 7(1), 15.
Birman, D./Simon, C. D./Chan, W. Y./Tran, N. (2014): A Life Domains Perspective on Acculturation and Psychological Adjustment: A Study of Refugees from the Former Soviet Union. In: American Journal of Community Psychology 53(1–2), 60–72.
Bogic, M./Njoku, A./Priebe, S. (2015): Long-Term Mental Health of War-Refugees: A Systematic Literature Review. In: BMC International Health and Human Rights 15(1), 29.
Bonanno, G. A. (2004): Loss, Trauma, and Human Resilience: Have We Underestimated the Human Capacity to Thrive after Extremely Aversive Events? In: American Psychologist 59(1), 20–28.
Cauce, A. M./Domenech-Rodríguez, M./Paradise, M./Cochran, B. N./Shea, J. M./Srebnik, D./Baydar, N. (2002): Cultural and Contextual Influences in Mental Health Help Seeking: A Focus on Ethnic Minority Youth. In: Journal of Consulting and Clinical Psychology 70(1), 44.
Correa-Velez, I./Gifford, S. M./Barnett, A. G. (2010): Longing to Belong: Social Inclusion and Wellbeing among Youth with Refugee Backgrounds in the First Three Years in Melbourne, Australia. In: Social Science & Medicine (1982), 71(8), 1399–1408.
Crosby, S. S. (2013): Primary Care Management of Non–English-Speaking Refugees who Have Experienced Trauma: A Clinical Review. In: JAMA 310(5), 519–528.
Cross, W./Singh, C. (2012): Dual Vulnerabilities: Mental Illness in a Culturally and Linguistically Diverse Society. In: Contemporary Nurse: A Journal for the Australian Nursing Profession 42(2), 156–166.
De Anstiss, H./Ziaian, T./Procter, N./Warland, J./Baghurst, P. (2009): Help-Seeking for Mental Health Problems in Young Refugees: A Review of the Literature with Implications for Policy, Practice, and Research. In: Transcultural Psychiatry 46(4), 584–607.

Dresen, A. (2019): The Practice of Newcomer Integration and Importance of Perspectives. In: S. K. Kehoe, E. Alisic and J.-C. Heilinger (eds.): Responsibility for Refugee and Migrant Integration. Berlin/Boston: de Gruyter, 183–192.

Dückers, M. L./Alisic, E./Brewin, C. R. (2016): A Vulnerability Paradox in the Cross-National Prevalence of Post-Traumatic Stress Disorder. In: The British Journal of Psychiatry 209, 300–305.

Eisenbruch, M. (1991): From Post-Traumatic Stress Disorder to Cultural Bereavement: Diagnosis of Southeast Asian Refugees. In: Social Science & Medicine 33(6), 673–680.

Ellis, B. H./MacDonald, H. Z./Lincoln, A. K./Cabral, H. J. (2008): Mental Health of Somali Adolescent Refugees: The Role of Trauma, Stress, and Perceived Discrimination. In: Journal of Consulting and Clinical Psychology 76(2), 184–193.

Etkin, A./Gyurak, A./O'Hara, R. (2013): A Neurobiological Approach to the Cognitive Deficits of Psychiatric Disorders. In: Dialogues in Clinical Neuroscience 15(4), 419–429.

Fazel, M./Wheeler, J./Danesh, J. (2005): Prevalence of Serious Mental Disorder in 7000 Refugees Resettled in Western Countries: A Systematic Review. In: Lancet 365(9467), 1309–1314.

Fleay, C./Hartley, L./Kenny, M. A. (2013): Refugees and Asylum Seekers Living in the Australian Community: The Importance of Work Rights and Employment Support. In: Australian Journal of Social Issues 48, 473–493.

Gordon, M. M. (1964): Assimilation in American Life. New York: Oxford University Press.

Guhan, R./Liebling-Kalifani, H. (2011): The Experiences of Staff Working with Refugees and Asylum Seekers in the United Kingdom: A Grounded Theory Exploration. In: Journal of Immigrant & Refugee Studies 9(3), 205–228.

Gupta, A./Leong, F./Valentine, J. C./Canada, D. D. (2013): A Meta-Analytic Study: The Relationship between Acculturation and Depression among Asian Americans. In: American Journal of Orthopsychiatry (2–3), 372.

Hobfoll, S. E./Watson, P./Bell, C. C./Bryant, R. A./Brymer, M. J./Friedman, M. J./ … Maguen, S. (2007): Five Essential Elements of Immediate and Mid-Term Mass Trauma Intervention: Empirical Evidence. In: Psychiatry: Interpersonal and Biological Processes 70(4), 283–315.

Kanagaratnam, P., & Asbjørnsen, A. E. (2007): Executive Deficits in Chronic PTSD Related to Political Violence. In: Journal of Anxiety Disorders 21(4), 510–525.

Kingsley, P. (2017): The New Odyssey: The Story of the Twenty-First Century Refugee Crisis. New York: Liveright Publishing.

Knipscheer, J. W./Kleber, R. J. (2006): The Relative Contribution of Posttraumatic and Acculturative Stress to Subjective Mental Health among Bosnian Refugees. In: Journal of Clinical Psychology 62(3), 339–353.

Lambert, J. E./Alhassoon, O. M. (2015): Trauma-Focused Therapy for Refugees: Meta-Analytic Findings. In: Journal of Counseling Psychology 62(1), 28–37.

Lustig, S. L./Kia-Keating, M./Knight, W. G./Geltman, P./Ellis, H./Kinzie, J. D./ … Saxe, G. N. (2004): Review of Child and Adolescent Refugee Mental Health. In: Journal of the American Academy of Child and Adolescent Psychiatry 43(1), 24–36.

Miller, K. E./Rasmussen, A. (2010): War Exposure, Daily Stressors, and Mental Health in Conflict and Post-Conflict Settings: Bridging the Divide between Trauma-Focused and Psychosocial Frameworks. In: Social Science & Medicine 70(1), 7–16.

Miller, K. E./Weine, S./Ramic, A./Brkic, N./Djuric-Bijedic, Z./Smajkic, A./... Worthington, G. J. (2002): The Relative Contribution of War Experiences and Exile-Related Stressors to Levels of Psychological Distress among Bosnian Refugees. In: Journal of Traumatic Stress 15(5), 377–387.

Mollica, R. F./Caridad, K. R./Massagli, M. P. (2007): Longitudinal Study of Posttraumatic Stress Disorder, Depression, and Changes in Traumatic Memories over Time in Bosnian Refugees. In: Journal of Nervous & Mental Disease 195(7), 572–579.

Mollica, R. F./Sarajlić, N./Chernoff, M./ Lavelle, J./Vuković, I. S./Massagli, M. P. (2001): Longitudinal Study of Psychiatric Symptoms, Disability, Mortality, and Emigration among Bosnian Refugees. In: JAMA: The Journal of the American Medical Association 286(5), 546–554.

Nguyen, A. M. D./Benet-Martínez, V. (2012): Biculturalism and Adjustment: A Meta-Analysis. In: Journal of Cross-Cultural Psychology 44(1), 122–159.

Nickerson, A./Liddell, B./Asnaani, A./Carlsson, J. M./Fazel, M./Knaevelsrud, C./ ...Rasmussen, A. (2017): Trauma and Mental Health in Forcibly Displaced Populations: An International Society for Traumatic Stress Studies Briefing Paper. International Society for Traumatic Stress Studies.

Parkinson, D. (2017): Investigating the Increase in Domestic Violence Post Disaster: An Australian Case Study. In: Journal of Interpersonal Violence, 0886260517696876.

Phinney, J. S. (1990): Ethnic Identity in Adolescents and Adults: A Review of Research. In Psychol Bull. 108(3), 499–514.

Phinney, J. S./Devitch-Navarro, M. (1997): Variations in Bicultural Identification among African American and Mexican American Adolescents. In: Journal of Research on Adolescence 7(1), 3–32.

Pirkis, J./Burgess, P./Meadows, G./Dunt, D. (2001): Access to Australian Mental Health Care by People from Non-English-Speaking Backgrounds. In: Australian and New Zealand Journal of Psychiatry 35(2), 174–182.

Porter, M./Haslam, N. (2005): Predisplacement and Postdisplacement Factors Associated with Mental Health of Refugees and Internally Displaced Persons: A Meta-Analysis. In: JAMA 294(5), 602–612.

Rose, S./Bisson, J./Churchill, R./Wessely, S. (2002): Psychological Debriefing for Preventing Post Traumatic Stress Disorder (PTSD). In Cochrane Database Syst Rev, 2(2), CD000560.

Sam, D. L. (2006): Acculturation: Conceptual Background and Core Components. In: D. L. Sam & J. W. Berry (eds.): The Cambridge Handbook of Acculturation Psychology. New York: Cambridge University Press, 11–26.

Substance Abuse & Mental Health Services Association (SAMHSA) (2018): Trauma-Informed Approach and Trauma-Specific Interventions. https://www.samhsa.gov/nctic/trauma-interventions (last accessed August 20, 2018).

Schwartz, S.//Unger, J. B./Zamboanga, B. L./Szapocznik, J. (2010): Rethinking the Concept of Acculturation: Implications for Theory and Research. In: The American Psychologist 65(4), 237–251.

Schweitzer, R./Melville, F./Steel, Z./Lacherez, P. (2006): Trauma, Post-Migration Living Difficulties, and Social Support as Predictors of Psychological Adjustment in Resettled Sudanese Refugees. In: Australian & New Zealand Journal of Psychiatry 40(2), 179–187.

Schick, M./Zumwald, A./Knöpfli, B./Nickerson, A./Bryant, R. A./Schnyder, U./ ... Morina, N. (2016): Challenging Future, Challenging Past: The Relationship of Social Integration and

Psychological Impairment in Traumatized Refugees. In: European Journal of Psychotraumatology 7(1), 28057.

Sijbrandij, M./Acarturk, C./Bird, M./Bryant, R. A./Burchert, S./Carswell, K./ … Ittersum, L. van (2017): Strengthening Mental Health Care Systems for Syrian Refugees in Europe and the Middle East: Integrating Scalable Psychological Interventions in Eight Countries. In: European Journal of Psychotraumatology 8(sup2), 1388102.

Silove, D./Sinnerbrink, I./Field, A./Manicavasagar, V./Steel, Z. (1997): Anxiety, Depression and PTSD in Asylum-Seekers: Associations with Pre-Migration Trauma and Post-Migration Stressors. In: The British Journal of Psychiatry, 170(4), 351–357.

Steel, Z./Chey, T./Silove, D./Marnane, C./Bryant, R. A./Ommeren, M. van (2009): Association of Torture and Other Potentially Traumatic Events with Mental Health Outcomes among Populations Exposed to Mass Conflict and Displacement: A Systematic Review and Meta-Analysis. In: JAMA 302(5), 537–549.

Steel, Z./ Momartin, S./Bateman, C./Hafshejani, A./Silove, D./Everson, N. … Mares, S. (2004): Psychiatric Status of Asylum Seeker Families Held for a Protracted Period in a Remote Detention Centre in Australia. In: Australian & New Zealand Journal of Public Health 28(6), 527–536.

Steel, Z./Silove, D./Phan, T./Bauman, A. (2002): Long-Term Effect of Psychological Trauma on the Mental Health of Vietnamese Refugees Resettled in Australia: A Population-Based Study. In: Lancet 360(9339), 1056–1062.

Stuart, G. W./Minas, H./Klimidis, S./O'Connell, S. (1998): The Treated Prevalence of Mental Disorder amongst Immigrants and the Australian-Born: Community and Primary-Care Rates. In: International Journal of Social Psychiatry 44(1), 22–34.

Summerfield, D. (1999): A Critique of Seven Assumptions Behind Psychological Trauma Programmes in War-Affected Areas. In: Social Science & Medicine 48(10), 1449–1462.

Tol, W. A./Barbui, C./Galappatti, A./Silove, D./Betancourt, T. S./Souza, R./ … van Ommeren, M. (2011): Mental Health and Psychosocial Support in Humanitarian Settings: Linking Practice and Research. In: The Lancet 378(9802), 1581–1591.

UNHCR (2001): Chapter 2.6: Fostering Independent Communication: Language Training Programs for Adult Resettled Refugees. In: Refugee Resettlement: An International Handbook to Guide Reception and Integration. Geneva: UNHCR.

UNHCR (2018): Global Trends: Forced Displacement in 2017. Geneva: UNHCR.

Van Minnen, A. /Hendriks, L./Olff, M. (2010): When Do Trauma Experts Choose Exposure Therapy for PTSD Patients? A Controlled Study of Therapist and Patient Factors. In: Behaviour Research and Therapy 48(4), 312–320.

Watkins, P. G./Razee, H./Richters, J. (2012): 'I'm Telling You … the Language Barrier Is the Most, the Biggest Challenge': Barriers to Education among Karen Refugee Women in Australia. In: Australian Journal of Education 56(2): 126–141.

Responding

Jan-Christoph Heilinger

Newcomer integration, individual agency, and responsibility

Abstract: This paper analyses the responsibility of well-off citizens in high-income countries for contributing to the social task of newcomer integration into their society, based on a moral outlook stressing the equal moral worth of all. It discusses moral reasons to overcome apathy and inaction, offers a multilayered justification of individual responsibility, and points towards the importance of collective action and institutional support.

1. A global challenge

The number of people forcibly displaced as a result of persecution, conflict, or violence reached a record high of close to 70 million in 2017 (UNHCR 2018). People fleeing from their place of origin have to stay away for ever-longer periods of time given the long duration of the conflicts or the persistence of the adverse circumstances that made them flee. Recently, substantial numbers of people also sought refuge in Europe, a process sometimes labelled the 'European refugee crisis'. However, the current situation would be more accurately described as a *global* challenge rather than a European one, for several reasons.

First, while there are significant numbers of people seeking refuge in Europe, this is part of a global phenomenon. The countries hosting the largest numbers of refugees are not the European ones; nor are the countries with the highest percentage of refugees in their populations. In absolute and relative terms, it is the low- and middle-income countries (LMIC) that are the most affected by incoming refugees.[1] The increase in displacement, but also in migration and mobility worldwide, affects, albeit to varying degrees, countries across the globe, either as countries of origin for migrants or as host countries receiving newcomers.

1 They are Turkey (3.5 million refugees), Pakistan (1.4 million), Uganda (1.4 million), Lebanon (998.800), Iran (979.300), followed by Germany (970.400), as the first European nation, Bangladesh (932.200), Sudan (906.600), Ethiopia (889.400), and Jordan (691.000). Highest numbers of refugees per 1.000 inhabitants are in Lebanon (164 in 1.000), Jordan (71), Turkey (43), Uganda (32), Chad (28) before Sweden (24), as the first European country, followed by South Sudan (23), Sudan (22), Malta (19), and Djibouti (18). Europe is involved only with a fraction of the number of refugees worldwide (UNHCR 2018).

https://doi.org/10.1515/9783110628746-010

Global migration is a fact of our time and its multiple effects become tangible in different world regions. Consequently, the complex social, political, and ethical issues raised by the large numbers of human beings seeking refuge or migrating worldwide, should ultimately be an issue of moral concern for *all humanity*, even if the impact of such movements becomes more palpable in particular regions. Finding successful strategies to support and secure the peaceful and constructive living together of people from different backgrounds thus constitutes an important, yet complex global challenge.

Second, the reasons prompting people to migrate to Europe are wide-ranging and often have a global dimension: Global economic inequalities and local conflicts often result from complex interactions that are not confined to local factors alone. Poverty and economic deprivation in certain world regions, for example in sub-Saharan Africa, are not only a result of exclusively local factors, but are influenced also by the global economy and its rules for international economic exchange. The fact that, for example, illegitimate leaders can sell natural resources or borrow money in the name of the country contributes to poverty and deprivation triggering migratory movements (cf. e.g., Lessenich 2016; Wenar 2016). Local conflicts, such as the Syrian civil war, similarly have external influences among their origins[2] and involve non-local agents (such as Iran, Turkey, Russia, and the *Combined Joint Task Force* which is composed of personnel from over thirty countries). For these reasons, any normative discussion about migration and its consequences calls for a global perspective transcending the confinements of an exclusively local or national perspective.

The large numbers of forcibly displaced people worldwide must not obscure the fact that migration involves individual lives and personal interactions in concrete and confined settings. The arrival of 'newcomers' – refugees, asylum-seekers, and other migrants[3] – triggers a complex set of local interactions involving multiple agents, including the newcomers themselves, public and political institutions, as well as the citizens and residents in the host community. From the perspective of *ethics*, it is important to look behind the statistics to see the actions and interactions of individuals as 'moral agents'. This chapter focusses on the role of individuals in the host countries and the responsibility they

2 For a discussion of the influence of the Sykes-Picot agreement on the current situation in the Middle East cf. Bâli (2016). For a discussion of the impact of anthropogenic climate change on the outbreak of the Syrian civil war cf. Kelley et al. (2015).

3 My focus is on people fleeing persecution, violence, or conflict; but many of the thoughts extend beyond this scope and call for the general realisation of integrated societies comprising of people with different backgrounds.

bear for contributing to the social task of integrating newcomers.[4] I offer a normative discussion of the responsibility of those who are already there towards those who had to flee and have just arrived. National citizens are a particularly important and large group in this context, but also important are other groups within the local population, namely permanent residents or former refugees who can, and in many ways are expected to, bear responsibility for the newcomers.

From the outset, I have to specify three presupposed background assumptions. *Firstly,* I assume that *all* humans have equal moral worth and have basic rights, such as those set out in the Universal Declaration of Human Rights. This is, fundamentally, a universalist and egalitarian outlook, which, since it encompasses all persons on the globe as forming a community of moral relevance, can be labelled 'cosmopolitan' (Brock 2013). I do not argue for this view here. *Secondly,* my discussion of individual responsibility for newcomer integration focusses on the perspective of individual citizens in high-income countries, despite migration to these countries representing only a fraction of global migratory movements and notwithstanding the fact that many other people and institutions also bear responsibility in this process. This focus does not imply that the responsibilities of other agents – e.g., newcomers, public institutions in the receiving societies, and states and the international community – should be reduced. Yet, they are beyond the scope of this paper. *Thirdly,* I stipulate that integration, as an ideal, should be understood as the peaceful and fair living together of different individuals and groups within a society. An integrated society allows for and supports the participation of and interaction among all people on a footing of equality.[5] It secures fair equality of opportunity, reduces and ultimately eliminates subordination, discrimination, and oppression. In an integrated society a sense of belonging is open to all and not dependent on issues of cultural, ethnic, religious, or national background.[6] I do *not* perceive integra-

4 Bearing responsibility means, in my understanding, to be subject to the demand to respond in a morally appropriate way to a given situation. Appropriate responses, for example, to someone having suffered an accident can include, depending on the context, calling the ambulance, coordinating with others to organise help, providing first aid, or offering mental support while waiting for help.

5 Full inclusion – as the opposite of segregated societies – consists in 'comprehensive intergroup associations on terms of equality' (Anderson 2010, 112).

6 For more on such a comprehensive social account of integration, cf. Anderson (2010), Foroutan (2015), and Ager and Strang (2008).

tion as a requirement to be met by newcomers who would have to unilaterally adapt to their new environment.[7]

Given this context, this chapter considers the role of those residing in the host community in the integration of refugees and newcomers; it defends the claim that they bear moral responsibility to contribute to addressing the local face of this global challenge. Apathy and inaction cannot be morally justified. This argument is presented in three sections. The first section explores the many ways that individuals and civil society initiatives actually support refugees and facilitate their integration. Large numbers of people contribute to this task and complement institutional activities or, as is often the case, make up for institutional shortcomings. This section thus shows a number of possible options to act. In the second section, I put forward a theoretical justification of such individual responsibility. Through a series of sub-questions, I take up the perspective of a citizen in an affluent country wondering why she should, as an individual, bear any responsibility for addressing the task of newcomer integration. The third section concludes with some reflections on the social and political context within which individual actions are located and stresses the importance of a division of labour between institutions and individuals in order to effectively realise the ideal of an integrated society.

Throughout the chapter, individual responsibility for refugee integration is considered from a normative perspective. I am fully aware that the views and arguments advanced here may contrast with many mainstream public debates, and I recognise that one should not overestimate the impact of philosophical reasoning in changing the deeply held convictions of those who disagree with the imperative of integration in what are rapidly becoming heated public debates. Nevertheless, it is important to spell out the implications of the fundamental equality of all (particularly in times when such views are increasingly subject to criticism and attack); and to promote the long-term project of realising a global society of equals.[8]

---

7 Earlier, integration was mostly discussed in this sense of a demand of the newcomer to assimilate to or integrate into the host society. Since nearly two decades the European Council on Refugees and Exiles (ECRE) has argued for the reciprocal nature of refugee integration as a "two-way" process making demands on both newcomers and the host communities (ECRE 1999, 29). For the distinction between assimilation and integration, cf. e.g., Anderson (2010, 114).

8 A more comprehensive account of my idea of relational equality and cosmopolitan responsibility can soon be found in Heilinger (forthcoming).

2. Taking responsibility for newcomer integration

Much public attention is currently being paid to the ugly responses to newcomers in the form of visible prejudice, xenophobia, outright racism, and violence; while the impressive range of contributions, projects, and initiatives undertaken by individuals and the civil society tend to receive little acknowledgement.[9] Many such initiatives exist in which individuals contribute to the social task of newcomer integration and often fill gaps left by existing policies. Yet, some recognition exists and the European Economic and Social Committee (2017), for example, awarded its Civil Society Prize to selected civil society organisations for their contributions in supporting refugees and migrants. The EESC distinguishes numerous types of interventions undertaken by individuals and civil society initiatives, covering all steps from the very first arrival of the newcomers on secure territory to the different challenges they face when starting a new life. Activities range from emergency help, which includes the rescue from danger at sea and the provision of first relief, food, clothes, and shelter, to advice and assistance in dealing with the legal and administrative processes in the host country. Other civil society initiatives ensure the newcomers' access to social and health services, or address the protection of human rights for the newcomers, e.g., by fighting against discrimination in its different forms. Some initiatives seek to raise awareness and increase understanding for the distinctive situation and the particular challenges faced by newcomers through information campaigns or the creation of meeting spaces allowing for encounters between long-term residents and newcomers. Yet others aim at promoting mutual understanding between people of different backgrounds and fostering the participation and integration of all. In this context, one must not underestimate how essential and effective the most basic human activities like sharing food or playing together can be. Another group of initiatives support training and education for newcomers and the provision of suitable and accessible information or individual mentoring to facilitate their integration into the labour market.

9 In the case of Germany, for example, cf. the data provided by the Institut für Demoskopie Allensbach on behalf of the federal German Bundesministerium für Familie, Senioren, Frauen und Jugend: A majority of the population (older than sixteen years) was personally engaged in the context of the refugee and newcomer arrival since 2015. And 11 per cent of the population are involved continually in activities with and for the newcomers. Most of those active in refugee work report that they see their contributions as immediately important, meaningful, and rewarding (Allensbach 2018).

The activities mentioned are not meant to constitute a complete list. Instead, they illustrate the numerous activities that large numbers of people actually engage with, often for long periods and with significant personal costs in terms of time and other resources. Moreover, they cast light on the task of newcomer integration as a complex social and moral challenge.

In the following section, I discuss moral reasons for such engagement from the perspective of a resident in the host community, and I contend that getting involved as an individual should not simply be considered as a matter of personal choice and benevolence, but also as a matter of moral responsibility.

3. Individual responsibility

A rather well-off person living in a high-income country facing the arrival of newcomers who fled situations wherein their basic rights were endangered or violated might raise several questions when considering his own role in this situation.[10] Questions about a possible demand for personal engagement present themselves even if one would generally prefer to assign responsibility for large-scale social tasks primarily to political and social institutions. Indeed, institutions surrounding welfare, education, and health can provide ways of addressing the social task of integration much better and more effectively than any individual,[11] but sometimes these institutions are absent or are unable or unwilling to do what is necessary or their action is insufficient. Under such conditions of institutional shortcomings and urgency, individuals ought to not only call for political and institutional reform but also get involved personally. They can respond flexibly, faster, and more directly to an important task than an institution, even though only on a relatively small scale and without solving the larger social or structural problem in general through their individual engagement. And even if, under more favourable circumstances, public institutions do address the current situation rather well, the actions of and interactions between individuals, who are not formally connected with such public institutions

10 Of course, the questions discussed here are necessarily selective and take up an individualistic and interactional perspective. I do not engage here with a general discussion of the right to seek refuge in another country (but cf. Carens 2013), nor do I discuss what would be, from an international perspective, the right way of distributing refugees between countries (but cf. Gibney 2015). I assume the perspective of a moral agent faced with the situation in which newcomers in need arrive in one's country and are likely to stay for a significant amount of time.

11 The international community can play an important role providing conditions that support and facilitate integration as well (Owen 2018).

are nevertheless integral to realising the ambitious goal of integration. After all, it is necessary though insufficient for integration that newcomers are treated well by public officials and that the laws and institutions are formally just, because integration hinges ultimately upon uncounted normal and informal everyday interactions between people on a footing of equality (Anderson 2010, 116). Private individuals and the civic society thus must play a role in realising integration.[12]

Three sets of questions seem particularly important. *Firstly*, what, if anything, creates a moral obligation for individual persons to accept responsibility for the challenge of realising newcomer integration? *Secondly*, why should one engage with the particular task of newcomer integration, even if it is morally important? Why not give preference to issues involving compatriots and why not contribute instead to addressing other problems in one's country or in this world? *Thirdly*, why should one sacrifice time and energy for something that promises only small results and will not be enough to solve the problem? The discussion of these questions will allow specifying individual responsibility in the context of newcomer integration.

The grounds of responsibility. In the case of refugee and migrant integration, in which different groups of people suddenly find themselves in a shared social context, two strategies for determining individual responsibility for the task of realising an integrated society can be distinguished: one universalist and the other connectivist. In this section I will move from more abstract and general grounds of responsibility to more specific and concrete ones. I claim that the universalist and the connectivist approach can complement each other in a multi-layered account of the grounds of responsibility.

Firstly, the fact that some humans suffer or live under circumstances where their basic needs and rights are not secured should trigger moral concern among all who think that the lives of all human beings matter. Such considerations can be called universalist because they contrast with views that restrict (full) moral concern to those who have, for example, a specific race, religion, sex, or nationality or stand in a particular (close) relationship to the person considering from a moral perspective what to do. Against such contrasting views, the universalist

12 Stressing individual responsibility in this chapter hence is no suggestion to *replace* the responsibility of governments and public institutions. Instead, both institutional and individual responsibility should mutually complement and support one another. This thought will also be included in the United Nation's *Global Compact for Safe, Orderly and Regular Migration*, to be adopted in December 2018: its objective 16 calls for the empowerment of migrants and societies to realise full inclusion and social cohesion and assigns also civil society an important role in this regard.

holds that if some are suffering from a preventable moral wrong, and if the person reflecting on what she should do does find herself in a position to end or alleviate this wrong, strong moral reasons speaks in favour of doing so. For some, knowledge about a case of preventable deprivation or suffering, combined with the ability to address it, is already sufficient to justify moral responsibility to act accordingly.[13] The need for protection of those in danger can hence provide one with moral reasons to support refugee support and also refugee resettlement; the need for integration of those having arrived can generate moral reasons to contribute to this task.

The universalist strategy, with its fast escalation from concern over reasons to responsibility and obligations, is straightforward. Yet, it might appear as not specific enough because it leaves several relevant aspects underdetermined. Among other things, it does not explain why particularly '*I*', as the deliberating moral agent, should address this particular problem by helping *these* people. Hence, to further strengthen individual responsibility beyond the universalist reasoning, it is helpful to point out several possible connections between 'me' and those towards whom 'I' might have a responsibility to support them. This will lead to a multilayered justification of responsibility.

Special relations and connections can come in many shapes and constitute the connectivist justification of individual responsibility. One can assume, as cosmopolitans do, that all humans form a morally relevant *community* across the globe. This community puts people into a specific relationship to each other, as '*citizens* of the world', similarly to the citizens in a country, where also a special relationship with corresponding responsibilities reigns. The numerous economic, political, and environmental connections between people establish such a global sphere of mutual influence and community, even if an overarching political authority as in the nation state does not exist (Beitz 1979; Brock 2013). Harms suffered by *some* then should trigger moral concern and some corresponding action to prevent and ease suffering among *all* 'global citizens'. In the present context, this could include providing refuge, security, and support to those who had to flee from one place to another due to disaster, deprivation, or war in a similar way as one would offer support to compatriots who had to flee from another region of one's country for similar reasons. This general cosmopolitan connection, however, still reads very much like the universalism already explained. So, one might look for more specific connections.

Additionally, specific connections often exist between those residing in the high-income countries in the Global North and those fleeing from zones of pov-

13 Cf. Singer (1972) and Heilinger (2012).

erty or crisis in the Global South. Many of the triggers of flight result from prior human action, or the failure of action, frequently involving representatives of the more affluent and politically powerful countries. Examples include global warming as a result of the massive greenhouse gas emissions from the industrialised world, which now makes living in several world regions, most often low- and middle-income countries, increasingly difficult (Althor, Watson et al. 2016); the systematic economic exploitation of poorer world regions to the economic advantage of the more powerful countries (Young 2006; Lessenich 2016; Wenar 2016); the legacy of colonialism (Lu 2011; Kehoe 2019); or combinations of these and additional factors.

In such cases, the connectivist reasoning goes, citizens in the affluent countries are part of a group (a collective agent like the nation state) that has caused harm in the past or that contributes to upholding an ongoing wrong. As an individual who is part of this collective, one bears also a personal share of – mediated and indirect, but nevertheless existing – responsibility to act, even though one did not necessarily cause the wrong in question or approve of it (Miller 2007; Young 2011). While this responsibility is constituted by establishing connections to past decisions and processes, it has an important present- and future-oriented focus; it points out the ongoing contributions of individuals to persisting problems and injustices, and it also conceives unjust benefitting from moral wrongs committed by *others* as relevant connections, which generate a forward-looking responsibility to contribute to addressing the problem or to dealing responsibly with its consequences (Butt 2007).

Yet an additional way to identify relevant connections starts from the status quo, once newcomers have arrived, find themselves in the host society, and are likely to stay. The jointly shared social setting of a nation state, a community, or a neighbourhood provides the frame within which its members are de facto connected, in which encounters and interactions will take place. Building on the ideal of an integrated society, newcomers deserve to be treated as moral equals and should receive, also through interpersonal interaction and individual engagement, all that is necessary and conducive to having their status as equals respected (Anderson 1999; 2010). Realising an integrated society will demand interactions shaped by mutual respect, openness, and general civic friendliness. Clearly, this will require abstaining from hateful and harmful acts leading to segregation and ostracism. Additionally, positive individual contributions are essential to realise this goal, such as a commitment to go beyond the minimal requirements and create and seize opportunities for interactions and connections to be established and deepened. Such connections – even if they result from ultimately contingent encounters – can gain in moral weight through increasing personalisation: Once one has met with refugees, learned about their personal stories, the formerly abstract knowledge gains a personal dimension and makes oneself a *witness* of what went on and what is needed.[14] Such deeper, significant connections and special relationships will generate weightier and more specific moral responsibilities to facilitate integration through different means.

The different connectivist arguments – joint membership in a global community on the one hand, and past or ongoing contributions to causing or upholding injustice on the other, combined with particular abilities, experiences and interactions – thus have the potential to add up and to specify and further strengthen the basic universalist strategy of justifying individual responsibility. This can be called a *multilayered justification* of individual responsibility. The implications of this view for newcomer integration are twofold. It can first justify and support the general acceptance of refugees to one's community; and, once they are there, it justifies the call to realising an integrated society in which all can interact with one another as equals.

Competing demands. Yet, even if one is willing to accept some responsibility to act for the needs of refugees and other migrants in a receiving community, it remains unclear how to weigh this particular responsibility against many other moral responsibilities a person may have. These can include obligations to respond to other global challenges (like climate change or world poverty, which also exposes large numbers of human beings to an existential threat), to other local challenges (like homelessness or need in one's city, where those affected may be mostly compatriots), or to the needs of those near and dear (one's children, parents, friends, and also oneself). All these factors generate moral demands. The widespread ease, however, with which we tend to assign greater weight, sometimes even exclusive weight, to our individual preferences, to those we love, or to compatriots, is not as easy to justify in the face of extremely severe harms and dire needs of others – who are, for example, expelled from their homes, persecuted, tortured, starved, bombed, etc. – as it is often assumed to be. Nevertheless, deciding between competing and often mutually exclusive demands is extremely difficult.

An extensive philosophical debate exists about the weighing of universal against special obligations (e.g., Scheffler 2001; Cottingham 2010). In this section, I want to address only one particular aspect of it that will be of relevance for the citizen deliberating about her moral obligations in the context of newcomer integration. Assuming that one has already determined the amount of per-

14 On the moral relevance of witnessing, cf. the contributions by Phipps (2019) and Grahle (2019) in this book.

sonal engagement (say, in terms of energy, time, and money) one is willing to commit to moral causes that expand beyond one's narrower circle of friends and family, how is one to decide among the different options – which all may have high urgency?[15] Should I become involved in supporting newcomers in my city? Should I participate in the fight against global warming and climate change? Should I work to reduce extreme poverty and child mortality in rural India? Or should I help to increase access to education for disadvantaged children in my neighbourhood? So many urgent needs exist that acknowledging them frequently leads to paralysis and inaction, instead of engagement. Inaction, however, is clearly the worst of all options and cannot be justified from a moral perspective (Cohen 2000). Yet, no convincing algorithm has been found to unambiguously determine or even calculate which (type of) engagement is morally demanded.[16] Instead, a personal decision is required, even some kind of an existential choice that has important implications for determining what kind of a person we ultimately will turn out to be (Williams 1981). Such a personal decision also takes into account contingent and individual factors: If I have, for example, some prior connection to, say, India, I might feel particularly inclined to contribute to addressing some social issue there rather than engaging in environmental protection activities elsewhere. Similarly, if I am moved by the images of refugees arriving at the train station in my city, if I have encountered some of the newcomers and heard their stories, I might take action as a volunteer there. If I come to the conclusion that global warming is possibly the largest threat to the existence of humanity, I might be motivated to donate money or time to help fight climate change.

My point is this: Individuals have significant discretion in how they assign priority to such incommensurable but important moral projects (always under the assumption that they *do respond* in a meaningful way to *some* of them). A moral person will understand a call for moral action in numerous cases, in

15 In other words, I do not discuss here *how much* of our available resources we should commit to moral causes, which would be a discussion of the challenge of moral overdemandingness (but cf. e. g., Scheffler 1992, ch. 2). Instead, here I simply assume that people should dedicate *some* of their available resources to moral causes and ask *how to decide among the many possible options* to do so.

16 Here I disagree with 'effective altruists' who attempt to do just this by calculating which types of action would generate the maximum impact in terms of lives saved or improved (Singer 2015). While outcomes and effectiveness certainly are relevant in deciding what to do, simply asking, 'How can I make the biggest difference I can?' (MacAskill 2015) seems to ignore both (a) the needs of those who happen not to be in the group of people who can be helped most effectively, and (b) the personal character of a moral agent invited to act and his contingent situation within which he might be confronted with a particular task.

many more cases than she actually can and will act. Making a choice and getting involved in only one or some of them is inevitable, given the limitations of human agency, and does not have to include denying the urgency and legitimacy of another. Under these circumstance, the personal choice, which takes into account also contingent, personal factors, is fully appropriate. Such discretion invites action while relieving the moral agent from the need to decide whether or not the global migration challenge and the call for integration is the only or the most serious moral challenge of our time. It is sufficient to see it only as among the important global challenges that stand in need of both political and individual responses. Consequently, engagement to address this issue is commendable and should be welcomed from a moral perspective – even if it inevitably comes at the expense of the road not taken.

The charge of futility. Many of the important moral challenges of our time, including the integration of newcomers and addressing climate change, are on such a massive scale that individual contributions seem pointless.[17] Who would think realistically that one's individual contribution has any tangible impact on solving so large a problem? Supporting, say, one refugee family in their new environment, or avoiding fossil fuels to reduce greenhouse gas emissions does not make any difference to the problem. So, if my personal engagement does not make any obvious difference, why should I do something about it at all? Would it not be better to avoid personal sacrifices and leave this task to politics and public institutions instead? Two arguments stand out in defending individual responsibility against this challenge. First, in the case of newcomer integration, one can make the obvious point that supporting even a single individual in navigating the new and difficult circumstances can make *all of a difference* for this person, even if it does not change or solve the general situation as a whole. Such an individualistic approach justifies direct personal engagement, even if it connects 'only' with

17 Cf. e. g., Peeters et al. (2015), Pinkert (2015), and Kagan (2011). Mentioning the different tasks of newcomer integration and addressing climate change in one breath might appear problematic. However, both phenomena share significant similarities. They are morally urgent insofar as omission to act affects – in a harmful way – the lives of large numbers of people. Both tasks result from the complex interplay of many agents and they have an important temporal dimension with some of the origins of the acute challenge lying in the past. Addressing the problems will require coordinated action, and – while many people are generally willing to contribute also personally to addressing the problem – many others deny responsibility and refrain from considering personal contributions. These structural similarities allow discussing such complex and large-scale moral challenges together, in spite of their obvious particularities.

a symptom of the challenge rather than confronting the origins of the large-scale problem.

The second argument in support of engaging with the seemingly peripheral elements associated with the global challenge stresses the *indirect* impact of personal engagement. Besides the positive impact on one person or on a small group of people, individual behaviour has an important social and communicative function. Thinking, talking, and acting in certain ways indicate concern and express commitment. Acts indicate that a situation is acknowledged as a problem requiring personal engagement, perhaps even some degree of personal sacrifices. Such commitments are the palpable expression of a moral ethos that is based on the acknowledgement of the equal moral worth of all; the visibility of corresponding action importantly and convincingly communicates one's moral judgement and commitment to others. Its possible effects thus reach beyond the – admittedly small – direct impact: one's actions also inform others in subtle ways about one's moral views and about the possibilities of engagement. Under favourable circumstances this can support the spread of ideas and commitments and encourage similar engagements among others. The effects of individual behaviour can spill over into the group and even promote a general demand for political and institutional responses.

In this context, the complex social dynamics in norm change and behavioural change in groups would deserve further attention.[18] Analysing how societies introduced novel practices that required changing normative and behavioural dispositions of large numbers of people – in cases as diverse as recycling of waste, or reducing gender injustice, etc. – shows that the role and influence of individuals (including but not restricted to first movers and trendsetters) must not be underestimated (Bicchieri 2016). This is not to say that all such engagements of individuals do always lead to success in achieving large-scale social change, but it is certain that without the engagement of individuals, norm change and political change will not occur.

The considerations presented so far have engaged with several arguments for and specifications of individual responsibility for the social task of newcomer integration. As I have shown, both universalist and connectivist arguments can justify individual responsibility, but people still have some discretion when deciding where and the degree to which they get involved with a particular moral. The different possible forms of personal engagement, including talking and acting in certain ways, are not only relevant because of their direct effects but also because of the indirect contribution they make to upholding or chang-

18 For the context of promoting cosmopolitan norms, cf. Cameron (2017).

ing patterns of behaviour, and because of their impact on social and political norms.

4. A division of moral labour and the interplay of individual and institutional responsibility

The preceding defence of individual responsibility for the integration of newcomers had a limited scope. It took the perspective of those who think on generally egalitarian grounds about their role in the (global) society and did not attempt to convince those who defend nationalism and parochialism as the appropriate guiding framework. With regard to the content of the responsibility of individuals, the ambition of the preceding arguments in this short paper was also limited: I have not attempted to develop an algorithm to determine exactly who should be doing what in order to address the challenge of newcomer integration. All I have tried to do here is make the case *that* individuals do indeed bear some personal responsibility which they can exercise in different ways.

However limited the scope of my argument, those who acknowledge *some* responsibility for addressing important challenges like global migration, be it through political engagement or through addressing its local symptoms, endorse – knowingly or not – an important change in thinking about responsibility altogether, a change that accommodates the realities of globalisation: Under the current circumstances of an interconnected globalised world, it seems important that individuals conceive of themselves as sitting within a larger context, as agents whose behaviour and choices are part of processes and developments extending beyond their immediate surroundings and direct influences. In this larger context, near effects matter as do remote effects; acts matter as do omissions; and individual effects matter as do group effects (Scheffler 2001, 38–46). However powerless individuals might frequently feel in the face of massive problems and horrendous injustices, it must not be forgotten that individuals can act, can generate effects, and they can coordinate and exercise political power. This power can and should be employed to address the major challenges of our time also from the perspective of an individual. This is the perspective of a *global political ethics* which demands individuals to accept moral responsibility for the world in which they live.

Such focus on individual agency and responsibility is certainly not meant to neglect the importance of social coordination and institutional responses. Instead, the two dimensions of institutional and individual responses should ideally complement each other. As individual behaviour can inform and invite other persons to act and can also create pressure for political and institutional responses, institutional arrangements can, conversely, also inform and invite personal action. I conclude this chapter with an inspiring example from Canada, which invites its citizens and permanent residents to take individual responsibility for newcomer integration in an institutionally recognised and supported way.

Since 1978, the Government of Canada grants its citizens and permanent residents the privilege of sponsoring a refugee or a refugee family who will, if certain criteria are met, be relocated to Canada.[19] Within this Private Sponsorship of Refugees Programme, small groups of people can sponsor a refugee family to come to Canada, even without (and this is an important difference to most of the existing sponsorship programmes elsewhere) any family connection. Basically, these groups "adopt" a refugee family for a limited amount of time and bear the responsibility for supporting the newcomers in their new home community.[20] The Government thus allows and encourages citizens to act individually to take people out of danger zones. In this case, public institutions and private individuals join forces, a process which neither denies nor reduces the responsibility of either side to contribute what is needed to respond appropriately locally to a moral challenge of global proportions.

Bibliography

Ager, A./ Strang A. (2008): Understanding Integration: A Conceptual Framework. In: Journal of Refugee Studies 21(2), 166–191.

Allensbach, I. F. D. (2018): Engagement in der Flüchtlingshilfe. Bundesministerium für Familie, Senioren, Frauen und Jugend. https://www.bmfsfj.de/blob/122010/d35ec9b f4a940ea49283485db4625aaf/engagement-in-der-fluechlingshilfe-data.pdf.

Althor, G./Watson, J. E. M./Fuller, R. A. (2016): Global Mismatch between Greenhouse Gas Emissions and the Burden of Climate Change. In: Scientific Reports 6, 20281.

Anderson, E. (1999): What Is the Point of Equality? In: Ethics 109(2), 287–337.

Anderson, E. (2010): The Imperative of Integration. Princeton, Princeton University Press.

Bâli, A. (2016): Sykes-Picot and 'Artificial' States. In: AJIL Unbound 110, 115–119.

19 Cf. Immigration, Refugees, and Citizenship Canada (2016). For a suggestion to introduce a similar programme within the EU, cf. Kumin (2015). For a critical discussion of private sponsorship, cf. Lenard (2016).

20 The programme is popular in Canada, and citizens' interests exceed the number of families that were selected for the programme by the Canadian authorities. Since its inauguration, more than 200.000 people were resettled through the programme. The people admitted through this programme do not count against the quota set by the Canadian government for other avenues of resettlement.

Beitz, C. (1979): Political Theory and International Relations. Princeton: Princeton University Press.
Bicchieri, C. (2016): Norms in the Wild. How to Diagnose, Measure, and Change Social Norms. Oxford/New York: Oxford University Press.
Brock, G. (2013): Contemporary Cosmopolitanism: Some Current Issues. In: Philosophy Compass 8(8), 689–698.
Butt, D. (2007): On Benefiting from Injustice. In: Canadian Journal of Philosophy 37(1), 129–152.
Cameron, J. D. (2017): Communicating Cosmopolitanism and Motivating Global Citizenship. In: Political Studies, 1–17.
Carens, J. H. (2013): The Ethics of Immigration. Oxford/New York: Oxford University Press.
Cohen, G. A. (2000): Political philosophy and personal behavior. In: G. A. Cohen (ed.): If You're an Egalitarian, How Come You're So Rich? Cambridge: Harvard University Press, 148–179.
Cottingham, J. (2010): Impartiality and ethical formation. In: B. Feltham and J. Cottingham (eds.): Partiality and Impartiality: Morality, Special Relationships, and the Wider World. Oxford/New York: Oxford University Press, 65–83.
European Economic and Social Committee (2017): How Civil Society Organisations Assist Refugees and Migrants in the EU: Successful experiences and promising practices from the 2016 EESC Civil Society Prize. Brussels: EESC.
European Council on Refugees and Exiles (1999): Good Practice Guide on the Integration of Refugees in the European Union. Brussels: ECRE. https://ec.europa.eu/migrant-integration/librarydoc/introduction-to-good-practice-guides-on-integration-of-refugees-in-the-european-union.
Foroutan, N. (2015): Integration als Metanarrativ. Kurzdossier: Integration in der postmigrantischen Gesellschaft. B. f. p. Bildung. Bonn: Bundeszentrale für politische Bildung.
Gibney, M. (2015): Refugees and Justice between States. In: European Journal of Political Theory 14(4), 448–463.
Grahle, A. (2019): Why Volunteers Should be Activists: Towards an Ethics of Ground Relationships. In: S. K. Kehoe, E. Alisic and J.-C. Heilinger (eds.): Responsibility for Refugee and Migrant Integration. Berlin/Boston: de Gruyter, 149–164.
Heilinger, J.-C. (2012): The Moral Demandingness of Socioeconomic Human Rights. In: G. Ernst and J.-C. Heilinger (eds.): The Philosophy of Human Rights: Contemporary Controversies. Berlin/Boston: de Gruyter, 185–208.
Heilinger, J.-C. (forthcoming): Cosmopolitan Responsibility. Berlin/Boston: De Gruyter.
Immigration, Refugees and Citizenship Canada (2016): Private Sponsorship of Refugees Program. http://www.cic.gc.ca/english/pdf/pub/ref-sponsor.pdf.
Kagan, S. (2011): Do I Make a Difference? In: Philosophy and Public Affairs 39(2), 105–141.
Kehoe, S. K. (2019): Historical Perspectives on Migrant Integration in Atlantic Canada. In: S. K. Kehoe, E. Alisic and J.-C. Heilinger (eds.): Responsibility for Refugee and Migrant Integration. Berlin/Boston: de Gruyter, 65–80.
Kelley, C. P./Mohtadi, S./ Cane, M. A./Seager, R./Kushnir, Y. (2015): Climate Change in the Fertile Crescent and Implications of the Recent Syrian Drought. In: Proceedings of the National Academy of Sciences 112(11), 3241–3246.

Kumin, J. (2015): Welcoming Engagement: How Private Sponsorship Can Strengthen Refugee Resettlement in the European Union. Brussels: Migration Policy Institute Europe.

Lenard, P. T. (2016): Resettling Refugees: Is Private Sponsorship a Just Way Forward? In: Journal of Global Ethics 12(3), 300–310.

Lessenich, S. (2016): Neben uns die Sintflut: Die Externalisierungsgesellschaft und ihr Preis. Berlin: Hanser.

Lu, C. (2011): Colonialism as Structural Injustice: Historical Responsibility and Contemporary Redress. In: Journal of Political Philosophy 19(3): 261–281.

MacAskill, W. (2015): Doing Good Better: Effective Altruism and a Radical New Way to Make a Difference. London: Faber.

Miller, D. (2007): National Responsibility and Global Justice. Oxford: Oxford University Press.

Owen, D. (2018): Refugees and Responsibilities of Justice. In: Global Justice: Theory Practice Rhetoric 11(1), 23–44.

Peeters, W./De Smet, A./Diependaele, L./Sterckx, S. (2015): Climate Change and Individual Responsibility: Agency, Moral Disengagement and the Motivational Gap. Basingstoke: Palgrave Macmillan.

Phipps, A. (2019): Bearing Witness: The Burden of Individual Responsibility and the Rule of Law. In: S. K. Kehoe, E. Alisic and J.-C. Heilinger (eds.): Responsibility for Refugee and Migrant Integration. Berlin/Boston: de Gruyter, 9–24.

Pinkert, F. (2015): What If I Cannot Make a Difference (and Know It). In: Ethics 125(4), 971–998.

Scheffler, S. (1992): Human Morality. Oxford: Oxford University Press.

Scheffler, S. (2001): Boundaries and Allegiances. Oxford: Oxford University Press.

Singer, P. (1972): Famine, Affluence, and Morality. In: Philosophy and Public Affairs 1(3), 229–243.

Singer, P. (2015): The Most Good You Can Do: How Effective Altruism is Changing Ideas about Living Ethically. New Haven: Yale University Press.

Wenar, L. (2016): Blood Oil: Tyrants, Violence, and the Rules that Run the World. Oxford/New York: Oxford University Press.

Williams, B. (1981): Moral Luck. Cambridge: Cambridge University Press.

Young, I. M. (2006): Responsibility and Global Justice: A Social Connection Model. In: Social Philosophy and Policy 23, 102–130.

Young, I. M. (2011): Responsibility for Justice. Oxford/New York: Oxford University Press.

André Grahle

Why volunteers should be activists: towards an ethics of ground relationships

Abstract: Much of the philosophical debate on the ethics of refugee reception focusses on the question of what states owe to refugees. The debate has only partially touched upon a whole range of ethical questions that become strikingly relevant on the ground. Here the reality cannot be fully understood in terms of a relationship between refugees and the state, but requires an additional account of responsibilities based on relationships between refugees and non-government personnel, as well as, and most importantly perhaps, between refugees and networks of volunteers and activists. In this chapter, the variety of relationships that are jointly constitutive of a certain volunteer- or activist-context, as well as the relationships formed by these contexts in reaching out to refugees, are referred to as *ground relationships*. Four reasons are explored as to why ground relationships merit philosophical attention within a wider project of a yet-to-be-developed ethics of flight and refugee arrival. Finally, a case is made for volunteers to become activists based on considerations of benevolence.

1. The ethical significance of ground relationships

Much of the philosophical debate on the ethics of refugee reception focusses on the question of what states owe to refugees. This question is typically spelled out in terms of the conditions under which states ought to grant refugees permission to reside in their territory, as well as of asking for the social and political rights that should be guaranteed to refugees and other migrants *once* they reside, or after a certain history of them residing, in their territory.[1] While these and related questions are important, it is odd that the debate has not yet gone into sufficient depth in analysing some of the main ethical complexities of current phenomena of flight, specifically where they are linked to the arrival of larger groups of refugees in (nominally) liberal states, as recently in Europe during what has devel-

1 The debate has become fairly comprehensive by now, but Walzer (1983, 31 ff.), Carens (1987; 2013, 192 ff.), Gibney (2004), Miller (2005; 2016, 76 ff.), Owen (2016), and Song (2016) provide useful examples for what I have in mind.

https://doi.org/10.1515/9783110628746-011

oped into the worse displacement crisis since World War II.[2] Crucially, the debate has only partially touched upon a whole range of ethical questions that become strikingly relevant *on the ground*, where the reality cannot be fully understood in terms of a relationship between refugees and the state (though the latter is, of course, powerfully present) but rather requires an additional account of responsibilities based on relationships between refugees and non-government personnel, as well as, and most importantly perhaps, between refugees and networks of *volunteers* and *activists*. So for example, with regard to the current crisis, in 2015, when most of the refugees now residing in Europe arrived, estimates are that up to 25 per cent of the German population actively volunteered in contexts of refugee support.[3]

I take the paradigm of a *volunteer* in refugee support contexts to be a person who intends to act, without remuneration, in some suitable context to the concrete benefit of refugees *given* the general structural conditions under which the latter have to move or live. The context can, but need not be institutionalised in any more narrow sense. Activities may include the provision of information in train stations, preparing and serving food in camps, assisting with bureaucratic requirements, teaching refugees the language of the country of arrival, offering translation services, organizing cultural events, and providing social spaces for people to get to know each other. I take the paradigm of an *activist* in this field to be a person who is committed to some form of political struggle aimed at the *improvement* of the structural conditions under which refugees have to move through or live in (one of) these countries of (potential) arrival. What comes to mind instantly are the struggles for safe passage and for open borders, the struggles against refugee detention and deportation, against camps and segregative city structures, and in general opposition to the prevailing tendencies of states to respond to displacement crises by way of restricting asylum laws to such an extent as to effectively criminalise flight. I also count as activism instances of protest and resistance against *particular consequences* of oppressive structures that may not (immediately) change or abolish the structure as such, as when activists prevent a deportation in their city or engage in (increasingly criminalised) sea rescue missions.

---

2 By "worst displacement crisis since World War II" I mean that this is the crisis with the greatest *number* of displaced people since World War II. This is according to a UNHCR (2015) report.
3 See BMFSFJ (2017, 11). The percentage refers to members of the population who were sixteen and over. Excluded are people who have only *donated* to refugees or refugee support groups. If we were to include the latter, the percentage rises to 55 per cent, according to the same study, which has been commissioned by the German Federal Ministry of Family Affairs, Senior Citizens, Women and Youth.

I call the variety of relationships that are jointly *constitutive* of a certain volunteer and activist group or context, as well as the relationships formed by these groups and contexts in *reaching out* to refugees, *ground relationships*. There are at least four reasons why ground relationships merit philosophical attention within a wider project of a yet-to-be-developed ethics of flight and refugee arrival. Firstly, ground relationships are sometimes more suitable and effective than various state policies, or may be able to co-contribute something distinct, when it comes to realizing certain *types* of goods that refugees arguably have a right to, particularly where these goods are linked to practices of inclusion to community life, the spontaneous recognition of personhood and personal achievements, or the acknowledgement of past and current experiences of injustices (Grahle 2019). Note that this is not an attempt to let the state off the hook. It amounts to the claim that the state's role with respect to a certain good might sometimes be better confined to the no-less-demanding role of *facilitating* the emergence and success of relevant ground relationships, e. g., by actively working against segregative city structures, than to try to deliver the relevant good directly. Moreover, my claim is compatible with the observation that the state often fails to live up to its responsibility by relying on volunteers to provide a certain good that it actually should provide, and would be better suited to provide, directly (e. g., assistance with its own bureaucratic procedures).

Secondly, in the absence of a properly functioning international system of refugee protection, ground relationships are often the best available source of resistance against injustices committed, or likely to be committed, by the state (or a union of states) against refugees. They are, positively, a place of voicing claims in favour of an improvement of the refugees' living conditions, including their legal status; negatively, they are a natural source of spontaneous or organised protest against coercive state policies. Moreover, ground relationships can often be the only available means of *defying* the execution of an injustice in a particular case. Think of the spontaneous, sometimes coordinated, and frequently successful efforts of people preventing the deportation of refugees to unsafe and otherwise deprived areas, by way of hiding refugees, shielding their homes, or even occupying airfields. In a similar vein, activists and volunteers have repeatedly coordinated the assistance of refugees crossing sea and land borders, by clearing away or helping to circumvent obstacles put in the way of refugees to prevent them from ever reaching the territories they are aiming for.

Thirdly, the activity of ground relationships is frequently necessary, sometimes sufficient in *enabling* people to migrate in the first place. This observation partly follows from the second one, as what enables people to move on is often the very act of resisting or defying an injustice. Yet, volunteering and activism also have a broader and more positive role to play in making the arrival of refugees possible. To see this point more clearly, we first have to question the prevalent ideology of refugee *intake*, where this notion refers to a state's allegedly benevolent act of admitting refugees to their territory and society. So for example, public international commentators have frequently assigned to Germany – and often to Angela Merkel personally – the achievement of having 'taken in' the greatest number of refugees of any European nation during the current crisis. Such a way of speaking and thinking about recent events of refugee arrival is, however, fundamentally flawed.

To stick with the German case, it is true that the state has provided some legal recognition (though often only subsidiary protection) to refugees who finally made it to its territory. Yet, in most cases, such provision is best understood as a subsequent response when the primary policy to which these refugees have been subjected has not been entirely effective. The primary policy of Germany and any other EU country is one of *keeping refugees away* from their territories and from participating in their societies. As *Médecins sans frontières* (2016) put it,

> [f]or years, the EU and European governments have chosen to invest in measures aimed at systematically sealing off borders and deterring refugees and migrants from seeking safety in Europe. These include: the building of fences at external and internal EU borders, stricter border controls aimed at 'fighting' irregular migration, the containment of migrants and refugees in countries of first arrival or in transit countries outside the EU, the increased use of immigration detention, and chronic substandard and insufficient reception conditions in countries of first asylum, primarily in Italy and Greece.

As the quotation indicates, the policy of keeping away is not even reducible to these governments' omission to assist, but must be understood as the 'positive' contribution of entertaining a system of obstacles set up to interfere with refugees' aim of moving forward and arriving in a place where a decent life is possible. Note further that we are talking here about policies linked to clear human rights violations (Amnesty International 2014) and increasingly based on explicit political agreements that raise serious doubts about whether Europe can meet its obligations under international human rights law (Welander 2018).

I argue that giving credit to a state like Germany, or some other European state, for 'taking in' refugees, is *ideological.* I contend that such a position upholds an injustice by distorting reality.[4] First take the element of distortion.

---

4 The way I use the term 'ideology' corresponds roughly with Sally Haslanger's (2017, 150) and other theorists' understanding, according to which, as Haslanger puts it, ideology 'functions to stabilize or perpetuate unjust power and domination, and does so through some form of masking or illusion'.

The only scenario intelligible as a state 'taking in' refugees is one in which refugees are provided with visas to enable them to use safe and comfortable transport (planes, ships, and trains). So whenever we speak as politicians, public commentators, lawmakers, philosophers, or participants of everyday conversations about recent events in terms of states 'taking in' refugees, we risk evoking in each other's minds a version of this specific scenario. But critical observers know that no safe passage has ever been granted to the great majority of refugees who have arrived in Europe in recent years. Moreover, by way of our speech distorting that aspect of reality it can prevent or undermine the moral clarity we need to initiate social and political change. We are more likely to fail to hold states accountable for the way they have damaged the life of human beings who have unavailingly sought their protection, but either died on their way (e.g., by drowning in the Mediterranean), or found themselves stuck in camps with utterly unacceptable conditions outside or inside Europe. Rather, such speech comes with the potential to further foster these injustices.

When it is not the state who 'takes in' refugees, the quantity and quality of ground relationships often serve as part of an explanation as to why refugees nevertheless keep on arriving. Yet, here again the ideology contributes to the prevention of an adequate moral acknowledgement of the achievement of the many networks enabling people to migrate and find their place in a new society against the forces that are actively trying to keep them out. The latter should count as an injustice in its own right, and it is specifically regrettable as many who are denied the acknowledgement of their moral achievements are refugees themselves.

This brings me to the fourth and final consideration as to why ground relationships ought to receive more philosophical attention. In ground relationships, refugees manifest their agency. A more detailed focus on ground relationships can therefore pave the way for proper acknowledgement of this agency. By contrast, the image of the state who either excludes or benevolently 'takes in' refugees and other migrants has little to offer in this regard. Here refugees and other migrants – the very subjects excluded or 'taken in' – seem to be deprived of their agency and are assumed to be passive victims reduced to their fate. Such a perspective only adds insult to injury.

To be sure, putting the emphasis on ground relationships does not necessarily protect us from committing a similar mistake, as we might still fall into the trap of assuming that volunteers and activists are *citizens* of the receiving societies. It is not conceptually necessary that they be so, and it is empirically likely that some are not.[5] I use the term 'citizen' here in the narrow and clearest sense as referring to *state* citizen in the country of arrival. There are less restrictive ways of using the term, of course, as sometimes long-term residents are subsumed under a wider concept of citizen as well. But this usage not only renders the term unnecessarily vague, it also glosses over important differentials of privilege, which can have important moral implications. The crucial observation here is that activists and volunteers can have different (including unclear) legal statuses in the country of arrival, and, most importantly, they can be refugees themselves, so that they would not even qualify as citizens according to the vague definition.

That refugees act as volunteers and activists while on the move is nowhere more apparent, perhaps, than in the case of large groups of refugees taking the same route at the same time. So for instance, with regard to the hundreds of thousands of refugees who arrived in Central Europe, taking the 'Balkan route' in 2015 and 2016, we have witnessed refugees constantly engaging in active solidarity, by assisting each other in the provision of basic needs. Observers were left with the impression that refugees cross borders only to turn around instantly in an effort to assist those following them. Moreover, as has been widely reported by the media, refugees frequently engage in coordinated and spontaneous acts of protest and resistance in an attempt to move forward. Refugee groups in Idomeni sewed their lips together and went on a hunger strike; others organised sit-ins and held signs, while singing and chanting 'Open the borders!' (Safdar 2015; Alderman/Bounias 2016). Another act of political disobedience that received worldwide media attention was the March of Hope, when thousands of refugees, stuck for days at Budapest Keleti train station, took the motorway towards Austria and Germany, by foot after days of planning and coordinating themselves, causing both states to effectively capitulate. Later, German migration scientists would find this and other events crucial in bringing the European border regime as it was organised at this time to an end (Hess et al. 2016). As such cases suggest, flight can be understood as being an activity of resistance in itself, when-

5 My impression is, however, that certain preconceptions and biases guiding public and scientific usage of the concept 'volunteer' manifest a tendency to link the term with the concept of 'citizen', or at least with the concept of 'long-term resident', even where scientists and journalists do not explicitly *define* the concept that way. Rather, drawing the link is part of the habitual way of thinking and speaking about the topic of volunteering in receiving societies, which makes such failure even harder to notice and correct. In contexts of refugee arrival it would be better not to speak in ways that present volunteering and activism too much in terms of the 'civil society' or *Bürgergesellschaft* (Beck 2016, 101), even though these terms may, in principle, be defined in more inclusive ways.

ever it includes the overcoming or abolishment of obstacles that states wilfully put in refugees' way.

Things are not much different after arrival. A significant amount of volunteering must again be understood as a matter of refugees turning around to assist those still to follow. The city of Munich provides a striking example of what I have in mind here, as there are at least two established Syrian-led support groups, تجمع السوريين في ميونخ (Syrians Gathering in Munich) and سوريين في ميونخ (Syrians in Munich), that effectively organise and coordinate practical assistance through social media networks that have over three thousand members.[6] Moreover, in activism, a good amount of it is led by refugees as well. In Germany alone, groups such as *Women in Exile and Friends, International Women's Space*, *The Voice*, *Afghan Refugee Movement*, *Caravan for the Rights of Refugees and Migrants*, and *Lampedusa* provide striking examples of a tendency towards political self-organization that began at least two decades ago. Other groups, such as *No Lager* or *We'll Come United*, pursue actively non-separatist agendas, with refugees, other migrants, and citizens working together, often embedded within larger transnational networks (Ataç/Steinhilper 2016; Steinhilper 2018).

Although it is surprisingly often ignored, refugees' active role in these matters is, of course, hardly surprising. Activism here is often a matter of self-defence. Refugees often have no choice but to protest border closure or to fight against their deportation. Second, even if acts could sometimes be taken over by state-citizens at lower risk, refugees are – especially while on the move – often the only agents *available* to assist or resist. Finally, refugees frequently

6 Some of the major empirical studies examining the German case have entirely neglected the role of volunteer networks set up by incoming refugees. So for example, one study that has received specifically wide media uptake (Karakayali and Kleist 2015, 2016), raises the question of *who* the many volunteers in Germany are. While the authors conclude that a disproportionally high percentage of volunteers (15.5%) have a 'migration background' (*Migrationshintergrund*), the official criterion in Germany to fall under this category is that either oneself or *one's parent* migrated to Germany without German state-citizenship at the time of arrival. This leaves the question of *refugee* participation entirely unanswered. Participants have also been asked whether they or members of their family have a history of displacement, but the reference to 'family' in that question clearly meant to include both conjugal and extended family. So even though a 'significant percentage' of the participating volunteers answered this question positively, no conclusion in terms of how many of them were themselves refugees (and, especially, how many of them were from groups of currently *incoming* refugees who immediately began to assist other incoming refugees) can be drawn from the data. As the authors admit, the question has mainly been raised to satisfy public interest in whether the history of German post-war displacement (the history of the *Vertriebene*) has motivated relevant parts of the German society to now volunteer for refugees. The question therefore was one put in the service of the self-understanding of Germans under some fairly narrow conception of German identity.

manifest greater competence at assisting and resisting than state-citizens of many receiving societies, partly because they can draw on virtues of political courage, resilience, and strategic wisdom acquired in the course of their struggles against oppression at home. It was in part by making use of previously acquired political virtues that people were able to succeed at crossing borders in the first place. So for example, among those who have planned and coordinated the March of Hope were young Syrian activists from al-Midan, the part of Damascus that saw the strongest anti-government protests in 2011 and 2012 (Dürr 2015). Moreover, after arrival, refugees can provide guidance to those who are still migrating by warning them about various risks from what is an experience-forged position of epistemic authority. In volunteering for other refugees, instructions and advice can be provided about complicated matters in the refugees' mother tongue, thereby significantly decreasing the risk of misunderstandings. To be sure, citizens and (other) long-term residents also have special competences that refugees tend to lack, including a tendency to know better about laws and bureaucratic procedures in the country of arrival, or at least of having what is often a more immediate access to relevant information at the time of arrival. These observations underscore the value of both groups working together to combine complementary resources of knowledge and practical competence.

2. Why volunteers should be activists

Given the way ground relationships already operate in certain, often publicly unnoticed moments of people actively defending refugees against the state, one question of philosophical interest is to ask for the conditions under which some such operating is morally permissible or even required. Clearly, the standard philosophical debate devoted to the question of whether (and if so, under which conditions) states are morally justified at excluding some migrants from their territory in the first place is relevant here as well.[7] Many philosophers today argue that states have no moral right to exclude migrants from their territories and societies, and so that borders must be open (e.g., Abizadeh 2008; Carens 2013; Bertram 2018); less often, it has been asked what migrants and citizens already living on this territory ought to do if states nevertheless close their borders, or forcibly remove non-citizens from their territory or deny them certain rights. The most notable exception perhaps is Javier Hidalgo (2015, 451), who ar-

7 Notice that this debate's focus is on migrants in general, not just on refugees, which is why I use the broader terminology here as well.

gues that if states have no moral right to exclude migrants from their territory, it is permissible for migrants to resist coercive attempts at such exclusion, even to the point of taking 'active steps to prevent state officials from successfully enforcing immigration law'. Moreover, Hidalgo (2016) argues that citizens are obliged to engage in acts of civil disobedience to counteract the state's exclusionary policies.[8] More moderately, Christopher Bertram (2018, 105) argues that 'it is surely permissible and indeed laudable for ordinary citizens to assist the unjustly excluded even at the risk of [...] punishment', but that it is also excusable if they do not.

The perspective I take in this paper is related, but in crucial respects different. I argue that volunteers should be activists according to my broad definition above, leaving to one side the question of the appropriate means such activism can take in a particular political context. Moreover, I suggest that there is something about being a volunteer in relation to refugees that may require one to become an activist, which I argue would be of particular relevance to volunteers who are not themselves refugees. Most importantly, however, my question is not just whether *the fact that border closure is a severe moral wrong* is sufficient to justify some form of active opposition. I fully believe that it is, but here I would like to show that there is even greater normative pressure for volunteers: There is something *about the specific relationship that volunteers (qua volunteers) have with refugees* that provides them with reasons for becoming activists as well as volunteers. I thereby speak to volunteers more directly, and specifically to the class of those who often wonder, 'Shall I also become an activist?', sometimes even put in terms of the question of, 'Shall I become political?' while thinking of volunteering in a putatively non-political or merely 'humanitarian' capacity. In providing an answer to this question, I speak mainly to volunteers privileged with state citizenship, as for the reasons cited above, many volunteers who are themselves refugees cannot even afford the luxury of raising this question. *Citizens* involved in volunteering during the current crisis, however, tend to be very familiar with this kind of question, so any plausible answer is likely to be of more than hypothetical ethical relevance.

The position I defend brings to light a distinct kind of reason for volunteers to challenge the social structures under which refugees have to move and live. This reason would be relevant over and above the reason volunteers arguably have anyway (e.g., qua citizens) to do the same thing, in which case they would be contributing to an even stronger case. Moreover, living in a world

8 For a decisively more moderate position, which nevertheless attributes value to non-compliance with migration laws under certain circumstances, see Yong (2018).

where there is a greater number of injustices than one could possibly struggle against in a single life, one's special reasons as a volunteer can lend some justification to what one might likely experience as a growing sense of special urgency to support the case of refugees in particular, even though it means that one could not at the same time get involved in any other political struggle. However, I have to leave this question open in the end. My main aim is more humble: to only show that there *are* such reasons based on one's special relationship one entertains towards refugees as a volunteer.

My argument is based on the simple assumption that good volunteering is acting towards refugees in ways that are motivated by benevolence. In other words, in volunteering relationships, any good volunteer's support activity is based on a desire to further the good of the refugees with whom they interact. To be sure, many volunteers will describe this benevolent motive as a component of a more complex motivational set underpinning their volunteering, or think of it as grounded in a more comprehensive ideal, such as a conception of lived solidarity, or a certain humanist or religious way of being. But at the core of any of these ideals or motivational sets lie motives of benevolence, in virtue of which they lend volunteers some guidance. Some may be tempted to say that what unifies these motivational sets or ideals is not benevolence, but love as some kind of moral emotion. In fact, love does not only inform certain religious ways of being, but has also been linked to secular notions of solidarity, specifically where the latter is understood to be an ingredient of personal relationships informed by support and understanding (cf. Ikäheimo 2012, 22; Cantillon and Lynch 2017, 175; Emerick 2016, 13). But benevolence as a virtue is even more basic than love, and while it might as such be sufficient in guiding good volunteering, it can also be identified as a core ingredient of love, which explains why people might take love to be central to good volunteering. In fact, what is widely taken to be a necessary constituent of any instance of proper love is a desire for the good of the person to whom one lovingly relates (cf. Frankfurt 1998, 7; Taylor 1976, 157; Rawls 1971, 190; Kolodny 2003, 152). Since not everyone might be ready to concede that love is what guides them as good volunteers, I take it to be an advantage of my argument that it only requires that benevolence guides good volunteering. That is, the volunteer primarily acts from a desire for the good of the refugees she relates to, where this desire has to be understood as a *disinterested* one, by which I mean that it does not stand or fall by whether acting on it benefits one's own good.

If good volunteering requires an agent to primarily act from a desire for the refugee's good, there might be some obvious ways of failing to really *be* a 'good' volunteer. Imagine, for instance, a white citizen-volunteer being motivated primarily by colonial sentiments, such as expectations of submissive forms of gratefulness that she experiences as pleasant insofar as they serve her self-perceived white saviour status. Another possible distortion (though the two are not mutually exclusive) is driven not so much by the desire to be thanked or affirmed by the refugees themselves as by an interest in being seen as noble in one's own privileged social context, where the image of nobility, even in its most superficial, deceitful manifestations may facilitate the accumulation of social capital. In Ma'an Moussli's film *Newcomers* (2018), a comprehensive collage of testimonies by refugees, the majority of whom arrived in Germany in 2015 during the 'long summer of migration' (Kasparek and Speer 2015), Medhat Aldaabal mentions such a character. Aldaabal describes her as motivated solely by the anticipated recognition of her social context that she knows will be granted to her, once she becomes sufficiently visible as 'helping refugees'. Unsurprisingly, he describes encounters with such people as essentially depersonalizing: 'She does not want to know you as a human being', he says.

The requirement of benevolence, however, also yields some less obvious implications that good volunteers have to live up to. A crucial one being actually that benevolent activity must not confine itself to the narrow realm of volunteering, in the first place. In other words, benevolence does not stop at the limits of what can be possibly realised *as a volunteer*. For, the benevolent agent simply desires to see refugees able to live good lives, and if social structures such as oppressive asylum law make that good life impossible, volunteers cannot at the same time be indifferent with regard to whether these structures persist. To be consistent, volunteers must want those structures to disappear or change and intent to actively challenge the structures that limit their ability to further the refugees' good. As these structures are found in most European countries today, volunteers in most countries should become activists.

Perhaps a comparison to friendship might be helpful here. As far as the desire to benefit each other is concerned, friends relate to each other in quite a similar way to how volunteers relate to refugees. To be sure, friendships are mostly more reciprocal, but this can change, as for instance if a friend begins to manifest a certain need that requires the other friend to substantially support them. Suppose a friend develops depression such that the other friend has to take special care of her. Suppose further that an obvious cause of her depression is that she is being bullied at work. It is clear that the good friend will put quite some effort into helping her friend through this situation. Her love will give rise to compassion, prompting her to listen and to provide solace. But her love will also give rise to some form of moral anger, directed at the bully as well as against the structural circumstances that fail to prevent bullying more efficiently. She will look more closely at her possibilities to make a difference and make use of those, even if they are limited. She may, for instance, sit down with her friend hoping that it will lead the bully to be held accountable or for the establishment of a better system under which bullying behaviour is prevented. In short, you also begin to work towards a change of the structure that *causes* your friend to suffer. If you fail to do this, even though you have the opportunity, you are a worse friend, and at worst it may mean that you are no friend at all.

Again, one may be tempted to say, 'Well, that's what *love* looks like, but benevolence is less demanding'. But while pure benevolence may be less complex phenomenologically, it is just as demanding in terms of its normative requirements. William Frankena (1987, 5) describes benevolence as 'a complex disposition (a) not to inflict evil or harm on others, (b) to benefit and do them good, and *also* (c) to prevent evil or harm coming to them and (d) to remove and remedy it when it does.' Frankena's list aims to capture action types that, when taken together, fully accounts for the idea of 'doing good' to others. In understanding that each of them is essentially related to that idea, any benevolent agent must take them equally seriously. In our context, it is (c) and (d) that require the benevolent volunteer to also oppose oppressive structures that cause harm to the refugees she relates to as a volunteer, and therefore to rise beyond her role as a volunteer and become an activist as well. In fact, if the volunteer deliberately confines herself to acting only as a volunteer, she does not only fail to be *more* benevolent than captured by (a) and (b), but in refraining from activism she undermines her own effort to be benevolent as a volunteer. In other words, her commitment to confining herself to her role as a volunteer would be weirdly self-contradictory.

What *in particular* volunteers should do in the field of activism requires additional reasoning. Looking only at the field of protest, it is already quite diverse. What it offers to a specific individual depends very much on the opportunities provided by the larger political context, as well as on personal abilities and resources. Some people are good at writing intervention pieces for newspapers, while for others street theatre or the coordination of marches is what they feel most comfortable doing. This said, activists may also face decisions as to whether to remain within structural limitations of legalised forms of activism in a given society or whether to go beyond them. While any active attempt to change and abolish the structures under which refugees have to move or live amounts to activism, the question about the general moral justifiability of acts intended to actively or passively resist current immigration law has its place here. Again, what I would like to show with the above argument is merely that there is, quite generally, strong reason for volunteers to seek structural change based solely on the way they relate as good volunteers to refugees, leaving open the question of how to morally evaluate the various political means available to them. In conclusion, then, I take it that in the absence of any stronger countervailing reasons, good volunteers should indeed, in order to live up to the requirements of benevolence, become activists.

3. Concluding remarks

As I have said above, citizen-volunteers might be more interested in these kinds of reasons than most refugee-volunteers are, who are often activists out of self-defence anyway. Moreover, it is precisely the fact that citizen-volunteers tend to have no similar reasons based on self-interest[9] that they are well-advised to actually *pay attention* to considerations of the nature of benevolence, if they want to avoid ethical failure. But would good volunteers make for good activists? Perhaps it is possible for them to see that in general they have *good reason* to become activists, but fail to be sufficiently equipped to act on these reasons. However, if we look carefully, we see that apart from refugees themselves, perhaps no group other than citizen-volunteers is better equipped with the knowledge and motivational potential needed to become activists, given that citizen-volunteers are direct *witnesses* of the suffering of the refugees they are trying to support.

As has been argued before (e.g., Harvey 2007; Bartky 2002), it may be possible to acquire correct beliefs about a certain group's oppression by reading credible newspaper or research articles. However, the quality and motivational impact of an understanding that arises from directly witnessing the harm done by oppressive structures targeting a certain group is of a higher moral order. Often it is only by way of attending to situations in which the oppression becomes salient, and by listening to first-personal accounts of members of the oppressed group, that one's understanding acquires the depth needed to guide meaningful projects of solidarity that really speak to the interests of those affected by an injustice.

In fact, such a process almost inevitably takes place in the course of the personal encounters that citizen-volunteers have on an almost daily basis with refugees, especially if their volunteering includes accompanying the latter in asylum-recognition procedures, searching for accommodation or jobs, or related bureaucratic requirements. As Ulrike Hamann and Serhat Karakayali (2016, 80) argue, based on an empirical study, most of the citizen-volunteers in Germany have middle-class background. Although these volunteers might have had

9 To be sure, they may have *some* such reasons, provided by additional facts of friendship or other personal relationships with refugees.

prior abstract knowledge about prevailing injustices affecting refugees, Hamann and Karakayali found that many of them witnessed for the first time in their lives the 'structural violence that people of foreign backgrounds with low professional profiles face in the German welfare system' (*ibid.*), which the authors interpret as both epistemically and practically valuable. They argue that 'these experiences raise the awareness of certain sections of the middle class in Germany about institutional racism, and therefore harbour the possibility of new alliances of solidarity' (*ibid.*). In a similar vein, Lisa Fleischmann and Elias Steinhilper (2017, 22) found that encounters between citizen-volunteers and refugees 'hold the potential for unveiling systemic contradictions within the European migration regime'. A number of additional studies the authors survey further indicate that there is a strong link between helping refugees and becoming more political in ways that include a desire to challenge structural injustices. Citizen-volunteers therefore might not only be specifically *aware* of the concrete manifestations of injustices that refugees face in a certain context; direct encounter with the oppressed also comes with an *increase in motivation* to actually act in ways that – as I hope I have shown – they have reason to act.[10]

Bibliography

Abizadeh, A. (2008): Democratic Theory and Border Coercion. In: Political Theory 36(1), 37–65.

Alderman, L./Bounias, D. (2016): Violence Erupts in Greece as Migrants Try to Cross into Macedonia. In: New York Times. February 29. https://www.nytimes.com/2016/03/01/world/europe/greece-macedonia-border-refugees--riots.html.

Amnesty International (2014): The Human Cost of Fortress Europe – Human Rights Violations against Migrants and Refugees at Europe's Borders. https://www.amnesty.org/download/Documents/8000/eur050012014en.pdf.

Ataç, I./Steinhilper, E.(2016): Escaping from Asylum to Act as Citizens: Political Mobilization of Refugees in Europe. In: Open Democracy. September 19. https://www.opendemocracy.net/ilker-ata-elias-steinhilper/escaping-from-asylum-to-act-as-citizens-political-mobilization-of-refuge.

Bartky, S. L. (2002): Sympathy and Solidarity and Other Essays. Lanham: Rowman & Littlefield.

Beck, S. (2016): Flüchtlingskrise als Renaissance der Bürgergesellschaft. In: Forschungsjournal Soziale Bewegungen 29(4), 101–106.

Bertram, C. (2018): Do States Have the Right to Exclude Immigrants? Cambridge: Polity Press.

10 My heartfelt thanks to James Camien McGuiggan, who sent me extensive written comments on earlier versions of this paper.

BMFSFJ (2017): Engagement in der Flüchtlingshilfe – Ergebnisbericht einer Untersuchung des Instituts für Demoskopie Allensbach. https://www.bmfsfj.de/blob/122010/d35ec9bf4a940ea49283485db4625aaf/engagement-in-der-fluechlingshilfe-data.pdf#page=11.

Cantillon, S./Lynch, K. (2017): Affective Equality: Love Matters. In: Hypathia 32(1), 169 – 186.

Carens, J. H. (1987): Aliens and Citizens: The Case for Open Borders. In: The Review of Politics 49(2), 251 – 273.

Carens, J. H. (2013): The Ethics of Immigration. Oxford: Oxford University Press.

Dürr, F. (2015): Days of Hope: Marsch der Syrischen Revolution nach Europa. In: Adopt a Revolution. https://www.adoptrevolution.org/march-of-hope-erlebnisse/.

Emerick, B. (2016): Love and Resistance: Moral Solidarity in the Face of Perceptual Failure. In: Feminist Philosophy Quarterly (2)2, Article 1.

Fleischmann, L./Steinhilper, E. (2017): The Myth of Apolitical Volunteering for Refugees: German Welcome Culture and a New Dispositif of Helping. In: Social Inclusion 5(3), 17 – 27.

Frankena, W. (1987): Beneficence/Benevolence. In: Social Philosophy & Policy 4(2), 1 – 20.

Frankfurt, H. (1998): Some Thoughts about Caring. In: Ethical Perspectives 5, 3 – 14.

Gibney, M. J. (2004): The Ethics and Politics of Asylum: Liberal Democracy and the Response to Refugees. Cambridge: Cambridge University Press.

Grahle, A. (2019): In the City's Public Spaces: Movements of Witnesses and the Formation of Moral Community. In: E. Cox, S. Durrant, D. Farrier, L. Stonebridge, A. Woolley (eds.): Refugee Imaginaries: Research Across the Humanities. Edinburgh: Edinburgh University Press.

Hamann, U./Karakayali, S. (2016): Practicing Willkommenskultur: Migration and Solidarity in Germany. In: Intersections: East-European Journal of Society and Politics 2(4), 69 – 86.

Harvey, J. (2007): Moral Solidarity and Empathetic Understanding: The Moral Value and Scope of the Relationship. In: Journal of Social Philosophy 38(1), 22 – 37.

Haslanger, S. (2017): Culture and Critique. In: Aristotelian Society Supplementary 91, 149 – 173.

Hess, S./Kasparek, B./Kron, S./Rodatz, M./Schwertl, M./Sontowski, S. (eds.) (2016): Der lange Sommer der Migration. Krise, Rekonstitution und ungewisse Zukunft des Europäischen Grenzregimes. In: Der Lange Sommer der Migration: Grenzregime III. Berlin: Association A, 6 – 24.

Hidalgo, J. (2015): Resistance to Unjust Immigration Restrictions. In: Journal of Political Philosophy 23(4), 450 – 470.

Hidalgo, J. (2016): The Duty to Disobey Immigration Law. In: Moral Philosophy and Politics 3(2), 165 – 186.

Ikäheimo, H. (2012): Globalising Love: On the Nature and Scope of Love as a Form of Recognition. In: Res Publica 18(1), 11 – 24.

Karakayali, S./Kleist, O. (2015): EFA-Studie: Strukturen und Motive der Ehrenamtlichen Flüchtlingsarbeit (EFA) in Deutschland. 1. Forschungsbericht: Ergebnisse einer explorativen Umfrage vom. November/Dezember 2014. Berliner Institut für empirische Integrations- und Migrationsforschung. https://www.bim.hu-berlin.de/media/2015 – 05 – 16_EFA-Forschungsbericht_Endfassung.p-.pdf.

Karakayali, S./Kleist, O. (2016): EFA-Studie 2: Strukturen und Motive der Ehrenamtlichen Flüchtlingsarbeit (EFA) in Deutschland. 2. Forschungsbericht: Ergebnisse einer explorativen Umfrage vom. November/Dezember 2015. Berliner Institut für empirische Integrations- und Migrationsforschung. https://www.bim.hu-berlin.de/media/Studie_EFA2_BIM_11082016_VÖ.pdf.

Kasparek, B./Speer, M. (2015): Of Hope. Ungarn und der lange Sommer der Migration. bordermonitoring.eu/ungarn/2015/09/of-hope.

Kolodny, N. (2003): Love as Valuing a Relationship. In: Philosophical Review 112(2), 135–89.

Médecins sans frontières (2016): Obstacle Course to Europe: A Policy-Made Humanitarian Crisis at EU-Borders. https://www.msf.org/sites/msf.org/files/msf_obstacle_course_to_europe_0.pdf.

Miller, D. (2005): Immigration: the Case for Limits. In: A. I. Cohen/C. H. Wellman (eds.): Contemporary Debates in Applied Ethics. Hoboken: Wiley-Blackwell, 193–206.

Miller, D. (2016): Strangers in Our Midst: The Political Philosophy of Immigration. Cambridge: Harvard University Press.

Owen, D. (2016): In *loco civitatis:* on the Normative Basis of the Institution of Refugeehood and of Responsibilities for Refugees. In: S. Fine/L. Ypi (eds.): Migration in Political Theory: The Ethics of Movement and Membership. Oxford: Oxford University Press, 269–290.

Rawls, J. (1971): A Theory of Justice. Cambridge: Harvard University Press.

Safdar, A. (2015): Refugees Sew Lips in Greece-Macedonian Border Protest. In Al Jazeera. November 24. https://www.aljazeera.com/news/2015/11/refugees-hunger-strike-greece-macedonia-border-151123152724415.html.

Song, S. (2016): The Significance of Territorial Presence and the Rights of Immigrants. In: S. Fine/L. Ypi (eds.): Migration in Political Theory: The Ethics of Movement and Membership, Oxford: Oxford University Press, 225–248.

Steinhilper, E. (2018): Mobilizing in Transnational Contentious Spaces: Linking Relations, Emotions and Space in Migrant Activism. In: Social Movement Studies.

Taylor, G. (1976): Love. In: Proceedings of the Aristotelian Society 76, 147–164.

UNHCR (2015): Global Trends: Forced Displacement in 2015. http://www.unhcr.org/576408cd7.

Walzer, M. (1983): Spheres of Justice: A Defence of Pluralism and Equality. New York: Basic Books.

Welander, M. (2018): Migration, Human Rights and Fortress Europe: How Far Will European Leaders Go to Protect the EU's Borders? https://www.law.ox.ac.uk/research-subject-groups/centre-criminology/centreborder-criminologies/blog/2018/07/migration-human.

Yong, C. (2018): Justifying Resistance to Immigration Law: The Case of Mere Non-Compliance. In: Canadian Journal for Law & Jurisprudence 31, 459–481.

Jet G. Sanders, Elizabeth Castle, Karen Tan, and Rob Jenkins

Applying behavioural science to refugee integration

Abstract: Successful refugee and migrant integration has been shown to generate novel opportunities for development, and to enrich countries economically, socially, and culturally. Nonetheless, integration is one of the most complex issues of our time. Here we review this problem from a behavioural science perspective. Behavioural science brings together insights from psychology, behavioural economics, neuroscience, and sociology to devise and improve population-level interventions and to develop more effective policies. One approach in behavioural science is commonly referred to as 'nudging'. Recently there has been a growing interest in nudge strategies among both practitioners and academics, in part because the strategies are cheap to implement. Here we provide an overview of such strategies and their applicability to refugee integration. By addressing two sectors of society where behavioural science is currently applied (education and employment), we examine how behavioural evidence may be used to bypass barriers and facilitate drivers of integration. Our review (i) reveals that few interventions aimed at refugee integration use a behavioural science approach, (ii) highlights areas in which this approach could be especially effective, and (iii) identifies some behavioural science techniques that may be counterproductive.

1. Introduction

Behavioural science aims to explain decision-making above and beyond what standard economic theory would predict, by integrating knowledge from psychology, behavioural economics, neuroscience, and social sciences. In this chapter, we examine the application of this approach to refugee integration. Some work in this area pertains to migrants, refugees, or asylum seekers specifically. Other work combines two or more of these groups, depending on its purpose and scope. Although we draw on a range of sources, our main interest is how behavioural science informs refugee integration in particular.

Integration efforts are most effective when they engage both host and refugee populations. Standard cost-benefit analysis would predict that both populations benefit economically in the long-term (Karakas 2015; European Commission 2016). For the host population, the refugee influx could lead to economic growth by addressing aging demographic trends, to take an example from the

https://doi.org/10.1515/9783110628746-012

EU. Refugees may also improve the ratio of active workers (European Commission 2016) and increase diversity, which has been shown to contribute to innovation, entrepreneurship, and GDP growth (Karakas 2015). For the refugee population, integration, in the long term, can benefit economic welfare, freedom, educational, and health outcomes (De Haas 2005).

According to standard economic theory, people should act to secure these long-term benefits. Instead integration is often resisted, in part because both host and refugee populations are focussed on short-term priorities such as first aid, shelter, and food, while postponing the provision and take-up of education or mental and primary health care (Fratzscher/Junker 2015; UNHCR 1997).

The tension between short-term and long-term thinking is core to one of the fundamental theories in behavioural science, the Dual System Theory (Kahneman/Egan 2011). This theory proposes that mental processing takes place on a fast, automatic, and intuitive level (System 1), as well as a slow, controlled, and reflective level (System 2). To optimise resource allocation, people operate in a System 1 state as much as possible. In the context of refugee integration, the proposal is that short-term approaches and attitudes are likely grounded in System 1 thinking. In contrast, long-term benefits are captured by System 2 thinking. This distinction applies to thinking in both host and refugee populations.

Dual System Theory offers a behavioural perspective on what may limit progress towards effective integration. Historically, the dominant strategy has been to engage host and migrant populations in their System 2 state, with information provided to illustrate the long-term benefits of integration (e.g., the European Commission's Refugee Awareness Project). Relaying such information is clearly important, but extensive research has shown that requiring people to function and make decisions in a reflective state is an unscalable, costly, and slow path to achieving behaviour change (see systematic review by Webb/Sheeran 2006). For example, knowing which food is healthy does not guarantee healthy food choices (e.g., Johnson et al. 2012).

In contrast, behavioural science strategies organise the environment so that the desired behavioural outcomes are as closely aligned as possible with System 1, sometimes bypassing System 2 altogether. This approach is also known as choice architecture (Johnson et al. 2012). A classic instantiation of choice architecture is the switch from a self-enrolment ('opt-in') to auto-enrolment ('opt out'), in line with the desired outcome. For example, Madrian and Shea (2001) showed that most people want to save for a pension and know that it is important. Yet out of inertia, many do not save. Changing the opt-in system to an opt-out system increased the proportion of workers saving towards a pension from 49 per cent to 86 per cent. To take another example, recent work suggests that merely changing the timing of a decision can affect the outcome (Artavia-Mora/Bedi/Rieger 2017; Ellis/Jenkins 2012; Sanders/Jenkins 2016).

A first step towards refugee integration is to identify System 1 biases and heuristics that affect host and refugee populations. Often, these will be situation dependent. However, we can begin by identifying some general ways in which a refugee population may differ from other populations.

Refugees generally face greater uncertainty than host populations (Aspinall/Watters 2010). The particular circumstances leading to relocation vary greatly (Hagen-Zanker 2008), as do circumstances of arrival. But common to many refugees is the prospect of 'starting again' (Agier 2008). Human capacity to envision a new start is rooted in experiences of the past or present (Bar 2011). Within displaced populations, the emerging situation may depart from previous experience in many ways (e.g., Berry 1997). For example, it may require understanding the local rental market, enrolling a child in school, or taking the subway. All of these tasks require extensive System 2 engagement (deliberative thinking), increasing cognitive load (Sweller 1988; Sweller/Van Merrienboer/Paas 1998). With System 2 occupied by everyday tasks, it falls to System 1 to handle effective integration.

In addition, many refugees and migrants must contend with a state of scarcity. Scarcity describes the condition of having insufficient resources to cope with demands (Lynn 1991). Many refugees arrive in a state of material scarcity, having travelled with minimal resources, often to countries where there are insufficient state provisions to accommodate the influx of people (Ratha/Mohapatra/Scheja 2011; UNHCR 2016). One insidious side effect of material scarcity is that it can lead to cognitive scarcity, entrenching the original position. Material scarcity tends to focus System 2 resources on immediate problems (Karau/Kelly 1992; Mullainathan/Shafir 2013). The resulting 'tunnel vision' can lead to desirable consequences for the problem at hand. However, it can also lead to undesirable consequences in the form of myopic or impulsive behaviour, with short-term gains being prioritised over long-term gains. In a laboratory demonstration of this effect, Tomm and Zhao (2016) allocated participants to a *poor* condition ($20 budget) or a *rich* condition ($100 budget) before presenting a restaurant menu. While poor participants spent more time than rich participants looking at prices, they spent less time looking at an 18 per cent discount on the bottom of the menu. Scarcity can induce neglect of non-focal information in the environment that could mitigate the scarcity itself. In the context of refugee integration, this might translate into financial worries obscuring job opportunities that could alleviate poverty. Thus, scarcity means not only a shortage of physical resources such as time and money, but also a shortage of cognitive resources such as attention and executive control.

The combination of uncertainty and scarcity is likely to leave refugees especially prone to System 1 thinking. The upside is that this provides an opening for System 1–aligned behavioural interventions.

2. Using behaviour change tools

Various behaviour change tools are available for developing behavioural interventions. The design process generally starts by mapping the current pathway towards the desired outcome – in this case, refugee integration. As integration is a highly complex issue, it is usually measured indirectly via behavioural proxies such as language acquisition, family self-sufficiency or employment, enrolment in education, and housing permanence, depending on the measurement tool that is used (see Sturm 2016 for an overview of tools).

In the early stages of planning an intervention, a behavioural analysis may be used to map the physical routes (e. g., schools/community centres), barriers (e. g., time), and drivers (e. g., finding work) of optimal engagement with these behaviours. For example, French et al. (2012) propose a four-step approach based around the following questions: Who needs to do what, differently? Using a theoretical framework, which barriers and enablers need to be addressed? Which intervention components (behaviour change techniques and modes of delivery) could overcome the modifiable barriers and enhance the enablers? And how can behaviour change be measured and understood? The analysis stage is often guided by a theoretical framework such as the Theoretical Domains Framework (TDF) (Cane/O'Connor/Michie 2012) or the COM-B model and Behaviour Change Wheel (BCW) (Michie/Stralen/West 2011). The TDF allows practitioners to think through a pathway systematically and to catalogue influences on the behaviours of interest.

COM-B and the BCW are used to identify drivers for those behaviours that may be most amenable to change. Ideally, this process can identify a series of new intervention opportunities that foster migrant integration for an entire system. For example, the behavioural analyses of antimicrobial resistance (Pinder et al. 2015) and climate change (Hallin/Hooper/Weyman-Jones 2017) both address problems on a global scale.

Once opportunities for behavioural intervention have been identified, the next step is to supplement, tweak, or restructure the existing pathway in service of the desired outcome. The traditional approach might involve launching an information campaign or a costly training programme. In contrast, a core principle of the behavioural science approach is that a small change, such as reversing the default option or simplifying an information letter, can yield disproportionate benefits. This allows interventions to be low cost and scalable to entire target populations if shown to be effective. Changing the default option is a prime example of a behavioural intervention that balances the level of intervention and the freedom of the individual. The Nuffield Ladder of Intervention (Nuffield Council on Bioethics 2015) characterises this balance by introducing various intervention options, from 'doing nothing' – where no state intervention occurs, to 'eliminating choice' – where the state removes the choice from the individual entirely. Table 1 illustrates this range of options for the case of smoking reduction.

Table 1: Nuffield ladder of intervention, applying different levels of intervention to smoking reduction.

RUNG OF LADDER	EXAMPLE
Eliminate choice	No smoking for minors
Restrict choice	No smoking in workplaces
Guide by disincentives	Taxes on cigarettes
Guide choice by incentives	Stop smoking during pregnancy
Guide choice by changing the default policy	Plain packaging requirements
Enable choice	Free 'stop-smoking' program enrolment
Provide information	Website, leaflets and adverts
Do nothing	

One concern about stronger interventions (eliminating or restricting choice) is that individuals may feel their freedom to choose is curtailed, causing upset and resistance if not managed carefully. The complementary concern about minimal intervention is that it does not guide the population towards the collectively beneficial choice. The middle strategies are frequently considered forms of nudging, 'ways of influencing choice without limiting the choice set or making alternatives appreciably more costly in terms of time, trouble, social sanctions, and so forth' (Hausman/Welch 2010, 126). Ideally, nudge strategies can be used to direct the population towards the collectively desirable option of refugee integration, without limiting individual choice and without placing unrealistic expectations on individual responsibility.

The potential of nudge to promote behaviour change across public domains for social good was popularised by Sunstein and Thaler (2008). Not long after, the British government created a 'Nudge Unit', the Behavioural Insights Team (BIT) (2014), which initially focussed on matters such as improving tax returns and increasing rates of organ donation (BIT 2014). Along with a number of trials that indicated strong potential for the approach, BIT devised several influential frameworks. First, BIT advocated that behavioural science in the public sphere should use randomised control trials (RCTs) –or other established research methods– to check for efficacy and to ensure that interventions have no adverse effects (see Test, Learn, Adapt framework by Haynes/Goldacre/Torgerson 2012). Second, they developed two frameworks to make behavioural science methods more accessible to policy makers and practitioners. In 2010, the MINDSPACE framework (Dolan et al. 2010) was introduced, capturing nine of the most effective behavioural insights techniques in mnemonic form to ease engagement (see Table 2, Dolan et al. 2010; Dolan et al. 2012).

Table 2: The MINDSPACE framework for behaviour change. Nine behavioural techniques that could promote behaviour change.

MINDSPACE CUE	BEHAVIOUR
Messenger	We are heavily influenced by who communicates information to us
Incentives	Our responses to incentives are shaped by predictable mental shortcuts
Norms	We are strongly influenced by what others do
Defaults	We 'go with the flow' of pre-set options
Salience	Our attention is drawn to what is novel and seems relevant to us
Priming	Our acts are often influences by sub-conscious cues
Affect	Our emotional associations can powerfully shape our actions
Commitments	We seek to be consistent with our public promises, and reciprocate acts
Ego	We act in ways that make us feel better about ourselves

Soon after, in 2014, the EAST framework was published. The EAST framework is less extensive than COM-B, BCW, or MINDSPACE, but simpler to use. It proposes that interventions are more likely to be effective if they are Easy, Attractive, Social, and Timely (BIT 2014; Figure 1).

A decade on from Sunstein and Thaler (2008), teams of behavioural scientists are employed in nearly all British government departments, as well as the governments of over thirty other countries, global organisations such as the UN and World Bank, and a range of international charities and specialist consultancies (Sunstein/Reisch/Rauber 2018). This global reach is matched by the range of projects in which behavioural science principles are applied, including global health pandemics such as obesity and air pollution, environmental issues such as climate change, and social issues such global poverty, gender inequality, tax evasion, violent crime, homelessness, and joblessness (Lourenço et al. 2016). Whatever techniques are used, behavioural science interventions must be accompanied by rigorous assessment methods. It is essential to establish the effectiveness of an intervention before rolling it out (Haynes/Goldacre/Torgerson 2012). RCTs have been recognised as the gold standard in testing medical interventions for over sixty years, partly because they allow researchers to dissociate treatment effects from changes over time. However, it is only recently that RCTs

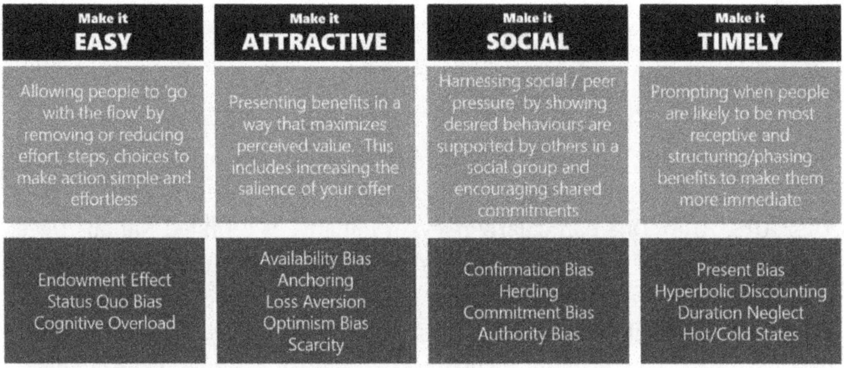

Make it EASY
Make it ATTRACTIVE
Make it SOCIAL
Make it TIMELY
Allowing people to 'go with the flow' by removing or reducing effort, steps, choices to make action simple and effortless
Presenting benefits in a way that maximizes perceived value. This includes increasing the salience of your offer
Harnessing social / peer 'pressure' by showing desired behaviours are supported by others in a social group and encouraging shared commitments
Prompting when people are likely to be most receptive and structuring/phasing benefits to make them more immediate
Endowment Effect
Status Quo Bias
Cognitive Overload
Availability Bias
Anchoring
Loss Aversion
Optimism Bias
Scarcity
Confirmation Bias
Herding
Commitment Bias
Authority Bias
Present Bias
Hyperbolic Discounting
Duration Neglect
Hot/Cold States

Figure 1: The EAST framework for behaviour change. Top row: Four behavioural principles; middle row: principles that support these; bottom row: some of the evidenced biases and heuristics that can be used to activate these principles. Image retrieved from https://bit.ly/2KqIQa0.

have entered mainstream social science and policy research. Slow adoption in this sector is partly due to the misapprehension that testing takes too much time and money (see Haynes/Goldacre/Torgerson 2012 for a review), and partly due to a reliance on common sense as a means of divining what will work. However, RCTs have been shown to overturn even very long-standing assumptions. For example, Scared Straight was a US crime reduction programme introduced in the late 1970s, which aimed to deter high school students from a life of crime through interaction with prison inmates. Early studies concluded that the intervention was highly effective in reducing crime rates (see Finckenauer 1982, for discussion), and similar programmes were trialled in at least six countries. It was only when an RCT was carried out, twenty-five years post-implementation, that the intervention was found to have *increased* crime rates all those years (Petrosino/Turpin-Petrosino/Buehler 2003). A background decrease in the crime rate over time had been wrongly attributed to the intervention. In a very different setting, the Behavioural Insights Team ran an RCT to test whether attendance at adult literacy classes could be improved by a financial incentive of £5 per session. Surprisingly, these payments actually *reduced* attendance relative to the control group – the very opposite of the expected effect (Brooks et al. 2008; see Festinger/Carlsmith 1959 for suppressive effects of reward). As these and many other examples illustrate, intuition is no substitute for evidence.

3. Relevant examples of behavioural interventions

Behavioural science interventions have been trialled by a number of global organisations, including United Nations and the World Bank (UNDP 2017; WB 2015, 2016, 2018). One particularly relevant initiative is a United Nations Development Programme intervention that aims to integrate Syrian refugees in Jordan via a skills exchange programme (UNDP 2016). This particular intervention is ongoing, and the results have not yet been published. However, several interventions have been conducted in related areas. Here we describe two examples – one in employment and one in education. Each example aligns with behavioural principles and techniques described in the EAST and MINDSPACE frameworks.

3.1. Employment

Employment is one of the most important issues in refugee integration. Gainful employment can increase economic independence, foster interactions between refugees and host populations, strengthen language skills, and develop self-esteem and self-reliance (Ager/Strang 2008). Here, we discuss two areas where behavioural science could be applied – employment rights and recruitment processes.

3.1.1. Employment rights

In the UK, individuals granted refugee status are permitted to work in any profession and at any skill level. Asylum seekers, on the other hand, are not permitted to work. A critical problem faced by people in this situation is the time taken to grant refugee status. Hainmueller, Hangartner, and Lawrence (2016) found a causal link between the length of time a refugee waits for a decision on their asylum claim and their subsequent economic integration. Each additional year of waiting from the moment of arrival reduced subsequent employment rates by four to five percentage points (16 to 23 per cent below the average rate). Even a small reduction in the time taken to decide an asylum seeker's status could reduce public expenditure and increase the economic and social integration of the refugee population. Below we explore two possible solutions to this challenge. *Intervention 1: Reducing cognitive load through simplification.* Simplification has been effectively used to encourage individuals to comply with a range of behaviours. In one study, simplifying letters from government departments resulted in a 5–10 per cent increase in response rate by making the behavioural request clearer (BIT 2014). Such interventions have typically targeted members of the public, for example, encouraging timely tax payments (BIT 2014) or increasing uptake of the NHS Health Check (Public Health England 2015). However, the same approach could be applied to government systems internally to streamline handling of asylum claims. If simplification improves communication, there is no reason why intra-government communication should be excluded.

Intervention 2: Changing the default. An example of a stronger nudge would be to change the default. A natural experiment in Germany provides empirical evidence for the impact of changing the default for asylum seekers and employment restrictions. In 2000, a court ruling prompted a reduction in the length of time asylum seekers must wait before seeking employment. Those arriving in Germany before 2000, on average, waited about nineteen months before they were permitted to seek employment. Individuals arriving after 2000, had to wait twelve months. Marbach, Hainmueller, and Hangartner (2017) found that employment rates were about twenty percentage points lower for those refugees who had to wait longer before entering the labour market. The employment gap between these groups persisted for ten years after the waiting period was reduced.

3.1.2. Recruitment processes

Refugees and asylum seekers often face multiple layers of discrimination. Unsurprisingly, forced migration can lead people to fall behind in education or work experience or both (World Health Organisation 2018). Racial discrimination may compound this disadvantage. Moreover, more than 80 per cent of the world's refugees are women and their dependent children, who tend to be victim to racial and gender discrimination (Pittaway/Bartolomei 2001). Most workplaces do not actively discriminate, but may harbour unconscious bias (Cortina 2008). Unconscious bias refers to automatic favouritism influenced by our background, cultural environment, and personal experiences, expressed through quick judgements and assessments of people and situations. There are a number of approaches to overcoming unconscious bias in the workplace. Here we outline two that are relevant to employment of refugees and migrants.

Intervention 1: Anonymous or blind applications. A review of the experimental evidence of the impact of anonymised job applications finds that anonymous hiring can reduce discrimination, but only if discrimination was in fact present

(Krause/Rinne/Zimmermann 2012). Anonymous hiring may have no effect if discrimination does not exist initially, as it can also prevent employers from applying measures such as affirmative action in the first stages of the recruitment process (White 2004). Specific to refugee and migrant populations, applications may be interpreted more positively if the identity of the candidate is available. For example, if recruiters are aware of an applicant's migration background, they may be better placed to understand the applicant's labour market experience or language skills. The use of anonymous job applications, therefore, crucially depends on the initial context of individual organisations.

Intervention 2: Priming values. A UK police force identified a test in their application process that appeared to disadvantage minority applicants. With a view to increasing diversity, they redesigned the wording that introduced the test. Specifically, they added the instruction, 'Before you start the test, I'd like you to take some time to think about why you want to be a police constable. For example, what is it about being a police constable that means the most to you and your community?' This new instruction primed applicants to reflect on their values and their contribution by representing the social identity of their community within the police force. The results showed a 50 per cent increase in the probability of passing the test for minority applicants in the treatment group, with no effect on other applicants. This simple intervention closed the racial gap in the pass rate without lowering the recruitment standard or changing the assessment questions (Linos/Reinhard/Ruda 2017).

3.2. Education

The educational needs of refugees are highly varied. Some may arrive with very little prior education. Others may be may be highly qualified but find that their qualifications are not recognised. While the specific needs of individuals will be very different, two general behaviours appear to promote refugee integration – integration into mainstream formal education systems and engagement in English for Speakers of Other Languages (ESOL) classes.

Integration into mainstream formal education. Quick access to quality education can equip refugees with the skills they need to succeed. Education is also an important channel for communicating the values of the host country, and supporting engagement with civic life. In short, education is central to successful integration (Bodwig 2015). However, refugees may find themselves facing education systems that are complex and unfamiliar. Uncertainties surrounding eligibility for services and how to engage with those services can become a significant barrier to effective integration. Evidence from service uptake in related areas suggests that simplifying enrolment procedures and providing enrolment support can overcome this barrier.

Bettinger et al. (2009) examined low uptake of financial aid for college enrolment in low- and middle-income families. Those who received professional help with the application form were significantly more likely to submit an application, and were 8 per cent more likely to enrol in college. However, the simplified form alone did not produce a significant effect (Bettinger et al. 2009). This research indicates that individuals, including refugees, may need support that goes beyond classic nudges (such as simplifying procedural documents). Extrapolating from this research, providing assistance to refugees in engaging with unfamiliar educational systems could be an effective and efficient approach to integrating people into mainstream formal education. Support for refugees would require broad knowledge of (i) educational provision from early years to adult learning, and (ii) eligibility criteria for access to these opportunities.

Learning the language of the host country. Learning the language of the host country is one of the most important behaviours for refugees to pursue (British Council 2016). It is considered a facilitator of refugee integration in nearly all measurement tools (Sturm 2016). Learning the host language increases refugees' ability to engage successfully with public services, leading to a range of benefits, including better health and well-being, education and employment, and social and civic integration (Casey 2016). All of these benefits rely on adequate funding for language course. In addition, behavioural science also highlights a non-structural barrier to engagement with language learning. Time discounting refers to the relative value an individual places on a given outcome at different points in time (Frederick/Loewenstein/O'Donoghue 2002). In general, immediate rewards are weighted more heavily than future rewards, and our preferences are often inconsistent over time (Laibson 1997). Educational decisions illustrate the tension between short- and long-term benefits. Short-term investment of time, money, and cognitive resource is required to secure longer-term, uncertain payoffs such as more highly paid employment (Cawley/Ruhm 2011). An important consequence of time-inconsistent preferences is that individuals may spend resources in the present that their future self would prefer to have conserved, despite knowing the same information.

Refugees face many competing demands on their resources. Despite the larger longer-term payoffs of language learning, immediate pressures may lead refugees to pursue behaviours with smaller short-term payoffs. For example, a highly qualified refugee may take up unskilled labour to achieve stability in the near term (Atwell/Gifford/McDonald-Wilmsen 2009). Although there is little evidence this is based on the refugee population specifically, behavioural approaches to increasing engagement with adult learning provide some insight. Of particular interest are interventions that exploit social drivers of behaviour. Below we provide two examples.

Intervention 1: Study supporters. Hume et al. (2018) asked learners to nominate a 'study supporter' (e.g., a parent, sibling, mentor, or friend) who would receive regular updates about the learner's studies via text. The update would encourage the supporter to engage the learner on study progress – for example, a recent topic or revision for an upcoming test. This simple intervention increased attendance by 4.1 per cent and attainment by 6 per cent, relative to a control group without study supporters.

Intervention 2: Buddy incentives. In a separate intervention, Hume et al. (2018) attempted to improve student attendance in Maths and English classes at Children's Centres by (i) providing a financial reward to parents if their children attended class, or (ii) randomly pairing each learner with another learner in the class. These intervention groups were compared to a control. Learners in each group received stamp card to monitor attendance. In the control and financial incentive group, these cards were used to monitor individual attendance. In the paired learner group, the card was shared between the two learners, and could only be stamped if both attended. Both interventions improved attendance compared to the control group. However, the buddy incentive, worked particularly well. Attendance increased from 43.6 per cent to 75.3 per cent in the buddy group.

These findings suggest that social incentives can be used to promote engagement in learning. In particular, a social incentive can provide an additional immediate reward to language learning and thereby motivate continued engagement. Potential interventions could include encouraging refugees to identify study supporters to discuss learning progress. Where social networks are not established, language learning providers could facilitate their creation by pairing each learner with a buddy. Where social networks are already in place, language engagement could benefit from being funnelled through them. In this space too, community role models could exemplify continued engagement and help to bring new learners on board. Beyond language learning, we expect that social approaches could promote well-being and integration more broadly.

4. Conclusion

In this review we have offered a background and overview of behavioural science, outlined how behavioural science principles may apply to refugee and host populations, and suggested possible paths towards applying behavioural science to refugee integration globally. To illustrate how a behavioural science approach functions, we provided specific examples of government aligned interventions in education and employment, using principles described in the MINDSPACE and EAST frameworks. Although we confine ourselves to education and employment in this chapter, the same principles could be applied to other aspects of refugee integration, such as housing or health and well-being. A useful next step would be to carry out a behavioural analysis to determine where progress could be made most efficiently. Once intervention areas are identified, implementing changes can be quite simple, unlocking disproportionate progress towards successful integration and all the benefits that flow from it.

In all of these areas, it is essential that behavioural science interventions be tied to rigorous assessments. RCTs have been widely adopted in the health sector as a means for evaluating medical interventions, and we suggest that behavioural science interventions should follow a similar path.

As a final point, we note that the use of nudge without consent has received widespread criticism from academics and members of the public. These criticisms tend not to concern a specific application (e.g., refugee integration), but rather the nature of the intervention itself. Much of the opposition stems from the ethical concern that nudging amounts to 'manipulating people's choices' (Mitchell 2004; Bovens 2009). Indeed, Sunstein and Thaler (2008) seem to subscribe to this view. A number of related criticisms have been advanced – that Libertarian Paternalism is an oxymoron (Mitchell 2004), that nudge is merely paternalism in disguise (Vallgårda 2012; Burgess 2012; Furedi 2011), and that nudging impairs autonomy (Furedi 2011; Bovens, 2009). Of course, nudge interventions are just one tool in the behavioural science toolkit. But given the high profile of such critiques, it is important to acknowledge that no truly neutral option exists. Consider a doctor discussing the risk of a treatment with a patient. The same information might be communicated in terms of a 90 per cent survival rate or a 10 per cent death rate, and these different framings will result in different rates of treatment uptake. Yet there is no way to abolish framing altogether. The doctor is obliged to pick something. This bind applies not only to word choice, but to countless other factors that influence each decision. To absorb this fact is to recognise that we are all nudgers and are always being nudged, whether we like it or not and regardless of anyone's intentions. Nudges are an inescapable feature of any decision-making context. The ethical question is not whether to nudge, but in which direction, and in whose interests.

Bibliography

Ager, A./Strang, A. (2008): Understanding Integration: A Conceptual Framework. In: Journal of Refugee Studies 21(2), 166–191.

Agier, M. (2008): On the Margins of the World: The Refugee Experience Today. Cambridge: Polity.

Artavia-Mora, L./Bedi, A.S./Rieger, M. (2017): Intuitive Help and Punishment in the Field. In: European Economic Review 92, 133–145.

Aspinall, P. J./Watters, C. (2010): Refugees and Asylum Seekers: A Review from an Equality and Human Rights Perspective. In: Research Report 52. Equality and Human Rights Commission.

Atwell, R./Gifford, S. M./McDonald-Wilmsen, B. (2009): Resettled Refugee Families and their Children's Futures: Coherence, Hope and Support. In: Journal of Comparative Family Studies 40, 677–697.

Bar, M. (ed.) (2011): Predictions in the Brain: Using Our Past to Generate a Future. Oxford: Oxford University Press.

Behavioural Insights Team (2014): EAST: Four Simple Ways to Apply Behavioural Insights.

Berry, J. W. (1997): Immigration, Acculturation, and Adaptation. In: Applied Psychology 46(1), 5–34.

Bettinger/Long, B. T./Oreopoulos, P./Sanbonmatsu, L. (2009): The Role of Simplification and Information in College Decisions: Results from the H&R Block FAFSA Experiment. NBER Working Paper.

Bodwig, A. (2015): Education Is the Key to Integrating Refugees in Europe. Future Development Blog.

Bovens, L. (2009): The Ethics of Nudge. In: Till Grüne-Yanoff and Sven Ove Hansson, (eds.): Preference Change: Approaches from Philosophy, Economics and Psychology. Theory and Decision Library A (42). Dordrecht: Springer, 207–219.

British Council (2016): Language for Resilience: Supporting Syrian Refugees. Retrieved from http://researchbriefings.files.parliament.uk/documents/CBP-7905/CBP-7905.pdf.

Brooks, G./Burton, M./Cole, P./Miles, J./Torgerson, C/Torgerson, D. (2008): Randomised Controlled Trial of Incentives to Improve Attendance at Adult Literacy Classes. In: Oxford Review of Education 34(5), 493–504.

Burgess, A. (2012): 'Nudging' Healthy Lifestyles: The UK Experiments with the Behavioural Alternative to Regulation and the Market. In: European Journal of Risk Regulation 3(1), 3–16.

Cane, J./O'Connor, D./Michie, S. (2012): Validation of the Theoretical Domains Framework for Use in Behaviour Change and Implementation Research. In: Implementation Science 7(1), 37.

Casey, Dame Louise (2016): The Casey Review: A Review into Opportunity and Integration, December.

Cawley, J./Ruhm, C. J. (2011): The Economics of Risky Health Behaviors. In: Handbook of Health Economics. Vol. 2. New York: Elsevier, 95–199.

Cortina, L. M. (2008): Unseen Injustice: Incivility as Modern Discrimination in Organizations. In: Academy of Management Review 33(1), 55–75.
CRASH Trial Collaborators (2005): Final Results of MRC CRASH, a Randomised Placebo-Controlled Trial of Intravenous Corticosteroid in Adults with Head Injury – Outcomes at 6 Months. In: The Lancet 365(9475), 1957–1959.
De Haas, H. (2005): International Migration, Remittances and Development: Myths and Facts. In: Third World Quarterly 26(8), 1269–1284.
Dolan, P./Hallsworth, M./Halpern, D./King, D./Vlaev, I. (2010): MINDSPACE: Influencing Behaviour for Public Policy.
Dolan, P./Hallsworth, M./Halpern, D./King, D./Metcalfe, R./Vlaev, I. (2012): Influencing Behaviour: The Mindspace Way. In: Journal of Economic Psychology 33(1), 264–277.
Ellis D. A.,/Jenkins, R. (2012): Weekday Affects Attendance Rate for Medical Appointments: Large-Scale Data Analysis and Implications. In: PLoS ONE 7(12), e51365. doi:10.1371/journal.pone.0051365.
Equality and Human Right Commission (2014): Employing Refugees: guidance for Employers
European Commission (2016): An Economic Take on the Refugee Crisis: A Macroeconomic Assessment for the EU. In: European Union, Institutional Paper 033.
Festinger, L./Carlsmith, J. M. (1959): Cognitive Consequences of Forced Compliance. In: Journal of Abnormal and Social Psychology 58, 203–210.
Finckenauer J. O. (1982): Scared Straight and the Panacea Phenomenon. Englewood Cliffs: Prentice-Hall.
Fratzscher, M./Junker, S. (2015): Integrating Refugees: A Long-Term, Worthwhile Investment. In: DIW Economic Bulletin 5(45/46), 612–616.
Frederick, S./Loewenstein, G./O'Donoghue, T. (2002): Time Discounting and Time Preference: A Critical Review. In: Journal of Economic Literature 40(2), 351–401.
French, S. D./Green, S. E./O'Connor, D. A./McKenzie, J. E./Francis, J. J./Michie, S./Buchbinder, R./Schattner, P./Spike, N./Grimshaw, J. M. (2012): Developing Theory-Informed Behaviour Change Interventions to Implement Evidence into Practice: A Systematic Approach Using the Theoretical Domains Framework. In: Implementation Science 7(1), 38.
Furedi, F. (2011): Defending Moral Autonomy against an Army of Nudgers. In: Spiked. https://www.spiked-online.com/2011/01/20/defending-moral-autonomy-against-an-army-of-nudgers/ (last accessed 05/09/2018).
Hagen-Zanker, J. (2008): Why Do People Migrate? A Review of the Theoretical Literature. Maastricht Graduate School of Governance Working Paper No. 2008/WP002.
Hainmueller, J./Hangartner, D./Lawrence, D. (2016): When Lives Are Put on Hold: Lengthy Asylum Processes Decrease Employment among Refugees. In: Science Advances 2(8), e1600432.
Hallin, S./Hooper, E./Weyman-Jones, T. (2017): Case Study Evidence and Behavioural Analysis of Residential Energy Consumption in the UK. In: Open Journal of Energy Efficiency 6, 14–40.
Hausman D./Welch B. (2010): Debate: To Nudge or Not to Nudge. In: Journal of Political Philosophy 18, 123–136.
Haynes, L./Goldacre, B./Torgerson, D. (2012): Test, Learn, Adapt: Developing Public Policy with Randomised Controlled Trials. Policy Paper. Cabinet Office.
Hume, S./O'Reilly, F./Groot B./Chande, R./Sanders, M./Hollingsworth, A./Ter Meer, J./Barnes, J./Booth, S./Kozman, E./Soon, X. Z. (2018): Improving Engagement and Attainment in

Maths and English Courses: Insights from Behavioural Research. Department for Education. https://bit.ly/2ArEPAx.
Johnson, E. J./Shu, S. B./Dellaert, B. G./Fox, C./Goldstein, D. G./Häubl, G./Larrick, R.P./Payne, J.W./Peters, E./Schkade, D./Wansink, B. (2012): Beyond Nudges: Tools of a Choice Architecture. In: Marketing Letters 23(2), 487–504.
Kahneman, D./Egan, P. (2011): Thinking, Fast and Slow. New York: Farrar, Straus and Giroux.
Karakas, C. (2015): Economic Challenges and Prospects of the Refugee Influx. European Parliamentary Research Service.
Karau, S. J./Kelly, J. R. (1992): The Effects of Time Scarcity and Time Abundance on Group Performance Quality and Interaction Process. In: Journal of Experimental Social Psychology 28(6), 542–571.
Krause, A./Rinne, U./Zimmermann, K. F. (2012): Anonymous Job Applications in Europe. In: IZA Journal of European Labor Studies 1(1), 5.
Laibson, D. (1997): Golden Eggs and Hyperbolic Discounting. In: The Quarterly Journal of Economics 112(2), 443–478.
Linos, E./Reinhard, J./Ruda, S. (2017): Levelling the Playing Field in Police Recruitment: Evidence from a Field Experiment on Test Performance. In: Public Administration 95(4), 943–956.
Lourenço, J. S./Ciriolo, E./Almeida S. R./Troussard, X. (2016): Behavioural Insights Applied to Policy. In: European Report 2016. EUR 27726 EN. doi: 10.2760/903938.
Lynn, M. (1991): Scarcity Effects on Value: A Quantitative Review of the Commodity Theory Literature. In: Psychology & Marketing 8(1), 43–57.
Madrian, B. C./Shea, D. F. (2001): The Power of Suggestion: Inertia in 401 (k) Participation and Savings Behavior. In: The Quarterly Journal of Economics 116(4), 1149–1187.
Marbach, M./Hainmueller, J./Hangartner, D. (2017): The Long-Term Impact of Employment Bans on the Economic Integration of Refugees. In: Science Advances 4(9), eaap9519.
Michie, S./Van Stralen, M. M./West, R. (2011): The Behaviour Change Wheel: A New Method for Characterising and Designing Behaviour Change Interventions. In: Implementation Science 6(1), 42.
Mitchell, G. (2004): Libertarian Paternalism Is an Oxymoron. In: Northwestern University Law Review 99, 1245.
Mullainathan, S./Shafir, E. (2013): Scarcity: Why having too little means so much. Macmillan.
Nuffield Council on Bioethics (2015): http://nuffieldbioethics.org/wp-content/uploads/2014/07/Public-health-Chapter-3-Policy-process-and-practice.pdf (last accessed June 2015).
Petrosino, A./Turpin-Petrosino, C./Buehler, J. (2003): Scared Straight and Other Juvenile Awareness Programs for Preventing Juvenile Delinquency. Campbell Review Update I. In: The Campbell Collaboration Reviews of Intervention and Policy Evaluations (C2-RIPE). Philadelphia: Campbell Collaboration.
Pinder, R./Sallis, A./Berry, D./Chadborn, T. (2015): Behaviour Change and Antibiotic Prescribing in Healthcare Settings. Literature Review and Behavioural Analysis. In: Public Health England 2014719.
Pittaway, E./Bartolomei, L. (2001): Refugees, Race, and Gender: The Multiple Discrimination against Refugee Women. In: Refuge: Canada's Journal on Refugees 19(6), 21–32.
Public Health England (2015): Low Cost Ways to Increase NHS Health Check Attendance: Results from a Randomised Controlled Trial.

Ratha, D./Mohapatra, S./Scheja, E. (2011): Impact of Migration on Economic and Social Development: A Review of Evidence and Emerging Issues. The World Bank.
Sanders J.G./Jenkins, R. (2016): Weekly Fluctuations in Risk Tolerance and Voting Behaviour. In: PLoS ONE 11(7), e0159017. doi:10.1371/journal. pone.0159017.
Sturm, D. (2016): Measuring Refugee Integration – The International Context (table), Research and Evaluation Manager, USCCB/MRS Oct. 21, 2016 (Draft). Retrieved from https://c.ymcdn.com/sites/usccb.site-ym.com/resource/group/085a874d-f909–48df-8f95–603bbf54c6c1/PAE_Refugee_Integration_Metr.pdf.
Sunstein, C. R./Reisch, L. A./Rauber, J. (2018): A Worldwide Consensus on Nudging? Not Quite, but Almost. In: Regulation and Governance 12(1), 3–22.
Sunstein, C./Thaler, R. (2008): Nudge: Improving Decisions about Health, Wealth, and Happiness. New Haven: Yale University Press.
Sweller, J. (1988): Cognitive Load During Problem Solving: Effects on Learning. In: Cognitive Science 12(2), 257–285.
Sweller, J./Van Merrienboer, J. J./Paas, F. G. (1998): Cognitive Architecture and Instructional Design. In: Educational Psychology Review 10(3), 251–296.
Tomm, B. M./Zhao, J. (2016): Scarcity Captures Attention and Induces Neglect: Eyetracking and Behavioral Evidence. In: A. Papafragou/D. GrodnerD. Mirman J. C. Trueswell (eds.): Proceedings of the 38th annual conference of the Cognitive Science Society. Austin: Cognitive Science Society, 1199–1204.
UNDP (2016): Behavioural Insights at the United Nations – Achieving Agenda 2030. United Nations Development Programme. http://www.undp.org/content/undp/en/home/library page/development-impact/behavioural-insights-at-the-united-nations-achieving-agenda-203.html.
UNHCR (2016): Mid-year Trends. http://www.unhcr.org/statistics/unhcrstats/58aa8f247/mid-year-trends-june-2016.html.
Vallgårda, S. (2012): Nudge: A New and Better Way to Improve Health? In: Health Policy 104(2), 200–203.
Webb, T. L./Sheeran, P. (2006): Does Changing Behavioral Intentions Engender Behavior Change? A Meta-analysis of the Experimental Evidence. In: Psychological Bulletin 132(2), 249–268.
White, J. V. (2004): What Is Affirmative Action? In: Scholarly Works. Paper 306.
World Bank (2018): Behavioral Science around the World: Profiles of 10 Countries. World Bank. Working draft of Mind, Behavior and Development Unit. http://documents.world bank.org/curated/en/710771543609067500/Behavioral-Science-Around-the-World-A-Pro file-of-10-Countries-Working-Draft.
World Health Organisation (2018): Migration and Communicable Diseases: No Systematic Association. http://www.euro.who.int/en/health-topics/health-determinants/migration-and-health/migrant-health-in-the-european-region/migration-and-health-key-is sues#292117.

Annemiek Dresen

The practice of newcomer integration and importance of perspectives

Abstract: In a personal interpretation of global individual responsibility, this essay explores practical issues concerning migration and refugees. It is by no means scientifically proven, nor does it intend to be: it is one person's interpretation of her role as a global citizen, and a tale of practical experiences and cultural encounters. It aims to make a case for a bottom-up approach when it comes to finding solutions, and creating policy, for refugee integration. It focuses on access to the European labor market, because having work is a key ingredient of successful integration. As such it explores work as an integration tool in the Netherlands, using case studies as experienced by NewBees, a local social enterprise.

1. One case of global individual responsibility

This is the story of my interpretation of global individual responsibility in the debate on migration and refugees. It is by no means scientifically proven, nor is it intended to be. It is one person's interpretation of her role as a global citizen. It aims to share practical experiences and cultural encounters, as well as to make a case for a bottom-up approach when it comes to finding solutions for refugee integration. It focuses on access to the European labour market, because having work is a key ingredient of successful integration. Without disregarding the importance of other vital aspects of integration, like the existence of a social network and access to healthcare, I will focus on work as an integration tool.[1]

2. Talent on the beach

I ended up on a beach in Lesbos in December 2015 because I wanted to do the right thing. Just like many people on that same beach, I had seen the news about

1 I refer to migrants and asylum seekers as 'refugees' and to shelters as 'refugee camps'. In some sections of this paper other terms such as 'newcomer' and 'asylum centre' may be more appropriate. However, I have chosen this wording in order to use consistent language and maintain clarity.

https://doi.org/10.1515/9783110628746-013

large numbers of refugees crossing the narrow stretch of Mediterranean Sea between Turkey and Greece that previous summer. As a European citizen I felt it was my duty to engage. I decided to travel to Greece and to lend my support on the beaches of Lesbos, where small dinghies packed with people arrived every morning. Once on Lesbos, I realised how many people had felt a similar pull. Beaches were packed with volunteers, with or without particular qualifications, helping people out of boats, handing out water, and using their small rental cars to transport recent arrivals to the closest refugee camp. It was quite something, this self-organizing semi-mess – that seemed to eventually serve its purpose – born from a collective ethos.

The reason I had decided to do something is simple: I feel very privileged to have been born into a world of opportunity, and I know not all of us are as lucky. I have a strong belief in equal opportunity and justice, which has been present throughout all of my career moves, and I could not escape it that winter of 2015. On the beach I met so many interesting and talented people among those who had just crossed the sea. The diversity in talent and strong will to make something out of life was surprising and even uplifting, despite the harsh reality of the situation. People were excited to start moving north and to begin their new lives. Their journey would still be a long one, however, filled with bureaucratic hurdles. The long road ahead of these refugees to find a new home, a new start, and a safe haven meant they had to travel far and long. But reaching Northern Europe would not be the end of their journey. In the Netherlands, for example, people piled up in refugee camps, waiting for a long asylum procedure during which work, study, and even volunteer work were not allowed. Talent was wasted. Because of systemic reasons embedded in policy, refugees had to wait outside our society until their asylum requests were granted, which could take months, or even years.

3. Purpose and participation

Having to wait, unable to do anything, being kept from contributing to the world around me is one of my worst nightmares. I enjoy action, work, and making myself useful to the world: I need a sense of purpose. The thought of having to sit in a refugee camp without anything to do scared me a little. Furthermore, I was disappointed that asylum seekers are frequently viewed as blank sheets of paper that have to learn everything all over again. Because of a cultural and a language barrier, past experiences and existing talents are often not noticed by people in host countries. On the beaches of Lesbos, I had seen the contrary and I wanted to show this. I was not a policymaker, nor did I want to decide who got to stay in the Netherlands and who did not, but I did feel I had an obligation to use my own talent for the benefit of both refugees and the Dutch society. So after my return from the beaches of Lesbos, I found purpose in making a case for participation during the asylum application. As an anthropologist I believed in being able to translate the systemic Dutch thinking to better match the perceptions of refugees. So I walked in to a refugee camp and started asking people questions about their backgrounds: what did they do before; what had they studied; what were their dreams in this new country. Responses were interesting and fun: many people very much enjoyed telling the story of what they could do, rather than talking about what they did not have. So I decided to start looking for companies and organizations in the neighbourhood that could make use of those skills, and I proposed refugees help them out as volunteers.

Even though the bosses and directors of these companies were quite enthusiastic, we had some bureaucratic hoops to jump through: any kind of participation was not allowed in the Netherlands at that time. With the support of the refugee camp's director – and a lot of patience – we managed to get our participation plans on the minister's desk, who eventually decided to 'not forbid it'. With our 'non-illegal plans',[2] I started running and quickly built a database of available vacancies in the area,[3] as well as available skills among residents of the refugee camp. An organization was born: NewBees. With NewBees I matched many refugees to fun and interesting voluntary jobs around the refugee camp, which allowed them to use their talents, add value, and get out of the camp into Dutch society. We had successfully created a dent in the systemic top-down policy, which did not allow refugees to participate in Dutch society at all, by offering a tangible bottom-up solution.

That practical bottom-up solution also came with practical lessons. The most recurring of these, it turned out, is the flexible concept of time. One of the organizations we worked with was a farm. Over the weekend, they needed help with a variety of activities, and in the camp I had met several North African men and women with agricultural knowledge who were excited to help out. We all agreed they would show up at 9 am on Saturday to spend the day helping and meeting Dutch people at the farm. I was quite pleased with the match. Come 10 am that Saturday, not a single person had shown up at the farm, even though I had gone through the trouble of showing them where it was, even making the trip the week before so that they would know how to get there.

---

2 It was still not legal, but in a very Dutch-tolerance kind of way, it was decided to allow us to continue.

3 Note that these were volunteer vacancies, as paid participation was very much illegal still. Our plans were waived because they entailed voluntary participation.

'They are late. See how those people do not keep their promises'? was one comment made by a Dutch volunteer. Together with one of my staff we tried to fix the situation, so he went to the camp, knocked on some doors, and woke people up. They were still quite excited but had not gotten out of bed yet. Life in the camp, as it turned out, was lived mostly at night and nobody was up before 10 am. After all, what would they be getting up for? 'But we had agreed to meet at 9 am!' 'And it would have been rude to say no,' was the response. In our Dutch world, it was rude to be late; in their world, it was rude to say no. This seemingly contradictory set of values would be a recurring cultural theme to be managed and explained to both refugees and Dutch companies.

4. Common misconceptions on perception

At the camp NewBees became a way for people to stop waiting and start doing, but that did not mean the wait was over. There would come a time when residents were granted their asylum (or not) and had to move to a different location to either await transport home or relocation to a Dutch municipality.[4] NewBees continued working at the camp and expanded its activities outside it, as former residents increasingly were granted asylum and appointed a home in a Dutch city. While the influx of refugees decreased following the Turkey Deal of March 2016[5] that did not mean our work was done. Many refugees from Syria, Eritrea, and a number of other countries were granted asylum and now had to start the integration process in the Netherlands. This process consists of learning the language and, eventually, finding work so as to no longer rely on government welfare. With a growing economy and increasing number of vacancies on the Dutch labour market, the task of finding work for people appeared to be simple: there is work, people can work, so done deal, right? From a Dutch perspective this top-down idea of supply and demand appears to make sense, but it is an interesting example of systemic thinking along one cultural line. Unfortunately, refugee integration in the Dutch labour market is more complicated than that.

Systemic thinking and a top-down approach, which are common in the Netherlands, and particularly in Dutch policymaking, are exactly what I believe make it difficult to create space for refugees in our society. In the Netherlands we

4 In the Netherlands, when granted asylum, refugees are appointed to a Dutch municipality which is then responsible for providing housing and welfare as refugees start the integration process.

5 I will not dive into the details or range of opinions on this particular deal, but instead describe the effect it had on the work NewBees does in the Netherlands.

are used to plan, think ahead, and build policy top-down around carefully crafted plans. In theory that makes a lot of sense, but in practice we deal with people who are individuals with their own perception of reality. And they do not view their own integration process in such systemic ways.

An example involves time once again. One of our participants, Hussam, was invited to meet with his contact person at the municipality, who had thought of a short course for him to do, to train for a job as a traffic controller. They had a meeting at 11 am. Hussam did not show up until 12 pm, to the great discomfort of his contact. Again, in the Netherlands it is rude to be late, and people who are left waiting often feel like they are not taken seriously. Furthermore, he needed to sign up Hussam for the course, which became difficult due to time constraints. Hussam, on his way to the municipality and fully intending to start the course proposed to him, had run into somebody he knew and stopped to chat. In his culture, it is very rude to not stop in the street for a chat, and people who are left in the street without having caught up often feel like they are not taken seriously. Both Hussam and his contact wanted to be polite, but their interpretation of this concept differed. The Dutch municipal clerk had thought out a process, planned it, informed Hussam, and expected it to go exactly as planned. Hussam, on the other hand, had accepted the plan and agreed on the meeting with every intention to participate, but he was open to the concept that plans sometimes change as one goes along. This distinct difference in cultural perception is often misunderstood by institutions focused on migration and potential employers alike, which leads to misunderstandings around the intentions of refugees.

Now, I do not want to make a case for being late (I am Dutch too and value punctuality), but in order for us to come closer together in our increasingly diverse society, it is of vital importance that we understand why we act the way we do and share it with each other. The devil really is in the detail when it comes to refugee integration on the labour market, and it is important that we reassess assumptions surrounding certain behaviour from a practical point of view.

5. Supply and demand in the healthcare sector

In order to demonstrate further how top-down policy sometimes fails us in the debate around migration and integration, I will explore the Dutch healthcare sector, in particular that of elderly care. With an aging population, this sector faces massive shortages and is predicted to have more than 120,000 vacancies in 2020 (ROC employee, interview with author, 13 June 2013). Among refugees, quite a number of people would be very interested in working with elderly people. Women, especially, who worked in education, or who were in charge of their households, have excellent skills as well as an interest in working in healthcare. Then why are we not succeeding in filling these vacancies? I will try to outline some factors that influence this.

First of all, many interested refugees have little or no tertiary education and it is difficult for them to access the Dutch education system. The system in the Netherlands is set up in such a way that its default means you enter at four years old, follow a certain path, and then come out of it as an adult with a degree or certified trade. For those who want to start somewhere halfway, it can be complicated to follow this journey, especially for those who have no diplomas from their home country that prove their skills and potential. The challenge is even more so, for those whose Dutch is far from perfect.

This brings me to the second point: in the Netherlands all refugees (and other immigrants for that matter) have to integrate and learn the Dutch language. In a wave of privatization in the 1990s, it was decided that integration was the responsibility of the migrant himself and language schools were privatised to promote a free-market economy. All other integration activities, as well as management of welfare and housing, lie with municipalities. In practice this means that there are several language institutions that use different methods and modules in the classroom, from which refugees have to choose. As such, people start at a certain school with little option to switch if they would want to, learning a language in that classroom, rather than in real life. Furthermore, students are trained to pass exams, and when they do, it does not necessarily mean they speak the language. So even though theoretically it makes sense to allow refugees their own decisions when working on integration, in practice we have learned that it can lead to confusion and sub-optimal outcomes.[6]

Furthermore, sitting in a classroom does not provide the most extensive view of the Dutch society and the possibilities on its labour market. For many people it is quite unclear what a realistic career path may be. A friend and former colleague once had a long discussion with a young Syrian man who aspired to become a sports commentator for radio and television. Trying to paint a realistic picture of his chances of reaching that goal, without tempering his enthusiasm, my friend asked him if there were any other careers he would be interested in, might his sports journalism one fall through. The young man replied that he actually really wanted to join the police force, but that, of course, was completely unrealistic. My friend was flabbergasted; in his Dutch mind, a career with the

6 As indicated in a note directed at the Dutch Senate d.d. July 2nd 2018, Dutch minister Koolmees (Social Affairs and Employment) announces changes to this system starting 2020.

police was so much more realistic than one in sports journalism. The Syrian boy had a different view on things: in his world the police force meant something completely different. In the case of elderly care, we need to keep this in mind as well: how will people know this is an option if you come from cultures where families take care of their own elderly? How would one aspire to work in elderly care if the existence of such a sector is completely unknown? It is of critical importance that we inform refugees of options they have, even if they seem all too obvious.

An example of somebody for whom working with elderly people was completely new is Bushra. In her home country of Syria Bushra was studying to become a children's teacher. But when given the chance to help a very different age group in her new hometown in the Netherlands, she accepted NewBees's idea to work at an assisted living centre for the elderly. Bushra now stays busy all day: whether she's serving coffee and tea to the tenants, helping them with their activities, or simply sitting down for a chat; there's always something to do. While she initially pursued volunteer work to grow her network and improve her Dutch, she's grown to enjoy the work itself: 'The atmosphere here is so nice,' she said. 'I like to help the people here.' Compared to her studies to become a teacher, working at the elderly home is completely new and different – but at the same time, some things extend across all age groups, such as the care for a fellow human being, the human interaction, and the mutual respect that are all so important in this line of work. It gave her the chance to work on herself, her communication, and the way she interacts with Dutch people. And after three months, she even decided she may like working with elderly people more than children. 'Working here has increased my self-confidence,' she said. 'I've become someone better. It's not always easy, but I always try. It's something new, and that's very nice.' Bushra is typically somebody who would love to pursue a career in healthcare but who would not have known about it had she not been told about the opportunity.

Then there are the sector-specific policy issues that stand in the way of including refugees in the workforce. Even though the healthcare sector is struggling with shortages, it works with a vulnerable clientele and is careful about whom they allow to work with them (with good reason). The most pressing shortage at the moment is that of high-educated nurses, who are certified to administer medicine and can execute a large variety of tasks so that is what most institutions are looking for. The qualifications to work in the sector are therefore quite extensive, which means that anybody new to the industry, like Bushra, would have to seriously invest in getting educated. As I already pointed out, this can be a significant challenge for refugees. Furthermore, the language barrier is particularly troublesome when it comes to elderly care, healthcare institutions say, because elderly people often speak no other language than Dutch, and it is important to understand precisely what they are saying, even when they speak unclearly. All of these are valid points, of course. However, they are also born from a line of thought that is stuck in its own systemic structure, allowing for little practical thinking outside the box.

Using this example of healthcare, we can identify a number of practical hurdles when it comes to refugee integration in the labour market. Language and education policy are designed in such a way that it is difficult for refugees to navigate the system. That system takes possibilities on the labour market for granted and does not explain well enough to refugees what possibilities they may have. Those possibilities, subsequently, are limited because of systemic standards within each sector, like certain qualifications in nurses. I like to believe we can overcome these challenges once we recognise them and focus on finding practical solutions. It is important that refugees are informed of their options, for example, in elderly care. That we offer fitting and more holistic education, perhaps letting go a little of the set systemic plan we are used to. That we incorporate language in that education, so that professional jargon is included and people can practice Dutch as they learn it. And I believe it is important that Dutch healthcare institutions investigate how they might become more flexible with their qualifications, thinking outside the box, without jeopardizing the care of their clients. A practical start can be a voluntary position, like Bushra has, which helps with language skills and learning about the sector, as well as with cultural differences such as punctuality. It may also help healthcare institutions see the skills and talents refugees bring to their work. Volunteering as preparation for work is a small step that does not immediately fit into the system, but which shows solutions can be found in bottom-up approaches to promote refugee integration.

6. An invitation to dance

Dutch policymakers tend to address a problem top-down, aiming to make a plan, institutionalise it, and then execute it. In the case of refugee integration and participation, I believe we would benefit from designing bottom-up solutions instead, together with those refugees. We need their point of view to be able to make integration a success, to understand the point of view of all participants in this debate, and to reassess assumptions. This is why I believe we need to invite both employers and potential employees to the discussion of integration more often and come up with practical solutions to practical problems, such a caring for our elderly people.

In her 1986 book, anthropologist Harrell-Bond quoted an African migrant who pointed out that 'refugees must not be settled, but must be allowed to try to settle themselves' (Harrell-Bond 1986, 300). At NewBees we aim to do exactly that. I started with the simple exercise of matching skills at a refugee camp and allocating them to the communities surrounding the camp where people could add value. Now that we have grown, we keep applying the same concept: we discuss with both refugees and employers what their needs are and try to find ways to address those needs in a practical way. With a team that consists of both Dutch people and refugees, we look for ways to open up the labour market to the talents and experiences refugees bring, using trial and error. In its first two years of existence, NewBees has matched more than four hundred people to purposeful participation positions, including volunteer work, internships, and work. This has helped people understand the Dutch system, learn about the necessary cultural code in the workplace, and increase language skills. Simultaneously, Dutch employers have learned how to appreciate diverse skills and how they may help to increase productivity in an inclusive workplace.

As a global citizen, I have shaped my personal responsibility in refugee integration by using an anthropological view to start a dialogue, bottom-up, between those participating in society and with those creating the policy to shape it. I have made it my purpose to show the diverse talents of refugees and to explain the importance of cultural details in the workplace. With NewBees I aim to open up the mindset of refugees, employers, and policymakers to see how the other thinks and to find a way to meet one another in the middle, on the work floor. It is how I successfully challenged the system by organizing volunteer work for refugees living in camps when that was not yet allowed. With NewBees we continue to show that the practical perception of integration and the tangible hurdles and challenges that come with it are real, no matter how minor or insignificant they may seem in theory. I feel it is my responsibility as a global citizen to continue on that path. One of my favourite well-known quotes is by Verna Myers: 'Tolerance is being invited to the party; inclusion is being asked to dance.'[7] I believe it is our role as global citizens to invite people to dance, and I urge everybody to do so.

---

7 Myers is an expert on inclusion and author of *Moving Diversity Forward: How to Go from Well-Meaning to Well-Doing* and *What If I Say the Wrong Thing? 25 Habits for Culturally Effective People.*

Bibliography

Harrell-Bond, B. E. (1986): Imposing Aid. Emergency Assistance to Refugees. Oxford: Oxford University Press.

Stephen Wordsworth

Perspectives on individual responsibility in the context of refugee and migrant integration

Abstract: Cara, the Council for At-Risk Academics, was established in the United Kingdom in 1933 in response to the crisis engulfing German academia following the Nazis' rise to power. The chapter outlines the history of this organisation and also its work today to help academics around the world to escape from persecution, violence and conflict, by working with university partners to provide safe places where they can continue their work until, as most hope, they can return home. The chapter also explains how Cara supports exiled academics through regionally-based programmes, and how it works with other partner organisations. For 85 years, Cara Fellows have gone on to enrich the scientific, intellectual and cultural life of Britain, and have been recognised for their ground-breaking work with Nobel prizes and other awards.

1. Policy and practice: Cara (the Council for At-Risk Academics)

> It seemed like a normal weekday, until my colleagues at my university picked me up to go to work, and one of them told me that we were being denounced in the newspapers. ...
>
> I was blacklisted by the Syrian government's security forces for my political views and for reporting on the Syrian Uprising in my hometown. I lost my father, brother, uncle, and many other friends during the military campaign and the subsequent evacuation. ...
>
> I really do not know what to do! For the opposition, I work with the regime, and for the regime, I belong to the opposition. In fact, I don't belong to any of them. I just happen to love my work as a researcher and lecturer.

These are the voices of just three academics who desperately needed help to get away to a place where they wouldn't face the risk of being arrested, beaten up, or even killed. Now they are safe, as Cara Fellows, and can get on with their academic work, with their families.

https://doi.org/10.1515/9783110628746-014

1.1. Cara's history[1]

Cara was set up eighty-five years ago, in 1933, by academics and scientists in the UK who came together to rescue their colleagues in Germany being forced out of their posts by the Nazis. William Beveridge, then director of the London School of Economics, was travelling in Austria in April of that year, and heard about the Nazi authorities' decree. He returned to the UK and set about enlisting the support of prominent academics, scientists, and others for an urgent rescue mission. The Academic Assistance Council (AAC) was launched in May. Its founders explicitly recognised that institutions were unlikely to be able to help, and that individuals therefore needed to take the initiative. As they put it in their founding statement,

> The financial resources of universities are limited and are subject to claims for their normal development which cannot be ignored. ... We have formed ourselves accordingly into a provisional Council for these two purposes. We shall seek to raise a fund ... and we shall seek to provide a clearing house and centre of information. ...("Founding Statement of the Academic Assistance Council" 1933)

Their declared aim set out in the founding document was to find 'means to prevent the waste of exceptional abilities exceptionally trained'.

Nobel Prize-winning chemist and physicist, Ernest Rutherford, was chosen as the first president. A. V. Hill, another Nobel Prize-winning scientist who went on to be Member of Parliament for Cambridge University, became vice-president. Hungarian physicist, Leo Szilard, who had met Beveridge in Vienna, moved to London and for a while also worked from the AAC offices in the Rooms of the Royal Society, at the top of Burlington House. He was never fully part of the AAC, as he saw his task mobilising an international, rather than primarily British, response to the crisis, but he influenced its early thinking before he left for the USA in 1937.

The AAC's founders, supported by the redoubtable Esther Simpson, who had been recruited as secretary by Szilard, threw themselves into their new task. Between May and August 1933, the AAC raised nearly £10,000 to get its work off the ground – around £350,000 in today's values – most of it from individual UK academics. The AAC was one of four organisations that came together as the Refugee Assistance Fund in October 1933 to hold a major fundraising event at the Royal

---

1 Much of the original content from Cara's website regarding Cara's history (see https://www.cara.ngo/who-we-are/our-history/) was written by Executive Director Stephen Wordsworth, and it is reprinted here with permission of same author.

Albert Hall. In his last public speech in Europe before leaving for the USA, Albert Einstein urged his audience to stand up for intellectual and individual freedom:

> If we want to resist the powers which threaten to suppress intellectual and individual freedom we must keep clearly before us what is at stake, and what we owe to that freedom which our ancestors have won for us after hard struggles. Without such freedom, there would have been no Shakespeare, no Goethe, no Newton, no Faraday, no Pasteur and no Lister. ... Most people would lead a dull life of slavery. ... It is only men who are free who create the inventions and intellectual works which to us moderns make life worthwhile. (Einstein 1933)

By 1936, it was clear that a new, more formal, structure was needed to take over the AAC's work. Rutherford explained the rationale in an open letter in *Science:*

> The council hoped that its work might be required for only a temporary period, but is now convinced that there is need for a permanent body to assist scholars who are victims of political and religious persecutions. The devastation of the German universities still continues; not only university teachers of Jewish descent, but many others who are regarded as "politically unreliable" are being prevented from making their contribution to the common cause of scholarship. (Rutherford 1936, 372)

As a result, he announced the creation of a permanent successor, the Society for the Protection of Science and Learning (SPSL). In a joint letter on the same page of the 1936 *Science* publication, Albert Einstein, Erwin Schrödinger, and Vladimir Tchernavin paid tribute to the work of the AAC in its three short years:

> The warm sympathy extended to all who approached the Academic Assistance Council has helped in hundreds of cases. ... The Academic Assistance Council is coming to an end in its emergency form, but we and our friends will endeavor to make it remain unforgotten. May we hope that the continuation of our scientific work – helped in no small measure by its activities – will be an expression of our gratitude?

At around the same time, the SPSL absorbed the staff and archives of the Zurich-based Notgemeinschaft Deutscher Wissenschaftler im Ausland (Emergency Association of German Scientists Abroad), which had been founded by the prominent German pathologist Philipp Schwartz in 1933 in a parallel effort to support German academics who were being forced out by the Nazis.

Between 1933 and 1939, the AAC/SPSL raised a further £100,000 from donors and universities, the equivalent of some £4 million today, and used it to support individuals and their families with grants and advice while they found new posts in universities in the UK or in other safe countries. A number of the AAC's founders and council members also personally provided places and/or funds to help individual academics. The AAC was also closely involved in the successful effort in 1933 to bring to London the Warburg Institute art library, which had been proscribed by the Nazis, and six of its staff. In all, some two thousand people were saved and helped to build new lives. Sixteen won Nobel Prizes; eighteen were knighted; and over one hundred became Fellows of the Royal Society or the British Academy. An unattributed article in *Nature* in 1938 set out clearly the underlying philosophy of the AAC/SPSL, based on individuals helping individuals:

> It [the SPSL] stands for the brotherhood of scientific endeavour, regardless of race and creed and politics: and it stands for it, not by passing pious resolutions or by putting out disguised political propaganda, but by trying to help colleagues in their need.(Science and Learning in Distress 1938, 1051)

And the SPSL didn't hesitate to take on their own government, when circumstances required it: in 1940, when many German academics were interned by the British authorities as part of a much wider round-up of 'enemy aliens', the SPSL worked tirelessly with specialist committees to get them released.

The contribution these people made to British scientific, intellectual, and cultural life was enormous. To give just a few examples: Ernst Chain, Nobel Prize in Physiology or Medicine, 1945; Hans Krebs, Nobel Prize in Physiology or Medicine, 1953; Max Born, Nobel Prize in Physics, 1954; Max Perutz, Nobel Prize in Chemistry, 1962; Lise Meitner, celebrated nuclear physicist; Nikolaus Pevsner, architectural historian and author; Marthe Vogt, prominent neuroscientist; Geoffrey Elton (born Gottfried Ehrenberg), Tudor historian and philosopher of history; Ernst Gombrich, the notable art historian, who was able to work as a Warburg Institute research fellow in London; Karl Popper, political and social philosopher; Ludwig Guttmann, neurologist at Stoke Mandeville, 'father' of the Paralympic movement. It was a unique effort; there was no parallel elsewhere in Europe. At a commemorative event at the House of Lords in 2012, Mrs Eva Loeffler, Sir Ludwig Guttmann's daughter, warmly thanked Cara for its vital role in obtaining visas for her family and for giving her father a grant to support his needs and to enable him to continue his research at the Radcliffe Infirmary in Oxford. Without Cara's help, she said, they would all have perished in the Nazi concentration camps. Instead, her father's dream of the Paralympics had come true.

The SPSL's work continued even after the Second World War had come to an end. Beveridge wrote in his *A Defence of Free Learning* (1959) that "though Hitler was dead, intolerance went on" (1959, 92), and concluded that continued needs and the possible future crises rendered the Society's services as necessary as ever, in Europe and across the world. In the 1940s and 1950s, the SPSL helped many academics seeking refuge from the Stalinist regimes in the USSR and Eastern Europe. As time passed, the SPSL's focus expanded to include, among others, those fleeing the apartheid regime in South Africa and juntas in Chile and Argentina. One of the most prominent South African exiles, whom the SPSL helped in 1966 and again in 1988, was the anti-apartheid leader Albie Sachs, later a justice in the South African Constitutional Court under Nelson Mandela. In 2012, he wrote of the importance of Cara's work:

> My story has been repeated a thousand times and more, with different details, but the same theme. An intellectual driven from his or her homeland by repression and intolerance, enabled by Cara to share ideas and values with welcoming hosts, improving skills ... Through living the principles of free enquiry we become natural apostles of peace and understanding and of internationalism at its best. Cara does more than provide succour for people in need. It helps keep alive the spirit of free enquiry. (Albie Sachs, personal communication to Cara's former chair Shula Marks, June 2012)

In 1999 the SPSL changed its name to the Council for Assisting Refugee Academics (Cara). This was modified again in 2014 to become the Council for At-Risk Academics, reflecting the fact that Cara helps many who are at great risk but do not see themselves as 'refugees', and instead still hope to return to their home countries when conditions allow.

1.2. Cara's work today

Cara's founders' mission, according to their 1933 Founding Statement – 'to prevent the waste of exceptional abilities exceptionally trained' – is still the organisation's inspiration today. Cara's horizons now may be much wider, as it works to help academics all around the world who fear for their freedom, their safety, even their lives, but it is still driven by its founders' conviction that science and learning have no geographical boundaries, that the world's academics are a single community, and that their freedom to research and to teach is vitally important for the future of our planet. Sadly, the dangers faced by academics around the world have changed little, if at all, in the years since 1933. Tyrants and extremists are as determined as ever to silence their enemies, and wars still rage. Those who say and write what they think can still be targeted. Peaceful protest alone can be enough to attract persecution, prison, or even murder. Those who want to survive are forced into self-censorship. Elsewhere, academics trying to continue their work against a background of conflict find their students staying away as normal study becomes impossible, or becoming radicalised as the divisions of the battlefield are brought into the lecture hall. Just moving around can involve a whole catalogue of risks – arrest, robbery or forced conscription at checkpoints along the route, being kidnapped for ransom, or injury or even death from crossfire or stray shells. For others, the danger can have very individual roots – someone may belong to the 'wrong' religion or ethnic group, or be of the 'wrong' sexual orientation in a society where being different risks getting beaten up, or even killed.

2. Cara's Fellowship Programme

Cara's Fellowship Programme has been developed in close partnership with a network of 117 UK universities that provide financial support for Cara and fee waivers and other support for Cara beneficiaries and acts as a lifeline to academics at risk, helping them to reach a place of safety where they can continue their work. Most are passionate about returning home when the situation allows, but they require support in the meantime to develop their skills and build the networks they will need when that day comes.

Most applicants first contact Cara by e-mail, a few by telephone. Cara staff direct them to the 'Get Support' function on the website home page (www.cara.ngo), which leads into the application process. This starts with some simple first-screening questions and then takes them into a detailed enquiry form. Here they can enter their personal data, explain their background and present circumstances, including the risks they face, provide details of their referees, and upload essential documents.

Cara staff check the applicants' background and qualifications and follow up on the references. Once they decide that the applicant is eligible for support, they assess the degree of risk the individual is facing, and prioritise accordingly. Each case is then taken on by an individual Programme Officer who works closely with the applicant to encourage them to identify a potential supervisor/host institution, if they have not already done so; helps to negotiate the placement; agrees with the university on the funding arrangements; and allocates any additional funding needed from Cara's own resources. Cara staff also make clear to the potential host university in each case that they must themselves interview the candidate, usually by Skype, to establish their academic suitability for the course or position under discussion – Cara staff cannot do this.

Cara Fellows, and any accompanying family members, do not come as asylum-seekers or refugees, but enter the UK on regular visas. The university is the visa sponsor, but experienced Cara staff work closely with the applicant and the university to try to ensure that everything goes smoothly, and stand ready to challenge any initial visa refusals by contacting Home Office staff or, when necessary, in the courts. In 2017, over 95 per cent of Cara Fellows were ultimately successful in their visa applications. Once the visa has been granted, Cara staff assist with the travel arrangements and liaise with the host university about the Fellow's arrival. Cara also requires the host institution, and the individual Fellow, provide regular reports back to Cara throughout the placement, to make sure that it is going smoothly or to make it possible for Cara to take remedial action if necessary.

In recent years, facing very high levels of applications because of overlapping crises in the Middle East in particular, Cara has been compelled to ask its UK university partners not only for full waivers of any course or bench fees but, wherever possible, to take on the full costs of each placement. This is a big commitment, as Cara normally grants support for two or three years as standard, sometimes even more. UK universities, however, have risen to the challenge, offering places, bursaries, and in-kind support for Cara Fellowships in 2017 worth nearly £6 m, up from £0.6 m in 2013 – a ten-fold increase in support in just four years, with strong support continuing in 2018. Cara also works with a small but growing number of universities abroad and had successful placements in 2017–18, with generous host university support, in Canada, Australia, France, Germany, Malaysia, Hong Kong, and Ethiopia (ICARDA).

As a result of this support, Cara has been able in recent years to increase significantly the number of academics it could get to safety. In 2017, Cara paid out over £1,350,000 on Fellowship awards (2016: £915,000) and committed over £583,000 more for disbursement in the following year (2016: £419,000). As of August 2018, Cara was providing support to over 290 academics (2017: 250; 2016: 160; 2015: 62), with some 350 dependants, from 28 countries, with some 70 further cases currently being taken forward with potential hosts.

At the same time, Cara never forgets that each Fellowship Programme 'case' involves an individual person, often with a family as well, going through a very stressful experience. For anyone who has not had the experience, it is hard to imagine how difficult it must be to leave behind one's home, family, friends, and career, and to face all the difficulties of settling in a new place and working in a foreign language. Cara staff keep in close touch with the applicants throughout the process of securing them a placement, answering their questions, and keeping them up to date with what can seem a mysterious and complex process. Once everything is in place, Cara makes all their travel arrangements and also arranges for those who come to the UK – the great majority – to visit the Cara offices soon after their arrival here, so everyone can finally all meet face-to-face. This is often a joyful occasion, with partners and children coming along too, and Cara staff see many Cara Fellows again as they travel around the country in the course of a year and can see the progress they are making and deal quickly with any problems that arise. Many go on to achieve good results in tough exams, while others make really important contributions as active members of advanced research teams.

Cara's relationship with its Fellows at universities outside the UK is inevitably less close, so Cara relies even more on the university hosts. Fortunately, Cara's partners around the world recognise the challenges that the Fellows will face and do their best to make everything as easy and welcoming as possible. Some things, of course, cannot easily be changed, as one Cara Fellow from the Middle East found in Canada: 'Unfortunately, I came in December when the snow was everywhere. The snowing weather had continued for three months.' But he was soon feeling more settled:

> I liked the underground markets, shops, and life. I liked the population diversity, multi cultures, nations, and languages. This mix, and the secure life gave me a feeling of safety. I felt like I am not foreign at all, but a part of this diversity. ... Professors, staff and students were like a small family, and they still are.

Two Cara Fellows in Australia commented similarly on how important a warm welcome can be:

> People are friendly, the city is vibrant and more importantly the country is kids-friendly. ... Through its staff and my supervisor, all were kind, helpful and more importantly smiling.
>
> The first few months were quite challenging, especially as I had to start building my network of friends and colleagues from scratch. Sorting out accommodation was particularly hard. But the community at my university was very welcoming. As I started to get my bearing around campus, I started feeling more at home.

Good working conditions can make up for a lot too:

> 'I remember being struck by the beauty and sophistication of the university's library and its automated retrieval system. I was told that the university contains more than 1.5 million items, which were all within any student's fingertips!'

A Cara Fellow in Malaysia also found that a friendly welcome made up for a lot:

> I faced some difficulties, but with good will and cooperation of the international office in my university I could overcome these. I have got many benefits in my new life, I have met professional scientists from different cultures and I have learned from their experience, especially from China, India, Pakistan and so on.

For most, returning home is the driving ambition, and each year some manage to do so. Over the past year, a few have even begun to return to Syria; despite all the problems there, some see a chance of picking up the threads of a normal life again. Elsewhere in the region too, the expulsion of 'ISIS' from most of the territory it so recently controlled has made it possible for people to take the first steps back to more normal life.

3. Cara's regional programmes

Regional initiatives allow Cara to provide innovative and effective support to academics who are working on in their country despite the risks or who have been forced into exile nearby.

In response to the violence that followed the 2003 coalition invasion of Iraq, Cara established its first regional programme, its Iraq Programme (2006–2012). Run through Cara's office in Amman, Jordan, this provided a wide range of co-operation activities designed to help rebuild Iraqi research and teaching capacities by bringing academics in Iraq together with those in Jordan and elsewhere, and with their counterparts in the UK. In particular, over seventy academics from sixteen UK and eleven Iraqi institutions came together within the framework of the Iraq Research Fellowship Programme (2009–2012) to deliver high-quality research outcomes, which influenced policy and practice within Iraqi ministries, the UN, and international agencies responding to the crisis, and promoted long-term collaborations. Cara also supported regional 'communities of interest' around themes of regional relevance, with a particular focus on the often-neglected social sciences, including gender issues and so forth.

Cara's second regional programme, its Zimbabwe Programme, was launched in 2009 in response to a marked increase in the number of academics fleeing Zimbabwe amid reports of a dramatic decline in the quality of higher education. The programme offered grants and fellowships to pay for vital equipment and supplies, and in 2012 established a 'Virtual Lecture Hall' at the University of Zimbabwe. This made it possible for Zimbabwean academics in exile and others to connect in real time with the colleges and faculties of health and veterinary sciences, to plug knowledge gaps identified by the relevant university deans, to improve standards of teaching and research, and to facilitate increased networking and collaboration. In response to demand, a second mobile system was installed in October 2013.

Drawing on this experience, in 2016 Cara launched its regionally based Syria Programme to provide support to academics affected by the Syria crisis. Most Syrian academics in exile, in Turkey, Lebanon, or elsewhere, intend to return to Syria when they can, but for now they urgently need opportunities to work and to continue to grow professionally through a very difficult time, so they will be able to help rebuild a better system of higher education when they do go back.

In the 2016 – 17 'pilot phase', with the active participation of UK, Turkish, and other universities, and many individual academics working on a *pro bono* basis, Cara organised workshops in Turkey on English for Academic Purposes (EAP) and Academic Skills Development (ASD) to lay the foundations for future research collaborations. The first Syria Programme Fellows were hosted by UK universities on short-term research incubation visits, and UK and Syrian academics and others worked together on research to help establish the true state of higher education in Syria, before and since 2011, to get a better sense of how exiled Syrian academics could be helped to prepare to return, when it is safe to do so.

Following the successful conclusion of the pilot phase, a much bigger second phase of the programme was launched in late 2017. This eighteen-month phase builds on the four 'activity strands' of the pilot programme – EAP, ASD, Research Incubation Visits, and a Cara-Commissioned Research Project – supplemented by a new fifth strand, a research funding initiative. This will offer small grants as seed-corn funding, followed by an 'open call' for research proposals of relevance to Syria or to Syrian refugee communities. Participating Syrian academics will need to be core research team members, working in partnership with experienced academics in posts in universities of international repute. The aim of the Cara Syria Programme is to nurture important discipline clusters, while allowing Syrian colleagues to develop an invaluable international resource on which to draw in the task of rebuilding higher education in Syria. The second phase is placing particular emphasis on the publishing of research as essential to a successful academic career.

4. Partnerships

Cara is the only organisation of its type in Europe but works with a wide range of like-minded international partners, including in particular its two US counterparts, the Scholars at Risk Network and the Institute of International Education's Scholar Rescue Fund, to help individual academics who are at risk and to support higher education in times of crisis. In 2017, Cara was again re-elected as Vice-Chair of the New York-based Global Coalition to Protect Education from Attack (GCPEA), a grouping of NGOs and UN agencies formed in 2010 to carry out research, monitoring, and advocacy to highlight the problem of targeted attacks on education at all levels, particularly during armed conflict. The Coalition's biggest single achievement so far has been the launch in 2013 of what became known as the *Draft Lucens Guidelines* for protecting schools and universities from military use during armed conflict. These ideas were subsequently developed under the leadership of Norway and Argentina into the *Safe Schools Declaration.* Work to persuade more countries to adopt the Declaration and accompanying Guidelines has continued throughout 2017 and 2018. By August 2018, seventy-nine states – well over one-third of the total UN membership and including a clear majority of NATO and EU states – had adopted both documents, with the UK and Germany both finally signing up in 2018. This process is already making, and will continue to make, a real difference to those caught up in conflict. Cara also worked with GCPEA partners in the preparation of *Education under Attack 2018*, the latest in a series of four yearly reviews of attacks on education around the world, at all levels, which was released in May 2018.

Cara has been delighted also, in recent years, to have had the opportunity to work with new initiatives in France and Germany. The Philipp Schwartz Initiative was launched in 2015 by the Alexander von Humboldt Foundation with backing from the German Foreign Ministry and other German foundations, and helps at-risk academics to find places at German universities. Cara has supported fourteen successful applications in the first three rounds, and a number of additional applications in the fourth round, which closed in May 2018. In November 2017, Cara took part in a meeting in Paris of the Programme d'aide à l'Accueil en Urgence des Scientifiques en Exil (PAUSE), which was established in January 2017 to award stimulus funding to higher education establishments and public research organisations in France that plan to host scientists at risk. Cara will continue its engagement with both organisations in 2018–19.

5. Conclusion

Eighty-five years since Cara was established, as the AAC and later the SPSL, its work is, sadly, still needed. The 'powers which threaten to suppress intellectual and individual freedom', about which Einstein spoke in 1933, are as active as ever. The threat to individual academics and to the precious knowledge which they carry in their heads – the intellectual and cultural capital of their societies – is still very real. Organisations such as Cara, and the many individuals who support them by personal donations and through their pro bono contributions to Cara programmes, cannot stop wars or overthrow tyrants. But they can help to ensure that, when the repression and fighting stop and sanity returns and rebuilding can start, the best-qualified people from those societies – those with 'exceptional abilities, exceptionally trained' – will be able to return and to help with the reconstruction of safer, better societies.

Bibliography

Beveridge, W. H. (1959): A Defence of Free Learning. London: Oxford University Press.
Einstein, A. (1933): Science and Civilization. In: Royal Albert Hall Programme. October 3, 1933. www.cara.ngo/wp-content/uploads/2016/11/Einstein-Speech-Albert-Hall-331003.pdf.
Founding Statement of the Academic Assistance Council (1933): London. May 22, 1933. www.cara.ngo/wp-content/uploads/2015/06/Cara-Founding-Statement.pdf.
Rutherford, E. (1936): The Society for the Protection of Science and Learning. In: Science 83(2155), 372.
Science and Learning in Distress (1938): In: Nature 142(3607), 1051.
Who we are: Our history (2018): In: Cara: A lifeline to academics at risk. https://www.cara.ngo/who-we-are/our-history/.

Jason Branford, André Grahle, Jan-Christoph Heilinger, Dennis Kalde, Max Muth, Eva Maria Parisi, Paula-Irene Villa, Verina Wild*

Cyberhate against academics

Abstract: Hate speech is endemic in digital space, and it does not spare academia. Especially scholars working in fields prone to political debate – from migration to climate change, from gender to refugee integration, and many more topics – find themselves increasingly attacked. With this chapter, we hope to raise awareness for the increasingly prevalent phenomenon of cyberhate targeting academics. Our intention is to shed light on some of its harmful effects, and, by providing some conceptual analysis, to contribute to individual and organisational prevention and coping strategies. We conclude that guarding against cyberhate is now part of academics' and their institutions' responsibility.

1. Introduction

Hate speech is endemic in digital space, and it does not spare academia. Especially scholars working in fields prone to political debate – from migration to climate change, from human rights to social inequality, from bioethics to vaccines, from sexualities to gender, and many more topics – find themselves increasingly attacked.[1] Some scholars and academic organisations have realised that cyberhate against academics is becoming a significant problem and are beginning to develop helpful defence strategies (e.g., AAUP 2017; Dutt-Ballerstadt 2018; Ferber 2018; Flaherty 2017; Grollman 2015; Wray et al. 2016).

With this chapter we hope to raise awareness of the increasingly prevalent phenomenon of cyberhate targeting academics.[2] Our intention is to shed light on some of its harmful effects, and, by providing some conceptual analysis, to contribute to individual and organisational coping strategies.

* equal contribution by each author

1 See for example Campbell (2017), who describes her experiences as an attacked ethnographer. Further semi-systematic accounts of recent attacks, such as 'cyberbullying' of academics especially in the USA, are discussed in Flaherty (2017).

2 A rather detailed analysis of the situation in the USA can be found in Ferber (2018). We are writing from the perspective of academics in a European democratic society. We are aware that cyberhate happens in many other places too, but we are not well-equipped to describe or evaluate the effects there.

https://doi.org/10.1515/9783110628746-015

Cyberhate against academics and accompanying practices such as cyberbullying or trolling are intimately linked to broader social developments and phenomena such as the general dynamics of online hate speech and new authoritarian movements, anti-Semitism, racism, sexism, anti-genderism, and anti-intellectualism (Hark/Villa 2015; Assimakopoulos et al. 2017; Stanley 2018b; Kuhar/Paternotte 2017). The further fact of universities falling under increasing economic and entrepreneurial pressures compounds the issue (Slaughter/Rhodes 2004; Jessop 2018). Even if this chapter can only briefly gesture towards this complex interplay, we would want to stress that the 'corporate university' model carries the risk of transforming scholars into output-oriented service-providers who are evaluated according to other than academic standards. The ethos of the marketplace includes, or maybe only reinforces, into academia the logic of popular demand, which is closely linked to populist media dynamics.

Matters are further complicated by the very limited specific conceptual or empirical research on cyberhate against academics presently available. The topic is often presented in narrative forms, field reports, in blog posts, or in journalism. In a similar vein, some parts of this chapter are also motivated by personal experiences. We think that these experiences – that unwillingly made some of us 'knowers' – helped us to better understand the phenomenon and its destructive and dangerous dimensions. Being knowers, and sharing knowledge and experiences, can have an empowering effect in building connections to others; it can also help build bridges to those who want or may need to understand without having had these experiences. Furthermore, as knowers we hope we are equipped to identify, promote, or develop constructive ways forward. We want this chapter to be instrumental in understanding the situation we live and work in and in preparing ourselves better for the matter of facts.

We begin this chapter by explaining the concept of cyberhate and arguing why it has to be taken seriously. We shall then explore cyberhate as a practice attacking academics and look at the more specific harm both to the individual scholar, as well as to universities and society at large. Finally, we introduce a few preliminary ideas on how academics and academic institutions should deal with cyberhate attacks.

2. The emerging phenomenon of cyberhate

The emergence of web 2.0 technology gave rise to a comprehensive and complex phenomenon of 'mass self-communication' (Castells 2007), most notably an increase of opportunities for individuals and groups to produce, access, and communicate information as private individuals. For most people, the advantages of this step in human history seem undeniable. Yet, as Nan Lin (1999) anticipated nearly two decades ago, despite the Internet's potential for facilitating the utilisation and accumulation of social capital, new 'tensions, conflicts, violence, competition, and coordination issues' (ibid., 237) arise. Today we see that web-based communication – specifically communication in social media – is often not characterised by respectful conduct, or even a spirit of mutual inclusion, but rather manifests strong and collective tendencies towards social exclusion and morally problematic conflict behaviour, including abusive commentary, and punctual or systematic spreading of misinformation about individuals and certain social groups (Jane 2014 and 2015; Whittaker/Kowalski 2014; Perry/Olsson 2009; Näsi et al. 2015).

In this chapter, we focus on one particularly regrettable problem also affecting academics: *cyberhate*. Cyberhate refers to a tendency of groups and individuals to express hateful sentiments and convictions targeting other groups and individuals, by way of using any textual, video-, or photographic means of communication available on the Internet.[3] Activities of cyberhate can be pursued through websites, social networks, dating sites, blogs, online games, messengers, and e-mail (cf. Anti-Defamation League 2010). Cyberhate is morally problematic for a number of reasons: it can establish forms of discrimination, abuse, intimidation, marginalizing, othering, dehumanisation, and humiliation.

Typically, haters have the *intention* of harming the other group or person and of exhibiting them as a viable object for further attacks, including physical attacks in the 'non-virtual' world. Yet we allow for the possibility of people *unintentionally* engaging in cyberhate, by communicating carelessly in ways that use expressions that are inherently abusive and exhibit others as a viable target of further attacks.

Cyberhate can be pursued by single individuals. More typically, however, cyberhate has a *movement character*. The phenomenon of hating publicly, thereby exhibiting one's target, simultaneously calls on other haters' attention, *encouraging* them to become active against the same or similar targets as well. Moreover, the collective activity of hating *together* can intensify the force of hate and the decisiveness of haters to cause damage to their targets. To a large extent, cyberhate is also a phenomenon of *mutual intoxication*.

---

3 Cyberhate is, as we see it, a specific form of the more general phenomenon of hate speech and related crimes. These have been extensively studied in a range of disciplines, e.g., legal studies, sociology, history, and philosophy. Cyberhate is, as we understand it, a mediawise specific variation of harmful articulations of hatred against groups or individuals, mainly along lines of social differences such as gender, sexuality, 'race', age, etc. Cf. Chakraborti and Garland 2015.

The tendencies of exhibition, mutual intoxication, and reflective attenuation, are irreducibly social phenomena. The same observation holds regarding the provision of *target selection criteria* and *semantic content* of cyberhate: typically, *whom* to hate and *what* to hate the target *for* are ideologically informed and constrained. Membership in some social groups constituted by ethnicity, 'race', religion, gender, political or sexual orientation, etc., whether perceived or self-identified, significantly increases the risk of becoming a target.[4] This strongly suggests that target selection criteria cannot be random or reduced to individual preferences, but are provided by ideologies of wider social significance. In other words, what guides cyberhaters (individuals or groups) in selecting their targets, are social practices, including properly institutionalised practices, but also ideologies, patterns of emotions, biases, and prejudices that are constituted historically. Various forms of sexism and racism, anti-Semitism, Orientalism, classism, anti-intellectualism, anti-communism, etc. are intersecting kinds of such ideologies. As to the semantic content of expressions of cyberhate, social practices, too, figure as the main resource of cyberhaters. Hate expressed against certain religious groups, for instance, frequently makes use of stereotypes that are not spontaneously invented, but are inextricably linked to historically established imaginaries that enjoy broader social acceptance in many, specifically Western, societies.

Finally, the wider social context in which cyberhate takes place is relevant also to the question of what, given the general ideological background conditions, *initiates* incidences or movements of cyberhate – that is, other than another instance of cyberhate. As it turns out, initiating causes are often linked to certain ideologically received social events in 'the real world'. So for instance, in times of increased refugee arrival being predominantly perceived and publicly represented from a distinctively ideological perspective, through discourse and pictures that come with racist and sexist assumptions, certain groups are rendered even more vulnerable to cyberhate than they already are. It seems as if the event and its ideological mode of presentation in many places, including parts of the mainstream media, encourages groups and individuals to come forward with their own hate online. This can take strategic, even organised forms. Reports from several NGOs (cf. Anti-Defamation League 2018; Kreißel et al. 2018) confirm this impression.

4 There is much evidence for this regarding (homo-)sexuality, gender (women), migrational status, 'race' (non-white), etc. Cf. the online library at the International Network for Hate Studies, http://www.internationalhatestudies.com/publications/.

In the light of these preliminary reflections, it comes as no surprise that most established institutions dealing with cyberhate today avoid unnecessary general accounts of the phenomenon. Rather, they attempt to capture more directly the social embeddedness of cyberhate by pointing at certain groups that are currently the most vulnerable in becoming targets of cyberhate. The International Network Against Cyber Hate (INACH), for instance, takes cyberhate to consist in discriminatory or defamatory statements aimed at people because of their (perceived) "race, ethnicity, language, nationality, skin colour, religious beliefs or lack thereof, gender, gender identity, sex, sexual orientation, political beliefs, social status, property, birth, age, mental health, disability, disease" (INACH 2018). While INACH's list is rather extensive, the Anti-Defamation League applies a slightly more narrow focus, describing online hate in relation to "anti-Semitism, anti-Muslim bigotry, racism, homophobia, misogyny, xenophobia", but also mentions "other forms of hate, prejudice and bigotry" (Anti-Defamation League 2018).

Linking cyberhate to specific groups is supported by our initial reflections on the relation between source ideologies and particular incidences of cyberhate. We believe, however, that lists should be kept open and be subject to possible augmentation. This chapter can be read as a plea for augmentation, as it focuses on the case of cyberhate *against academic*s in an age of increased anti-intellectualism, minding of course that this field covers many intersections, as female academics, black academics and academics of colour, academics with working-class backgrounds, leftist academics, etc., can face different kinds and dimensions of cyberhate.

3. Cyberhate in society

The aggressive and active nature of cyberhate has the potential to inflict drastic social damages.[5] The movement character of cyberhate illuminates the manner in which it may come to *infect* societal interaction writ large. Broadly speaking, the spread of cyberhate risks eroding, altering, or destroying social norms regarding public behaviour, attitudes of democratic culture, and the value of reason and scientific inquiry.[6] What is at stake is a specific form of society which promotes and displays particular kinds of values and norms that have been

5 The harms to the individual, specifically individual academics, will be discussed below.

6 We suggest that the phenomenon of cyberhate should itself be understood as an effect of specific forms of social erosion – or what Buchanan and Powell (2018, ch.7) call 'moral regression' – that can increasingly be witnessed in democratic societies.

the hallmark of liberal democracies (e.g., inclusion, tolerance, equality, and public reason).

The frequency and the effects of cyberhate contribute to its spread and normalisation. It is often either picked up by others and imitated, applauded, or ignored rather than challenged. People are quick to collectively adopt behaviours they believe are accepted by others, giving cyberhate what was noted above as a *movement character.* Subsequently, communities tied together by hateful and oppressive convictions may develop and possibly have a snowball effect on other social groups. For example, reports following the election of leading political figures who openly vilified particular social groups and incited hatred towards them in their campaigns, as well as those following the "Brexit" vote where its proponents employed hate rhetoric against immigrants leading up to the vote, show how these incidents produced a 'new normal' that has led to further increases in hate speech and hate crimes (Crandall et al. 2018; Okeowo 2016; Kenyon 2016; Mindock 2017).

Ishani Maitra and Mary Kate McGowan (2012, 6) identify four ways in which 'consequential harms' can follow from hate speech: (1) it helps persuade witnesses to believe negative stereotypes that lead them to engage in other harmful conduct; (2) it shapes, over time, the preferences of witnesses so that negative stereotypes become more persuasive to them; (3) it conditions and alters the social environment in a way that normalises (often unconsciously) the expression of negative stereotypes and subsequent discrimination of those persons; (4) it ultimately can lead to witnesses imitating the hateful behaviour. Consequently, cyberhate can, over time, incite a social climate of boundaries and exclusion, fearmongering, intolerance, and the increasingly accepted use of hate rhetoric. Such a climate filled with distrust and animosity is, therefore, unstable and prone to violence (Brown et al. 2018).

The *mutual intoxication* may breed situations whereby many members of society are brought into the folds of hate. Even those firmly against hateful action may find themselves drawn into inciting hate themselves against the original haters merely to defend themselves and, as such, become entangled in spirals of hate that stem from the first instance. In fact, this is one of the aims of cyberhate which follows from the tactic of utilising emotional bait to evoke the anger of targets, enabling them to argue that the original hate was justified. This tactic can undermine the debate culture by misdirecting the focus of disagreement, by simplifying or by distorting the facts of the debate to discredit the target.[7]

---

7 The 'poisoning of debate culture' whereby force comes to prevail over reason is a population-

The culture of hate runs contrary to that of enlightened liberal democratic culture (Baer 2018). Jeremy Waldron emphasises this and argues that hate and discrimination undermines the 'assurance that every community member is entitled to; namely, that they may go about their business unimpeded by assaults on their social standing, their entitlement to be treated as equals, and their dignity' (2012, 5). Consequently, the social harms of cyberhate can ultimately lead to the realisation of unenlightenment and, as such, the destruction of civilised society, as Waldron puts it. It is for this reason that the concern over the harms of hate speech is not stymied merely by protecting victims of hate from sporadic wounds but, rather, by 'securing, in a systematic fashion, a particular aspect of social peace and civic order under justice' (ibid., 103–104).

4. Cyberhate against academics: anti-intellectualism

Quantitative data on cyberhate against academics is scarce. As stated above, our considerations on cyberhate in academia are based mostly on individual reflections found in blog posts. Some of the individual cases testify to the detrimental effect of cyberhate on the lives of the scholars (Ferber 2018). One exemplary experience is described in a 2018 blog post, written by a professor of cognitive and education psychology from a university in the United States (Cuevas 2018). His story began with an online discussion of an article about the role of the Electoral College after the 2016 presidential election. He referenced some right-wing comments in these discussions and was verbally attacked by a reader for his views. After a brief exchange and the decision to block the reader, the professor experienced several orchestrated hate waves against him. A dreadful litany of attacks then followed on social media, through e-mail and phone calls, and via the website ratemyprofessors.com from an invisible mob on the web involving students and their parents. This created a major issue for the university administration and for some politicians. He writes:

> Their stated goal was to see that I was fired. This, apparently, was the type of opportunity they relished: find a person to harass, maybe by drawing him or her into a political argument, locate any information they could find online, and then coordinate attacks in an attempt to damage the person as much as possible. (ibid., 26)

---

level harm that cannot be overstated and is one of the primary reasons for focusing on the impacts of cyberhate on academics.

He also points out that

> among many on the right there is a palpable hostility toward the basic concept of higher education, as if college attendance made one part of a liberal conspiracy, and professors have come to be viewed as the embodiment of what many resent in American culture: political correctness, diversity, willingness to look to science for answers, secularism, feminism, intellectualism, socialism, and a host of other 'isms'. (ibid., 24–25)

Other academics have written about similar experiences and note a general tendency in some parts of the population to view education and research in negative terms (Pew Research Center 2017). The American Association of University Professors has acknowledged that attacks on academics are a serious problem and has issued a statement (AAUP 2017). Other academic associations, including the American Philosophical Association (APA 2016), have also issued statements regarding bullying of and hate speech against scholars. At some universities in Europe similar discussions are taking place.[8]

While general anti-academic and anti-intellectual stances have a long history in all sorts of populisms, and are also core to well-established mainstream conservatism (cf. Blakely 2017 for the US case), it seems that those who are more active and more visible in presenting their research do expose themselves to a higher degree of vulnerability (Kaakinen et al. 2018). Incidences of cyberhate can be more prevalent among academics who also belong to one or more excluded groups, for example in relation to ethnicity, gender, or religious minorities. Those working in politically charged disciplines or on politically contested topics are more vulnerable to attacks (Ferber 2018). Views that were until recently considered rather uncontroversial, such as those defending human rights or calling for higher environmental standards, are increasingly targeted by hate speech. While disagreement and dissent are unavoidable and, in fact, essential in the pursuit of knowledge about matters not yet settled, and while science is always also about debate regarding concepts, methods, normative perspectives, etc.,

8 The recent case of the Hungarian government undermining the constitutional right of academic freedom by removing the two master's degrees in Gender Studies from the list of accredited subjects – without any professional or academic review – is a rather extreme example of institutional anti-intellectualism paired with authoritarian and illiberal policies. The meagre explanation given to the measure was that Gender Studies did not seem to generate employability and were a danger for traditional family and moral values. Besides this being wrong in an objective sense, such reasoning shows a clear anti-intellectual and anti-academic stance. University degrees and curricula are seen as market-driven assets, not as knowledge- and research-related forms. Cf. from the many protest notes and media comments http://hungarianspectrum.org/2018/11/14/information-strike-at-elte-for-gender-studies/.

there are acceptable and established methods for doing so. The public waves of hate and personal attacks towards those whose research might question ideological common sense or specific political views have nothing to do with legitimate disagreement and debate. On the contrary, they subvert and undermine them, and multiple harms can follow, not only for the individual but also for the population more broadly.

Now, above we have argued that target selection criteria employed by cyberhaters are unlikely to be random, but tend to be provided by ideologies of wider social significance. An interesting hypothesis about why academics are attacked *as academics* is that anti-intellectualism as an ideology is on the rise again. Anti-intellectualism can be understood to be a general disregard or willingness to attack those "who seek to show the truth in its full complexity" (Stanley 2018b). Jason Stanley (2018a, 64 f.) looks at anti-intellectualism as essential to fascist politics which, as he reminds us, 'seeks to undermine public discourse by attacking and devaluing education, expertise, and language.'

Actually, anti-intellectualism is part of all sorts of illiberal, fundamentalist, or populist political dynamics. As Peters (2018) works out in a research overview, there are right- and left-wing anti-intellectual positions, there are those motivated by religion or, on the contrary, by dogmatic positivists, etc. Furthermore, the production of so-called 'alternative facts' is a growing problem because where alternative facts are taken seriously, earnest academics, with their efforts to identify the truth about complex issues, will be presented as naive, ignorant, or even ideologically biased.

> The particular character of anti-intellectualism in the era of post-truth politics is associated with 'strongman politics', anti-immigration sentiments, anti-globalization and local protectionism, anti-women, anti-environment and a kind of national populism that swings on emotion and belief rather than fact, reason or argument. (Peters 2018, 6)

Stanley (2018a, 85 ff.) cites various cases of state and non-state actors currently pursuing anti-intellectual agendas, from the influential American right-wing radio host Rush Limbaugh's frequent condemnations of academia and science to the Hungarian president Viktor Orbán's drastic measures against schools and universities in an attempt to redefine the purpose of education. During the writing of this paper, for example, the Orbán regime has abolished Gender Studies as an academic discipline in Hungarian universities.[9] The discipline has been criticised by government members as undermining 'the foundations

9 For the relation between anti-genderism, right-wing populism, and cyberhate see Hark/Villa (2015) for the German case, and Harsin (2018) for the French case.

of the Christian family' and not being relevant for the labour market (ZEIT Online 2018). Such acts of state repression come with an additional top-down pressure on ordinary citizens to follow. Cyberspace provides an easy outlet for those who endorse such views – for whatever reasons.

While it is important and timely to look at anti-intellectualism as an element of populist politics, we also believe that anti-intellectualism starts to emerge before it becomes part of such politics. Most importantly, the populist ideology can confine itself to cultivating disregard for the necessity of seeking to explore the complexities of facts and norms. Naika Foroutan (Dernbach 2018) has studied German political contexts that would think of themselves as liberal and clearly distance themselves from the far-right hate against intellectuals and academics. She describes anti-intellectualism as an anti-elitist attitude currently cultivated in social contexts that reaches clearly beyond far-right politics,[10] which includes disregard for intelligence and usage of academic language. While it may be used to convince people of how 'down to earth' they are, it actually serves to smother the kind of critical reflection needed to deliver societal progress. In general, all sorts of populisms and illiberal political articulations can adhere and promote anti-intellectual positions since the latter work especially well within antagonist political dynamics, that is, such operating in dualistic us/them, we/they, people/elite, common sense/counter-intuitive, reasonable/radical, etc.

In light of the Hungarian case regarding Gender Studies, but also beyond it, it seems sound to suggest that the anti-intellectualism coming with the academic capitalism is an additional force in rendering academics vulnerable to cyberhate. By way of powerful voices publicly moralizing about individuals' failure to care for their own, the latter are exposed as a potential target of social disdain, which, again, can be expressed through cyberhate with the lowest possible costs. Academics and intellectuals whose projects are hardly commodifiable and require public funding and support are therefore at greater risk of being targeted or silenced. Moreover, it is no surprise, therefore, that those academics working in the humanities or social sciences, areas often deemed 'useless' or a pure luxury, are vulnerable when they come to the defence of groups such as refugees.

---

10 In fact, the social scientist Naika Foroutan describes this anti-intellectual attitude in terms of a social tendency that she accuses the moderate-left German Social Democratic Party (SPD) to be too welcoming of (Dernbach 2018).

5. Harmful effects for the individual scholar

Besides possibly eroding, altering, and destroying the accepted norms of liberal democracies in defence of individuals' dignity and equal status, cyberhate can have a detrimental impact on the lives of individual scholars.[11] We focus on two dimensions regarding the impact of cyberhate on individual academics: first, how it affects their lives *as private persons*; and second, the way in which it undermines their lives *as scholars* pursuing academic projects.[12]

Consider how cyberhate can make its targets experience a wide range of negative emotions such as fear, anxiety, distress, isolation, self-alienation, and shame (see e.g., Campbell 2017). These effects are often immediate and emerge as a result of a bombardment of insults and threats of violence against themselves or people close to them (Williams/Pearson 2016). The initial reaction can alter and is likely to translate into long-term consequences. Targeted individuals may become progressively aware of their own vulnerability: they may not solely feel threatened in the acute moment when receiving attacks, but also start to identify themselves in a generalised and lasting way as targets of possible harm. This may shape individuals' perceptions of themselves and make them question and/or regret the choices and behaviours that exposed them to harm, such as sharing information, pictures of themselves, or work in progress online. They may feel that they themselves and not their aggressors bear responsibility for what is happening to their life. Such feelings of guilt and regret can compromise the victims' self-esteem, which may already be weakened by virtual insults endured, insults that have taken aim also on physical appearance, ethnic origin, religious beliefs, linguistic proficiency, etc. This may compromise someone's capacity to interact with others without fear and mistrust.

Beyond the private is the professional life, and cyberhate against academics threatens to undermine their reputation both in society and in academia. By collecting, distorting, and spreading information on their targets with the intent to undermine, ridicule, and embarrass them publicly, cyberhaters undermine academics' *social and professional standing* (Waldron 2012, 5). As Waldron empha-

11 Here, the idea that hate speech harms the individuals who perpetuate it is not explored. Cf. Matsuda et al. (1993, 92–93) who argue that 'bigotry harms the individuals who harbor it by reinforcing rigid thinking, thereby dulling their moral and social senses and possibly leading to a "mildly ... paranoid" mentality.'

12 Although this distinction might be helpful to understand the different types of harm cyberhate might cause to persons, it is not clear-cut, as academics indivisibly are private persons and professionals.

sises, cyberhaters 'besmirch' the basics of academics' reputation 'by associating ascriptive characteristics like ethnicity, or race, or religion with conduct or attributes that should disqualify someone from being treated as a member of society in good standing' (ibid., 5).

These harms are not limited to academics – they can affect other targeted individuals as well. Perhaps a more distinctive harm in relation to academic work is the way in which the attacks threaten the continuation of academic research as an endeavour connected with one's identity and giving meaning and purpose to one's life (cf. Betzler 2013, 112). By threatening them because of their research, cyberhate may have the effect of forcing academics to question their approaches, withdraw from public and private debates, and to stop researching, publishing, and commenting on topics that could expose them to further hate.[13]

Additionally, silencing can be a harm for academics when accompanied by victim blaming. When cyberhate stops academics from expressing themselves as scholars, some become exposed to unjustified (self) blame for 'having let themselves being silenced' or 'being weak', as if the targets of hate, as opposed to the haters, should be blamed.

6. Undermining academia

The previous sections have raised the general problem of silencing and the harmful effects of cyberhate on academics as individuals. The harms against academia and academic research that result from silencing require further exploration, as well. Ideally, science and academic research can be understood as being a collective pursuit for truth and knowledge through questions that directly or indirectly matter to human lives (Kitcher 2001). We recognise that this is the ideal and not always the reality, but this is precisely why we need to keep asking which practices support or damage the endeavour.

If certain views defended by scholars are systematically attacked by waves of cyberhate, the possibly resulting silencing of these views can lead to a significant epistemic distortion that must be considered problematic: As raised above in the mentioning of anti-intellectualism, cyberhate against academics can be an instance of 'bullying away' intellectual thinking and results of re-

13 In a study of 5050 participants in Norway researchers found that 7.2 per cent had received hate messages on social media (more immigrants than national citizens). A quarter of those who received hate speech also experienced the feeling of having been 'silenced', with women three times more likely than men to be silenced (Fladmoe/Nadim 2017).

search. It can create a hostile environment which dissuades further such academic research, but also undermines rational debate and methodological, systematic inquiry generally. Such damage goes well beyond the university as such.

In no way should our focus on academia here be misunderstood as diminishing the gravity of the harms or impact of silencing on other individuals and groups. Generally speaking, the social harms of silencing are the same whether an individual is an academic or not – the problems of a population which is too fearful to resist oppression or raise their voices in the name of humanity are clear. However, given the topic of this paper, we explore in somewhat more detail the specific nature of academics in relation to society.

Academics – especially those working on social issues – often play an important social and civic role.[14] Martin (1984, 19) calls their work 'social action', and it fundamentally involves informing social debates and policy making.[15] Downs and Manion (2004) go further in highlighting the manner in which much academic work serves as either social critic or social informer. Specifically, they explain that the kind of work in which some academics engage, what they label 'sites of activism', produces knowledge that 'informs progressive social change.'[16] This is one of the main arguments for the protection of academic freedom and tenure (Blessinger/de Wit 2018).

Researchers might act as social *critics*: They often do so since research is exactly a form of questioning common sense or political ideologies in a methodologically controlled manner. Thus, academics have the tools for informing policies or debates aimed at improving social conditions. When targeting

---

14 Obviously, the role academics should or should not play in modern, highly differentiated democratic societies is much disputed. While some may argue, that since doing research is invariably social practice and since such practices are invariably constituted by normative textures and frames impregnated by political dynamics such as inequality or dominance, others defend the genuinely modern differentiation between distinct subsystems such as economy, politics, research, arts, etc. In our view, there is no simple and unambiguous position on this issue. Rather, we consider both ethics and critical reflexivity crucial aspects of any academic activity. At the same time, we consider academic activities and political activism to be actually distinct. They may be related and mutually informed, but we do see a risk in collapsing both logics (cf. Couture 2017; Flood/Martin/Dreher 2013).

15 Such capacity derives from academics' being 'trained and experienced in [cutting] to the root of problems.' Further, academic freedom should enable 'unfettered creative thinking and bold experimentation towards the solution of social problems'. Finally, they are supposed to be 'self-reflective, and hence able to critically examine their own ideas and actions' (Martin 1984, 19).

16 Several valuable publications exist for those who seek to heighten the social impact of their work or are interested in how academic work can instigate change (cf. Collins 2013; Badgett 2015).

academics, cyberhate threatens the ability for teachers and researchers to carry out this intellectual endeavour.

The Professors Watchlist is a particularly striking example of a tool utilised for publically targeting academics. These kinds of sites support the normalisation of shaming, defaming, and persecuting certain scholars. In this particular case, it targets mostly academics who are critical of conservative thinking and, to quote their mission statement, 'advance leftist propaganda in the classroom' (Professor Watchlist 2018), but defamation against academics holding other views is, of course, equally problematic. George Yancy, whose powerful *New York Times* essay was a response to him being placed on the list, argues that such tools of oppression can 'have the impact of the philosopher Jeremy Bentham's Panopticon – a theoretical prison designed to create a form of self-censorship among those imprisoned.' In line with our description of silencing, this list and other similar methods can 'install forms of psychological self-policing to eliminate thoughts, pedagogical approaches and theoretical orientations that it defines as subversive' (Yancy 2016).

7. Responding to cyberhate against academics

The growing prevalence of cyberhate against academics is worrying. We want to end this chapter with a brief, more practical and constructive outlook about possible individual and institutional responses to cyberhate and ways of preventing it or limiting the damage it causes. We leave untackled the broader, moral and political question as to whether hate speech itself should be sanctioned by the state, or whether the state should also be able to sanction Internet companies – especially social media companies – if they do not effectively prevent hate speech on their platforms. By focusing on cyberhate against academics, we look at what those scholars could do in response whose primary institutional context is the university. There are, we believe, in fact various ways for scholars to prevent harmful effects of cyberhate.

In the event of an attack there are ways to support targeted colleagues or oneself. One of the most detailed overviews of advice is included in Eric Anthony Grollman's essay 'Scholars under Attack' (2015). Grollman distinguishes three levels: 1) Individual Level strategies: Here he gives detailed advice what to say and do if a colleague comes under attack, e.g., asking what kind of help is needed, instead of praising the person 'for doing something right' or telling the person 'to just turn off the computer and ignore it'. 2) Department and University Level strategies: Here it is emphasised to demand for university guidelines and standard procedures in case of an attack, for university funds for lawyers, and also how and what to teach students in relation to using social media. 3) Discipline and Professional Level Strategies: This level covers, for instance, the role and potential of professional associations, the possibility to organise conferences on the use of social media or the link to political action. Further strategies, such as those outlined in the 'No Hate' movements, which are not primarily related to the scholarly context, can also be useful. For example, the No Hate Speech campaign which was initiated by the European Council,[17] now has many branches worldwide. It provides readers with knowledge about hate speech, shows ways to counter hate speech online, for example with gifs, memes, and messages, and it provides creative ideas on how to network, support dissemination of knowledge, raise awareness, and activate communities. Similar initiatives are increasing in number in response to cyberbullying and hate.[18]

All these strategies are based on an obvious, but often overseen first step: communicating the issue. In order to act, and when evaluating coping and response strategies, communication with others is crucial. Strategies need networks, even if only to assess the dimension and nature of the problems that are dealt with. For others to be supportive and for the organisation to be able to react, those others need to know that a colleague, a student, a co-researcher, etc., is under attack. But since, due to a variety of reasons, such as shame, naivety, trauma, academic pressure, many of those affected do not mention their experiences, strategies fail to even be addressed. As with sexual harassment, cyberhate – which, as we pointed out above often contains racial slurs, obscenity, violent threats, anti-Semitism, etc. – is frequently kept private and confined to the intimate, private sphere by those attacked. In light of this problem, and following all relevant studies so far, we encourage affected scholars to share their experiences with others in their field. This could be through social media, for example, in Facebook groups to be trusted, or in personal and direct contact. It might be in more formal settings, such as departmental meetings, or in a less formal way, such as lunch or coffee with colleagues. Second, we suggest that all academic institutions create sustainable protocols for allowing such sharing of experiences. Protocols should include safe and trustworthy paths of reporting, routines for the recording of such communications, the instalment and funding of trained and specialised experts, especially regarding legal matters.

For the prevention of harm, raising awareness of it as an issue might be crucial. Knowing that an attack can happen, and that individual attacks are part of

17 See https://no-hate-speech.de/en/.

18 Very detailed further advice can also be found here https://othersociologist.com/sociology-public-harassment-prevention-policies/.

a wider phenomenon, is extremely helpful, but this needs to be accompanied by the development of response strategies. Implementing protocols, organisational routines, and proven strategies increase the ability to react against cyberhate, and to stay in control. This, again, reduces helplessness, isolation, and vulnerability.[19] Such foresight and collegial solidarity may even result in some academics feeling more capable of speaking about and working on the kind of topics which triggered an attack. It may stimulate a sense of meaning, strength, and self-empowerment, and help to uphold the values of truth, facts, and knowledge, while advocating respectful, constructive, and non-discriminatory engagement.

Another, potentially very powerful way of counteracting cyberhate is to build peer groups within universities. This can help reduce trauma in acute situations of attack. The attacked person will know who to speak to in confidence and can receive immediate emotional support and relief. Such support groups can also work on developing infrastructures that can be activated on demand. This can be a list of confidants who answer social media, telephone, and e-mail for a while for the attacked person, a list of lawyers and therapists who can be contacted, and funding mechanisms to pay these professionals for their support. In building such support systems, the people involved will exchange ideas, experiences, and thoughts. Thus, peer groups can even create an increased sense of belonging and trust among individuals, possibly promoting structural change within universities and the wider society that may mitigate further attacks.

The university as an academic institution must also play a role because it has ‘top-down' responsibilities when it comes to protecting staff from cyberhate. Earlier it was argued that the ideal function of research institutions was to inquire after truth, to explore and test accepted standards, and to push on our social intuitions. In order to fulfil this function, such institutions have to act in different ways. As employers, they must work to prevent the occurrence of cyberhate against academics and then offer appropriate and public support for those targeted by it. They need to see their role as having two functions: 1) to protect employees from individual harm, and 2) to preserve the institution of academic research as a whole and push against anti-intellectualism. In other words, the university has a vested interest to take a stand against cyberhate in order to maintain its own validity.

---

19 If the minimal impact of this chapter is to make those working in this field aware of the possibility that their work might make them targets, this may prove to make a world of difference. It would then, in the very least, have helped prevent them from being caught off guard and allow for preemptive preparation on their part, and hopefully more open dialogue about the issue with their own institutions.

Another ground which motivates action on behalf of the university is related to the practicalities of being an academic in these digital times, where academic success is often measured in the publicity of academics.[20] Apart from the 'impact factor', which grades the size of the audience a publication reaches and the influence it has over them, it has also become increasingly necessary for academics to maintain public professional profiles. They are expected to be involved in interviews and give public talks which are often recorded for sharing on the internet. Sara Perry explains that

> higher education professionals increasingly work at the interface of the academic and the public worlds, invested in research impact, community engagement and public intellectualism; this means that our workspace is expanding. Digital technology makes our workspace more accessible and more immediate, creating a perfect environment for cybercreeps. (Perry 2014)

Given the growing pressure to have a public online presence,[21] and the fact that this greatly increases the likelihood of being targeted for cyberhate, the university is responsible for managing the fallout in the event of a cyberhate attack and protecting its researchers.

8. Conclusion

In this chapter, we have begun to analyse the phenomenon of cyberhate and its harmful effects for society in general and for scholars and academic work more specifically. When studying a socially contested issue such as the integration of newcomers into society, there is a risk of becoming a target of cyberhate. The increasing phenomenon of such attacks calls for various responses. As part of a general social trend, addressing the origins of cyberhate more broadly would require measures beyond the scope of this paper. The individual, collective, and institutional strategies briefly noted in the previous section underscore our conviction that increased *awareness* and *knowledge* about the phenomenon of cyberhate, as well as the existence of some institutional and collective *support structures* in the context of academia can lessen significantly the negative impact of cyberhate on academics. The sad reality is that guarding against cyberhate is now part of the responsibility for academics.

---

20 For interesting literature on the increasingly digitised nature of academia cf. Daniels/Thistlethwaite (2016), Stein/Daniels (2017), and Carrigan (2016).
21 Cf. Mitchell (2013) and Parr (2013).

Bibliography

AAUP (2017): American Association of University Professors. Targeted Online Harassment of Faculty. Statement January 2017. https://www.aaup.org/file/2017-Harassment_Faculty_0.pdf (last accessed 12 October 2018).

Anti-Defamation League (2010): Responding to Cyberhate. Toolkit for Action. https://www.adl.org/sites/default/files/documents/assets/pdf/combating-hate/ADL-Responding-to-Cyberhate-Toolkit.pdf (last accessed 12 October 2018).

Anti-Defamation League (2018): Best Practices for Responding to Cyberhate. https://www.adl.org/best-practices-for-responding-to-cyberhate (last accessed 12 October 2018).

APA (2016). American Philosophical Association. Statement on Bullying and Harassment. https://cdn.ymaws.com/www.apaonline.org/resource/resmgr/Docs/Statement_on_Bullying_and_Ha.pdf (last accessed 12 October 2018).

Assimakopoulos, S./Baider, F. H./Millar, S. (2017): Online Hate Speech in the European Union: A Discourse-Analytic Perspective. Cham: Springer.

Badgett, M. V. L. (2015): The Public Professor: How to Use Your Research to Change the World. New York: NYU Press.

Baer, S. (2018): More Than Welcome: A Berlin Call for University Ethics. https://www.scholarsatrisk.org/wp-content/uploads/2018/05/SBaer-Remarks-2018-SAR-Global-Congress.pdf (last accessed 12 October 2018).

Betzler, M. (2013): The Normative Significance of Personal Projects. In: M. Kühler/N. Jelinek (eds.): Autonomy and the Self. Philosophical Studies Series 118, Springer Science +Business Media Dordrecht 2013, 101–126.

Blakely, J. (2017): A History of Conservative War on Universities: The GOP tax bill is the latest example of an anti-intellectualism that's been brewing for decades. In: The Atlantic 17 December. online https://www.theatlantic.com/education/archive/2017/12/a-history-of-the-conservative-war-on-universities/547703/ (last accessed 24 November 2018).

Blessinger, P./de Wit, H. (2018): Academic Freedom Is Essential to Democracy. In: University World News 500, 6 April http://www.universityworldnews.com/article.php?story=20180404101811251 (last accessed 12 October 2018).

Brown, R./Walters, M./Paterson, J. (2018): How Hate Crime Affects a Whole Community. In: BBC, 12 January. https://www.bbc.com/news/uk-42622767 (last accessed 12 October 2018).

Buchanan, A./Powell, R. (2018): The Evolution of Moral Progress: A Biocultural Theory. New York: Oxford University Press.

Campbell, E. (2017): 'Apparently Being a Self-Obsessed C**t Is Now Academically Lauded': Experiencing Twitter Trolling of Autoethnographers. In: Forum Qualitative Social Research 18(3), 1–19.

Carrigan, M. (2016): Social Media for Academics. Los Angeles: Sage Publication.

Castells, M. (2007): Communication, Power and Counter-power in the Network Society. In: International Journal of Communication 1(2007), 238–266.

Chakraborti, N./Garland, J. (2015): Hate Crime: Impact, Causes and Response. London: Sage.

Collins, P. H. (2013): On Intellectual Activism. Philadelphia: Temple University Press.

Couture, S. (2017): Activist Scholarship: The Complicated Entanglements of Activism and Research Work. In: Canadian Journal of Communication 42(1), 143–147.

Crandall, C. S./Miller, J. M./White, M. H. (2018): Changing Norms Following the 2016 U.S. Presidential Election: The Trump Effect on Prejudice. In: Social Psychological and Personality Science 9(2), 186–192.

Cuevas, J. A. (2018): A New Reality? Far Right's Use of Cyberharassment Against Academics. Academe (Jan–Feb 2018), 24–28. https://onefacultyoneresistance.org/wp-content/uploads/2018/01/Cuevas-article.pdf (last accessed 12 October 2018).

Daniels, J./Thistlethwaite, P. (2016): Being a Scholar in the Digital Era: Transforming Scholarly Practice for the Public Good. New York: Policy Press.

Dernbach, A. (2018): Migrationsforscherin Naika Foroutan: 'Es ist unser Land, verteidigen wir es gemeinsam.' In: Der Tagesspiegel, 22 July. https://www.tagesspiegel.de/politik/migrationsforscherin-naika-foroutan-es-ist-unser--land-verteidigen-wir-es-gemeinsam/22830476.html (last accessed 7 September 2018).

Downs, J./Manion, J. (eds.) (2004): Taking Back the Academy! History of Activism, History as Activism. New York: Routledge.

Dutt-Ballerstadt, R. (2018): What to Do When You Are an Academic under Attack. In: Inside Higher Ed blog, entry 2 March (last accessed 24 November 2018).

Ferber, A. L. (2018): 'Are You Willing to Die for This Work?' Public Targeted Online Harassment in Higher Education: SWS Presidential Address. In: Gender & Society 32(3), 301–320.

Fladmoe, A./Nadim, M. (2017): Silenced by Hate? Hate speech as a social boundary to free speech. In: A. H. Midtbøen/K. Steen-Johnsen/K. Thorbjørnsrud (eds.): Boundary Struggles: Contestations of Free Speech in the Norwegian Public Sphere. Cappelen Damm Akademisk/NOASP.

Flaherty, C. (2017): Belly of the Beast: Sociologists Seek Systematic Response to Online Targeting of and Threats against Public Scholars. In: Inside Higher Education blog, entry 14 August (last accessed 24 November 2018).

Flood, M./Martin, B./Dreher, T. (2013): Combining Academia and Activism: Common Obstacles and Useful Tools. In: Australian Universities' Review 55(1), 17–26.

Grollman, E. A. (2015): Scholars under Attack. In: Inside Higher Ed. 9 July. https://www.insidehighered.com/advice/2015/07/09/essay-how-support-scholars-under-attack (last accessed 12 October 2018).

Hark, S./Villa, P.-I. (2015): Anti-Genderismus: Sexualität und Geschlecht als Schauplätze aktueller politischer Auseinandersetzungen. 2. Auflage. Bielefeld: transcript.

International Network Against Cyber Hate (2018): Cyber Hate Legislation. http://www.inach.net/cyber-hate-legislation/ (last accessed 12 October 2018).

Jane, E. A. (2014): 'Your a Ugly, Whorish, Slut': Understanding E-Bile. In: Feminist Media Studies 14, 531–46.

Jane, E. A. (2015): Flaming? What Flaming? The Pitfalls and Potentials of Researching Online Hostility. In: Ethics of Information Technology 17, 65–87.

Jessop, B. (2018): On Academic Capitalism. In: Critical Policy Studies 1(12), 104–109.

Kaakinen, M./Keipi, T./Oksanen, A./Räsänen, P. (2018): How Does Social Capital Associate with Being a Victim of Online Hate? Survey Evidence from the United States, the United Kingdom, Germany, and Finland. In: Policy & Internet 10(3), 302–323.

Kenyon, P. (2016): After Brexit Vote, U.K. Sees A Wave Of Hate Crimes and Racist Abuse. In: National Public Radio. https://www.npr.org/sections/parallels/2016/06/29/484038396/

after-brexit-vote-u-k-sees-a-wave-of-hate-crimes-and-racist-abuse?t=1539359427272 (last accessed 12 October 2018).

Kitcher, P. (2001): Science, Truth, and Democracy. Oxford: Oxford University Press.

Kreißel, P./Ebner, J./Urban, A./Guhl, J. (2018): Hass auf Knopfdruck. Rechtsextreme Trollfabriken und das Ökosystem koordinierter Hasskampagnen im Netz. https://www.isdglobal.org/wp-content/uploads/2018/07/ISD_Ich_Bin_Hier_2.pdf (last accessed 12 October 2018).

Kuhar, R./Paternotte, D. (2017): Anti-Gender Campaigns in Europe. Mobilizing against Equality. Lanham: Rowman & Littlefield.

Lin, N. (1999): Building a Network Theory of Social Capital. In: CONNECTIONS 22(1), 28–51.

Maitra, I./McGowan, M. K. (eds.) (2012): Speech and Harm: Controversies over Free Speech. Oxford: Oxford University Press.

Martin, B. (1984): Academics and Social Action. In: Higher Education Review 16(2), 17–33.

Matsuda, M. J./Iii, C. R. L./Delgado, R./Crenshaw, K. W. (1993): Words That Wound: Critical Race Theory, Assaultive Speech, and the First Amendment. 1st edition. Boulder: Westview Press.

Mindock, C. (2017): Number of Hate Crimes Surges in Year of Trump's Election. In: Independent, 14 November. https://www.independent.co.uk/news/world/americas/hate-crimes-us-trump-election-surge-rise-latest-figures-police-a8055026.html (last accessed 12 October 2018).

Mitchell, A. (2013): Take Back the Net: Institutions Must Develop Collective Strategies to Tackle Online Abuse Aimed at Female Academics. In: LSE Impact Blog, 24 July. http://blogs.lse.ac.uk/impactofsocialsciences/2013/07/24/take-back-the-net-female-academics-online-abuse/ (last accessed 12 October 2018).

Näsi, M./Räsänen, P./Hawdon, J./Holkeri, E./Oksanen, A. (2015): Exposure to Online Hate Material and Social Trust among Finnish Youth. In: Information Technology & People 28(3), 607–622.

Okeowo, A. (2016): Hate on the Rise After Trump's Election. In: The New Yorker, 17 November. https://www.newyorker.com/news/news-desk/hate-on-the-rise-after-trumps-election (last accessed 12 October 2018).

Parr, C. (2013): Academics Face the Cybercreeps Alone. In: Times Higher Education Supplement, 21 November. https://www.timeshighereducation.com/news/academics-face-the-cybercreeps-alone/2009183.article#survey-answer (last accessed 12 October 2018).

Perry, B./Olsson, P. (2009): Cyberhate: The Globalization of Hate. In: Information & Communications Technology Law 18(2), 185–99.

Perry, S. (2014): Cyber-Abuse of Academics – It's Time for Action. Times Higher Education. https://www.timeshighereducation.com/comment/opinion/cyber-abuse-of-academics-its-time-for-action/2011187.article (last accessed 24 November 2018).

Peters, M. A. (2018): Anti-intellectualism Is a Virus. In: Educational Philosophy and Theory, 1–7.

Pew Research Center (2017): Sharp Partisan Divisions in Views of National Institutions: Republicans Increasingly Say Colleges Have Negative Impact on U.S. http://www.people-press.org/2017/07/10/sharp-partisan-divisions-in-views-of-national-institutions/ (last accessed 12 October 2018).

Professor Watchlist (2018): About Us: Turning Point USA, a 501(c)3 Non-Profit Organization. https://www.professorwatchlist.org/about-us/ (last accessed 12 October 2018).
Slaughter, S./Rhoades, G. (2004): Academic Capitalism and the New Economy: Markets, States, and Higher Education. Baltimore: Johns Hopkins University Press.
Stanley, J. (2018a): How Fascism Works: The Politics of Us and Them. New York: Random House.
Stanley, J. (2018b). How Propaganda Works, Precis. In: Philosophy and Phenomenological Research 96(2), 470–474.
Stein, A./Daniels J. (2017): Going Public: A Guide for Social Scientists. Chicago: University of Chicago Press.
Waldron, Jeremy (2012): The Harm in Hate Speech. Cambridge: Harvard University Press.
Whittaker, E./Kowalski, R. M. (2015): Cyberbullying via Social Media. In: Journal of School Violence 14(1), 11–29.
Williams, M./Pearson, O. (2016): Hate Crime and Bullying in the Age of Social Media. Conference Report. https://orca-mwe.cf.ac.uk/88865/1/Cyber-Hate-and-Bullying-Post-Conference-Report_English_pdf.pdf (last accessed 12 October 2018).
Wray, M./Daniels, J./Fetner, T. (eds.) (2016): Promoting Sociological Research: A Toolkit. Washington, DC: American Sociological Association.
Yancy, G. (2016): I Am a Dangerous Professor. In: The New York Times, 30 November 2016. https://www.nytimes.com/2016/11/30/opinion/i-am-a-dangerous-professor.html (last accessed 12 October 2018).
ZEIT Online (2018): Ungarn verbannt Geschlechterforschung aus den Unis. https://www.zeit.de/politik/ausland/2018-10/gender-studies-ungarn-studienfach-abschaffung-universitaeten-viktor-orban (last accessed 20 November 2018).

Alison Phipps

Day 1

The room is grasping
after words
in an English
which hovers over German
over French
over Kiswahili
over Arabic
over Dutch
over
over
over

we interpellate
and are interpellated

the language
of Rights is
is
is
is...somehow
insufficient

Metaphors spin.
First there are 'bridges,'
then weapons for 'cultural survival',
there are 'routes',
a 'social organism' is 'threatening'
the 'seat of culture'
migration is 'strengthening
and weakening the organism'
the power.

And that is just in Canadian history.

They are 'blank sheets'
They are 'instruments'

They are ‘beggars.’
Then come the ‘inhabitants of colours’
dwellers in a new land
‘agents’ of ‘freedom’
‘resisters’
‘refusers’
‘witnesses’
‘listeners’
‘story tellers’
the ‘empirical
victims’ dissolve into
norms of human agency
at its surviving best.

Under traumatic conditions
we simply behave.

And breathe.

Love becomes a moral
notion.

And that is the theory
And that becomes the practice.
For this, a peace-making moment
in time.

The listening deepens.
The agency is enacted
The stories are told
again,
again.

They are not legalised,
or theorised,
or medicalised,
or standardised.

The structures of
the academy

flake
become porous.

It is war time.

Hate's violence threatens
the ideals and practices of
justice, solidarity, dialogue.

But here and now,
An ethos of responsibility
is being made.

There is silence and silencing
They are not the same.
They are sisters.

Love, we are told, is disarming.
Humour brings change.
Love, is disarming.

List of contributors

Yahya Al-Abdullah PhD student, L'École des Hautes Etudes en Sciences Sociales, Paris, France

Eva Alisic Associate Professor, Child Trauma and Recovery, Melbourne School of Population and Global Health, University of Melbourne, Australia

Jason Branford PhD student, Munich Center for Ethics, LMU Munich, Germany

Elizabeth Castle Behavioural Insights Research Analyst, Public Health England, London, UK

Annemiek Dresen Founder & Director, NewBees, Amsterdam, The Netherlands

Yves Frenette Canada Research Chair in Migrations, Transfers and Francophone Communities, Université de Saint-Boniface, Manitoba, Canada

André Grahle Research Fellow, Practical Philosophy and Ethics, Philosophy Faculty, LMU Munich, Germany

Jan-Christoph Heilinger Academic Director, Munich Center for Ethics, LMU Munich, Germany

Rob Jenkins Reader in Psychology, Department of Psychology, University of York, UK

Dennis Kalde PhD student, Practical Philosophy and Ethics, Philosophy Faculty, LMU Munich, Germany

Dzenana Kartal Research Specialist, Phoenix Australia Centre for Posttraumatic Mental Health, University of Melbourne, Australia

Debora Kayembe Lawyer and founder of Full Options, Edinburgh, UK

S. Karly Kehoe Canada Research Chair in Atlantic Canada Communities, Saint Mary's University, Halifax, Canada

Niamh McLoughlin Postdoctoral Research Associate, Wheelock College of Education and Human Development, Boston University, USA

Max Muth Journalist, Süddeutsche Zeitung, Munich, Germany

Nasar Meer Professor of Race, Identity and Citizenship, School of Social and Political Science, University of Edinburgh, UK

Harriet Over Senior Lecturer, Department of Psychology, University of York, UK

Eva Maria Parisi PhD student, Munich Center for Ethics, LMU Munich, Germany

Alison Phipps Professor, Languages and Intercultural Studies, UNESCO Chair in Refugee Integration through Languages and the Arts, University of Glasgow, UK

Jet G. Sanders LSE Fellow, Department of Psychological and Behavioural Science, London School of Economics and Political Science, UK

Karen Tan Behavioral Insights Lead, International Rescue Committee's Airbel Center, New York, USA

Paula-Irene Villa Professor, Sociology and Gender-Studies, LMU Munich, Germany

Verina Wild Lecturer, Institute of Ethics, History and Theory of Medicine, LMU Munich, Germany

Stephen Wordsworth Executive Director, Council for At-Risk Academics (Cara), London, UK

Index

www.ingramcontent.com/pod-product-compliance
Lightning Source LLC
Chambersburg PA
CBHW030733280326
41926CB00086B/1275
* 9 7 8 3 1 1 0 7 3 6 8 6 1 *